Nutshell Series

of

WEST PUBLISHING COMPANY

P.O. Box 3526

St. Paul, Minnesota 55165

May, 1983

I

NUTSHELL SERIES

NUTSHELL SERIES

Debtor-Creditor Law, 2nd Ed., 1980, 324 pages, by David G. Epstein, Professor of Law, University of Texas.

Employment Discrimination—Federal Law of, 2nd Ed., 1981, 402 pages, by Mack A. Player, Professor of Law, University of Georgia.

Energy Law, 1981, 338 pages, by Joseph P. Tomain, Professor of Law, Drake University.

Environmental Law, 1983, approximately 332 pages by Roger W. Findley, Professor of Law, University of Illinois and Daniel A. Farber, Professor of Law, University of Minnesota.

Estate Planning—Introduction to, 3rd Ed., 1983, 370 pages, by Robert J. Lynn, Professor of Law, Ohio State University.

Evidence, Federal Rules of, 1981, 428 pages, by Michael H. Graham, Professor of Law, University of Illinois.

Evidence, State and Federal Rules, 2nd Ed., 1981, 514 pages, by Paul F. Rothstein, Professor of Law, Georgetown University.

Family Law, 1977, 400 pages, by Harry D. Krause, Professor of Law, University of Illinois.

Federal Estate and Gift Taxation, 3rd Ed., 1983, 509 pages, by John K. McNulty, Professor of Law, University of California, Berkeley.

Federal Income Taxation of Individuals, 3rd Ed., 1983, approximately 425 pages, by John K. McNulty, Professor of Law, University of California, Berkeley.

Federal Income Taxation of Corporations and Stockholders, 2nd Ed., 1981, 362 pages, by Jonathan Sobeloff, Late Professor of Law, Georgetown University and Peter P. Weidenbruch, Jr., Professor of Law, Georgetown University.

Federal Jurisdiction, 2nd Ed., 1981, 258 pages, by David P. Currie, Professor of Law, University of Chicago.

Future Interests, 1981, 361 pages, by Lawrence W. Waggoner, Professor of Law, University of Michigan.

Government Contracts, 1979, 423 pages, by W. Noel Keyes, Professor of Law, Pepperdine University.

Historical Introduction to Anglo-American Law, 2nd Ed., 1973, 280 pages, by Frederick G. Kempin, Jr., Professor of Business Law, Wharton School of Finance and Commerce, University of Pennsylvania.

Injunctions, 1974, 264 pages, by John F. Dobbyn, Professor of Law, Villanova University.

Insurance Law, 1981, 281 pages, by John F. Dobbyn, Professor of Law, Villanova University.

Intellectual Property—Patents, Trademarks and Copyright, 1983, approximately 410 pages, by Arthur R. Miller, Professor of Law, Harvard University, and Michael H. Davis, Professor of Law, University of Tennessee.

International Business Transactions, 1981, 393 pages, by Donald T. Wilson, Professor of Law, Loyola University, Los Angeles.

Introduction to the Study and Practice of Law, 1983, approximately 400 pages, by Kenney F. Hegland, Professor of Law, University of Arizona.

Judicial Process, 1980, 292 pages, by William L. Reynolds, Professor of Law, University of Maryland.

Jurisdiction, 4th Ed., 1980, 232 pages, by Albert A. Ehrenzweig, Late Professor of Law, University of California, Berkeley, David W. Louisell, Late Professor of Law, University of California, Berkeley and Geoffrey C. Hazard, Jr., Professor of Law, Yale Law School.

Juvenile Courts, 2nd Ed., 1977, 275 pages, by Sanford J. Fox, Professor of Law, Boston College.

Labor Arbitration Law and Practice, 1979, 358 pages, by Dennis R. Nolan, Professor of Law, University of South Carolina.

Labor Law, 1979, 403 pages, by Douglas L. Leslie, Professor of Law, University of Virginia.

Land Use, 1978, 316 pages, by Robert R. Wright, Professor of Law, University of Arkansas, Little Rock and Susan Webber, Professor of Law, University of Arkansas, Little Rock.

Landlord and Tenant Law, 1979, 319 pages, by David S. Hill, Professor of Law, University of Colorado.

Law Study and Law Examinations—Introduction to, 1971, 389 pages, by Stanley V. Kinyon, Late Professor of Law, University of Minnesota.

Legal Interviewing and Counseling, 1976, 353 pages, by Thomas L. Shaffer, Professor of Law, Washington and Lee University.

Legal Research, 3rd Ed., 1978, 415 pages, by Morris L. Cohen, Professor of Law and Law Librarian, Yale University.

Legal Writing, 1982, 294 pages, by Dr. Lynn B. Squires, University of Washington School of Law and Marjorie Dick Rombauer, Professor of Law, University of Washington.

Legislative Law and Process, 1975, 279 pages, by Jack Davies, Professor of Law, William Mitchell College of Law.

Local Government Law, 2nd Ed., 1983, approximately 345 pages, by David J. McCarthy, Jr., Professor of Law, Georgetown University.

Mass Communications Law, 2nd Ed., 1983, 473 pages, by Harvey L. Zuckman, Professor of Law, Catholic University and Martin J. Gaynes, Lecturer in Law, Temple University.

Medical Malpractice—The Law of, 1977, 340 pages, by Joseph H. King, Professor of Law, University of Tennessee.

Military Law, 1980, 378 pages, by Charles A. Shanor, Professor of Law, Emory University and Timothy P. Terrell, Professor of Law, Emory University.

Oil and Gas, 1983, approximately 365 pages, by John S. Lowe, Professor of Law, University of Tulsa.

NUTSHELL SERIES

Personal Property, 1983, approximately 318 pages, by Barlow Burke, Jr., Professor of Law, American University.

Post-Conviction Remedies, 1978, 360 pages, by Robert Popper, Professor of Law, University of Missouri, Kansas City.

Presidential Power, 1977, 328 pages, by Arthur Selwyn Miller, Professor of Law Emeritus, George Washington University.

Procedure Before Trial, 1972, 258 pages, by Delmar Karlen, Professor of Law, College of William and Mary.

Products Liability, 2nd Ed., 1981, 341 pages, by Dix W. Noel, Late Professor of Law, University of Tennessee and Jerry J. Phillips, Professor of Law, University of Tennessee.

Professional Responsibility, 1980, 399 pages, by Robert H. Aronson, Professor of Law, University of Washington, and Donald T. Weckstein, Professor of Law, University of San Diego.

Real Estate Finance, 1979, 292 pages, by Jon W. Bruce, Professor of Law, Vanderbilt University.

Real Property, 2nd Ed., 1981, 448 pages, by Roger H. Bernhardt, Professor of Law, Golden Gate University.

Regulated Industries, 1982, 394 pages, by Ernest Gellhorn, Dean and Professor of Law, Case Western Reserve University, and Richard J. Pierce, Professor of Law, Tulane University.

Remedies, 1977, 364 pages, by John F. O'Connell, Professor of Law, Western State University College of Law, Fullerton.

Res Judicata, 1976, 310 pages, by Robert C. Casad, Professor of Law, University of Kansas.

Sales, 2nd Ed., 1981, 370 pages, by John M. Stockton, Professor of Business Law, Wharton School of Finance and Commerce, University of Pennsylvania.

Law, Lewis and Clark College, Northwestern School of Law.

Wills and Trusts, 1979, 392 pages, by Robert L. Mennell, Professor of Law, Hamline University.

Hornbook Series

and

Basic Legal Texts

of

WEST PUBLISHING COMPANY

P.O. Box 3526

St. Paul, Minnesota 55165

May, 1983

IX

of Law, University of Illinois and Peter Hay, Dean and Professor of Law, University of Illinois.

Constitutional Law, Nowak, Rotunda and Young's Hornbook on, 2nd Ed., Student Ed., 1983, approximately 1100 pages, by John E. Nowak, Professor of Law, University of Illinois, Ronald D. Rotunda, Professor of Law, University of Illinois, and J. Nelson Young, Professor of Law, University of North Carolina.

Contracts, Calamari and Perillo's Hornbook on, 2nd Ed., 1977, 878 pages, by John D. Calamari, Professor of Law, Fordham University and Joseph M. Perillo, Professor of Law, Fordham University.

Contracts, Corbin's One Volume Student Ed., 1952, 1224 pages, by Arthur L. Corbin, Late Professor of Law, Yale University.

Contracts, Simpson's Hornbook on, 2nd Ed., 1965, 510 pages, by Laurence P. Simpson, Late Professor of Law, New York University.

Corporate Taxation, Kahn's Handbook on, 3rd Ed., Student Ed., Soft cover, 1981 with 1982 Supplement, 614 pages, by Douglas A. Kahn, Professor of Law, University of Michigan.

Corporations, Henn's Hornbook on, 3rd Ed., Student Ed., 1983, approximately 1167 pages, by Harry G. Henn, Professor of Law, Cornell University.

Criminal Law, LaFave and Scott's Hornbook on, 1972, 763 pages, by Wayne R. LaFave, Professor of Law, University of Illinois, and Austin Scott, Jr., Late Professor of Law, University of Colorado.

Damages, McCormick's Hornbook on, 1935, 811 pages, by Charles T. McCormick, Late Dean and Professor of Law, University of Texas.

Domestic Relations, Clark's Hornbook on, 1968, 754 pages, by Homer H. Clark, Jr., Professor of Law, University of Colorado.

Environmental Law, Rodgers' Hornbook on, 1977, 956 pages, by William H. Rodgers, Jr., Professor of Law, University of Washington.

Estate and Gift Taxes, Lowndes, Kramer and McCord's Hornbook on, 3rd Ed., 1974, 1099 pages, by Charles L. B. Lowndes, Late Professor of Law, Duke University, Robert Kramer, Professor of Law Emeritus, George Washington University, and John H. McCord, Professor of Law, University of Illinois.

Evidence, Lilly's Introduction to, 1978, 486 pages, by Graham C. Lilly, Professor of Law, University of Virginia.

Evidence, McCormick's Hornbook on, 2nd Ed., 1972 with 1978 Pocket Part, 938 pages, General Editor, Edward W. Cleary, Professor of Law Emeritus, Arizona State University.

Federal Courts, Wright's Hornbook on, 4th Ed., Student Ed., 1983, 870 pages, by Charles Alan Wright, Professor of Law, University of Texas.

Federal Income Taxation of Individuals, Posin's Hornbook on, Student Ed., 1983, approximately 421 pages, by Daniel Q. Posin, Jr., Professor of Law, Hofstra University.

Future Interest, Simes' Hornbook on, 2nd Ed., 1966, 355 pages, by Lewis M. Simes, Late Professor of Law, University of Michigan.

Income Taxation, Chommie's Hornbook on, 2nd Ed., 1973, 1051 pages, by John C. Chommie, Late Professor of Law, University of Miami.

Insurance, Keeton's Basic Text on, 1971, 712 pages, by Robert E. Keeton, Professor of Law Emeritus, Harvard University.

Labor Law, Gorman's Basic Text on, 1976, 914 pages, by Robert A. Gorman, Professor of Law, University of Pennsylvania.

Law Problems, Ballentine's, 5th Ed., 1975, 767 pages, General Editor, William E. Burby, Late Professor of Law, University of Southern California.

Legal Writing Style, Weihofen's, 2nd Ed., 1980, 332 pages, by Henry Weihofen, Professor of Law Emeritus, University of New Mexico.

Local Government Law, Reynolds' Hornbook on, 1982, 860 pages, by Osborne M. Reynolds, Professor of Law, University of Oklahoma.

New York Practice, Siegel's Hornbook on, 1978, with 1981–82 Pocket Part, 1011 pages, by David D. Siegel, Professor of Law, Albany Law School of Union University.

Oil and Gas, Hemingway's Hornbook on, 2nd Ed., Student Ed., 1983, approximately 507 pages, by Richard W. Hemingway, Professor of Law, University of Oklahoma.

Poor, Law of the, LaFrance, Schroeder, Bennett and Boyd's Hornbook on, 1973, 558 pages, by Arthur B. La-France, Dean and Professor of Law, Lewis and Clark College, Northwestern School of Law, Milton R. Schroeder, Professor of Law, Arizona State University, Robert W. Bennett, Professor of Law, Northwestern University and William E. Boyd, Professor of Law, University of Arizona.

Property, Boyer's Survey of, 3rd Ed., 1981, 766 pages, by Ralph E. Boyer, Professor of Law, University of Miami.

Real Estate Finance Law, Osborne, Nelson and Whitman's Hornbook on, (successor to Hornbook on Mortgages), 1979, 885 pages, by George E. Osborne, Late Professor of Law, Stanford University, Grant S. Nelson, Professor of Law, University of Missouri, Columbia and Dale A. Whitman, Dean and Professor of Law, University of Missouri, Columbia.

Real Property, Burby's Hornbook on, 3rd Ed., 1965, 490 pages, by William E. Burby, Late Professor of Law, University of Southern California.

Real Property, Moynihan's Introduction to, 1962, 254 pages, by Cornelius J. Moynihan, Professor of Law, Suffolk University.

Remedies, Dobb's Hornbook on, 1973, 1067 pages, by Dan B. Dobbs, Professor of Law, University of Arizona.

Sales, Nordstrom's Hornbook on, 1970, 600 pages, by Robert J. Nordstrom, former Professor of Law, Ohio State University.

Secured Transactions under the U.C.C., Henson's Hornbook on, 2nd Ed., 1979, with 1979 Pocket Part, 504 pages, by Ray D. Henson, Professor of Law, University of California, Hastings College of the Law.

Torts, Prosser's Hornbook on, 4th Ed., 1971, 1208 pages, by William L. Prosser, Late Dean and Professor of Law, University of California, Berkeley.

Trial Advocacy, Jeans' Handbook on, Student Ed., Soft cover, 1975, by James W. Jeans, Professor of Law, University of Missouri, Kansas City.

Trusts, Bogert's Hornbook on, 5th Ed., 1973, 726 pages, by George G. Bogert, Late Professor of Law, University of Chicago and George T. Bogert, Attorney, Chicago, Illinois.

Urban Planning and Land Development Control, Hagman's Hornbook on, 1971, 706 pages, by Donald G. Hagman, Late Professor of Law, University of California, Los Angeles.

Uniform Commercial Code, White and Summers' Hornbook on, 2nd Ed., 1980, 1250 pages, by James J. White, Professor of Law, University of Michigan and Robert S. Summers, Professor of Law, Cornell University.

Wills, Atkinson's Hornbook on, 2nd Ed., 1953, 975 pages, by Thomas E. Atkinson, Late Professor of Law, New York University.

Advisory Board

XIV

ENVIRONMENTAL LAW

IN A NUTSHELL

By

ROGER W. FINDLEY
Professor of Law
University of Illinois

and

DANIEL A. FARBER
Professor of Law
University of Minnesota

ST. PAUL, MINN.
WEST PUBLISHING CO.
1983

COPYRIGHT © 1983 By WEST PUBLISHING CO.
50 West Kellogg Boulevard
P.O. Box 3526
St. Paul, Minnesota 55165

Printed in the United States of America

Library of Congress Cataloging in Publication Data

Findley, Roger W.
Environmental law in a nutshell.

(Nutshell series)
Includes index.
1. Environmental law—United States. I. Farber, Daniel A., 1950–
II. Title. III. Series.
KF3775.Z9F56 1983   344.73'046   83-6764
                      347.30446
ISBN 0-314-73633-6

For Suzy, Dianne, Sheila,
Steve, Joey and Sonia

*

PREFACE

Like our Casebook on *Environmental Law*, this book is organized around several pervasive issues which underlie environmental laws and doctrines. These issues relate generally to the process of integrating environmental policies into a social system which evolved with little regard for such matters. The process involves implementing environmental policies through a legal system which stresses administrative discretion, judicial restraint, and respect for the authority of different levels of government. It also involves accommodating environmental values with the economic realities of our society, with traditional property rights, and with national energy policy.

Chapter 1 considers the role of the courts in controlling environmental decisionmaking under the federal Administrative Procedure Act and National Environmental Policy Act. Chapter 2 examines the structure of major federal pollution statutes; the extent to which problems of economic and technological feasibility operate as constraints on environmental protection; and ways in which government can create countervailing economic incentives to encourage environmental protection. Directly related to the first two chapters is Chapter 3 on toxic substances. It analyzes the strains placed upon the mechanisms of administrative rulemaking and judicial review by the scientific uncertainty which characterizes toxic chemicals regulation. Chapter 4 then considers important regulatory limitations attributable to intergovernmental conflicts within our federal system. The problems considered in these four chapters arise under virtually any regulatory scheme, whether it relates to air pollution, water pollution, nuclear power, or some other environmental problem.

In the final two chapters the focus shifts away from the internal dynamics of the environmental protection process. Instead, these chapters consider the external relationships between environmental law and other social policies concerning resource management. Chapter 5 examines the relationships between environmental regulation and energy policy. Chapter 6 considers law and policies pertaining to the preservation of natural areas, including both private and federally owned lands.

As part of the Nutshell series, this book does not offer an exhaustive treatment of the subject of environmental law. For further helpful information the reader may consult R. Findley and D. Farber's Casebook on *Environmental Law* (1981); W. Rodgers' Hornbook on *Environmental Law* (1977); D. Currie, *Air Pollution: Federal Law and Analysis* (1981); and J. Nowak, R. Rotunda and J. Young's Hornbook on *Constitutional Law* (2d ed. 1983).

PREFACE

Preparation of the manuscript for this book was completed in May, 1983. As this book went to press, the Supreme Court handed down its decision in Baltimore Gas and Electric Co. v. NRDC, — S.Ct. — (1983), upholding the NRC rule governing EIS discussion of nuclear waste disposal. The opinion stresses the limited purpose of the rule and the deference due the agency's expertise. Unfortunately, the decision was announced too late for inclusion in the text. We want to express our special appreciation to Norma Roberts and Harriett Carlson for their outstanding assistance in word processing.

ROGER W. FINDLEY
DANIEL A. FARBER

Champaign, Illinois
Minneapolis, Minnesota
June, 1983

*

OUTLINE

TABLE OF CASES

References are to Pages.

TABLE OF CASES

TABLE OF CASES

TABLE OF CASES

TABLE OF CASES

*

ENVIRONMENTAL LAW

IN A NUTSHELL

*

CHAPTER 1

CONTROL OF ENVIRONMENTAL DECISIONMAKING BY FEDERAL AGENCIES

Almost all environmental litigation involves disputes with governmental agencies, rather than disputes between private parties. Such litigation typically takes one of two forms. First, the claim may be made that in implementing an environmental statute, an agency such as the EPA has acted improperly. Second, the claim may be that in implementing some non-environmental statute, the agency has improperly threatened the environment. Both kinds of claims often raise general issues about the procedural restrictions on suits against the government. The second kind of claim also raises the issue of what substantive limitations exist on government action which threatens the environment. The first set of issues is addressed by the Administrative Procedure Act (APA). The second set of issues is addressed by the National Environmental Policy Act (NEPA). This chapter will consider both sets of issues.

A. THE JUDICIAL ROLE IN ENVIRON-
MENTAL LAW

Apart from the political process, the only check on agency action is found in the courts. Because of the importance of government agencies in environmental law, it is important to understand the circumstances under which courts will intervene in environmental decisionmaking. We can break this problem down into three issues. First, when will a court hear a case challenging agency action? Second, if the court does hear the case, what standards will it apply in reviewing the agency's action? And third, what remedies will the court impose?

We will begin with the first of these issues, the restrictions on a court's ability to hear environmental cases. It is quite possible to conceive of a legal system in which any individual could bring suit to halt any government action that violated the law. It is also possible to conceive of a system in which the only redress against illegal government action would be at the ballot box. American law has taken an intermediate position. Courts can hear some, but not all, claims that a government agency has acted illegally. A plaintiff who seeks to bring such a claim must demonstrate that he is a proper individual to challenge the government action, and that the issues he is raising are issues that the court is authorized to

[2]

consider. The requirement that the suit be brought by the proper individual is known as the doctrine of "standing." The requirement that the issues be suitable for judicial resolution raises instead the problem of "reviewability." The standing issue has given rise to a great deal of litigation in environmental cases.

1. STANDING

The Supreme Court has had occasion to consider the standing issue in three major cases. The first of these cases was Sierra Club v. Morton, 405 U.S. 727 (1972). This case involved a decision by the Forest Service to approve a plan by Walt Disney Enterprises to build a $35,000,000 resort in the Mineral King Valley, which the Court described as "an area of great natural beauty nestled in the Sierra Nevada Mountains." Construction of the huge resort was opposed by the Sierra Club on the ground that the Forest Service had violated several federal statutes. The Sierra Club did not base its lawsuit on the claim that it would be directly injured by the construction of the resort. Instead, it based its lawsuit on its status as a public interest group with a long-standing, special interest in preservation of the environment.

Although some lower courts had indicated a willingness to confer standing based on similar allegations, the Supreme Court refused to do so.

[*3*]

Instead, it relied on earlier cases establishing a general test for standing under the APA. This test, known as the *Data Processing* test, requires that the plaintiff seeking judicial review of agency action show two things: (1) an "injury in fact"; and (2) an interest "arguably within the zone of interests to be protected or regulated" by the statute that the agency is claimed to have violated. The "injury in fact" requirement has proved to be the more important of these two elements of the *Data Processing* test.

In *Sierra Club* the Court held that a mere allegation of a general interest in a problem, even if the interest has been active and long-standing, is not enough to constitute injury in fact. The practical importance of this decision, however, was diminished by the Court's holding that the Sierra Club could establish injury in fact to itself merely by alleging that some of its members used the area in question for recreational purposes. The esthetic injury suffered by these members, who would no longer be able to hike through an unspoiled wilderness if the project was built, was sufficient to constitute an injury in fact not only as to themselves, but also as to the organization to which they belonged. Obviously, there was little doubt that the Sierra Club could satisfy this requirement, so the ultimate effect of the Court's holding was simply to require an amendment to the pleadings.

[4]

The next Supreme Court case showed how easy it can be to satisfy the *Sierra Club* requirements. United States v. Students Challenging Regulatory Agency Procedures, 412 U.S. 669 (1973) *[SCRAP I]*, involved a challenge to an ICC decision in a railroad rate case. The railroads had sought permission for an across-the-board rate increase in order to increase their revenues and to cover expenses. The plaintiffs, who had formed an association in order to bring the case, alleged that the existing rate schedule unfairly discriminated against recycled goods. As a result of this rate discrimination, they alleged, recycled goods were used in lower amounts than they otherwise would be. The plaintiffs' theory was that the situation would only be made worse by an across-the-board rate increase. They alleged that the result of this increase would be to further discriminate against recycled goods, thereby further diminishing the use of recycling, thereby increasing the amount of litter on a nationwide basis, and thus causing an increase in the amount of litter in the parks near Seattle, Washington where the plaintiffs lived. In short, their theory was that the ICC's approval of the railroad rate increase would ultimately have the effect of making their visits to local parks less pleasant because of an increase in litter. They also alleged that the decrease in recycling would cause an increase in mining and logging in the region. (A complicating factor in the case was the fact that the ICC

[*5*]

had not given final approval to the rate increase, but had merely refused to issue an interlocutory order suspending the increase pending investigation.) Despite the somewhat tenuous chain of causation alleged by the plaintiffs, and the fairly minimal injury which they claimed as a result of this chain of causation, the Supreme Court held that they did have standing to challenge the ICC's action.

The *SCRAP* decision clarifies several elements of the law of standing. First, the Court made it clear that standing "is not to be denied simply because many people suffer the same injury." As the Court pointed out, to deny standing to individuals who are injured simply because many others are also injured, would mean that the "more injurious Government actions could be questioned by nobody." Second, the Court held that the test for standing was qualitative, but not quantitative. Thus the magnitude of the injury in fact makes no difference so long as some injury in fact exists. As the Court said, quoting Professor Davis, "the basic idea that comes out in numerous cases is that an identifiable trifle" is enough to establish standing.

Following the *SCRAP* decision, a number of Supreme Court decisions in non-environmental cases seemed to take a restrictive view toward standing. In particular, the Court scrutinized quite suspiciously the causal chain allegedly connecting an illegal government action and the injury to the plaintiffs. In several cases, plausible claims of injury were rejected by the Court as being too speculative. The Supreme Court's most recent decision in the environmental area, however, makes it clear that at least in this area the test for standing remains liberal. That case, Duke Power Co. v. Carolina Environmental Study Group, Inc., 438 U.S. 59 (1978), involved a chain of causation as tenuous as that in the *SCRAP* case. The plaintiffs in *Duke Power* challenged the constitutionality of the Price-Anderson Act. That statute limits the liability of the nuclear industry for damages resulting from a single nuclear accident. The plaintiffs claimed that without this limitation on liability, reactors would not be built, and that this in turn would spare them immediate environmental injuries such as injury to fishing. Their claim on the merits, however, did not relate to these immediate environmental injuries. Instead, it related to the possible limitation on liability if and when a reactor in their vicinity became involved in a nuclear accident. They contended that if they were injured and their damages exceeded the amount allowed by the statute, the statute would constitute an unconstitutional taking of property without compensation. Thus, their contention was that, as a result of a statute which might be unconstitutional if it ever were applied to them in the future, they were suffering an immediate environmental injury today. Despite the tenuousness of the chain of causation, the Court held that there was a "substantial likelihood" that the nuclear plants near the plaintiffs' homes would not be completed or operated without the statute. This was held to be a sufficient basis for standing. The defendants had also attacked the plaintiffs' standing because the injury which they were using to establish their standing had no logical relationship to their claims on the merits. The Court held, however, that such a nexus between the plaintiffs' injury and the claim on the merits was unnecessary.

Thus, the Supreme Court has taken a liberal view of standing in environmental cases. The reason does not seem to be sympathy with the plaintiffs in these cases. Almost without exception, plaintiffs who have won standing in the Supreme Court have lost on the merits of their claims. Rather than sympathy for the plaintiffs, the reason for the Supreme Court's attitude is more likely to be found in the nature of environmental claims. The plaintiff in an environmental case is not challenging the government's general social policies or seeking to base standing on some interest in the general welfare of society. Rather, the environmental plaintiff is making a claim that the government has injured his physical environment. Such physical injuries are more similar to the kind of injuries traditionally redressed by courts than are injuries simply ad-

[*8*]

dressing the general legality of government decisionmaking. The environmental lawsuit is simply
an extension of the common law action of nuisance and thus presents courts with a kind of litigation familiar to them. Also, environmental litigation typically asks the Court to apply some
federal statute rather than seeking judicial intervention on the basis of the Constitution. In constitutional cases, the Court is often required to
fashion the norms governing its decision with
very little help from the text or history of the
Constitution. It is not surprising that courts
should be reluctant to undertake this difficult
task in cases where the plaintiff's claim of injury
is weak. On the other hand, in environmental
cases, the Court is merely being asked to apply a
norm created by Congress. Because intervention
by the Court involves only routine issues of statutory construction, rather than the more difficult
task of construing the Constitution, it is not surprising that the Court is more willing to act. In
combination, these factors may explain the
Court's relative willingness to grant standing to
plaintiffs in environmental cases.

To summarize the law of standing, the Supreme Court has required plaintiffs to prove that
they have suffered an injury in fact. In environmental cases, this requires the plaintiff to allege
the existence of a chain of causation between the
allegedly illegal government action and an injury

to some portion of the environment used by the plaintiff. It is not necessary to allege any physical injury to the plaintiff or any economic damage; esthetic injury is enough. To obtain standing, the plaintiff need only demonstrate a "substantial likelihood" that judicial relief directed at the illegal government action would have the effect of reducing the plaintiff's environmental injury. In applying this test, at least in environmental cases, the Court has shown a willingness to tolerate attenuated claims of causation. Thus, while standing is often raised as an issue by the government in environmental cases, the government is rarely successful in having cases dismissed on this basis.

2. REVIEWABILITY

The existence of standing does not mean that the plaintiff will necessarily get a hearing on the merits of his case. Standing involves the relationship between the plaintiff and the issue he seeks to litigate. Although the plaintiff may stand in the proper relationship to an issue, the issue itself may not be suitable for judicial resolution. If anyone could litigate the issue, the plaintiff would be the proper person to do so, but some issues simply cannot be litigated by anyone at all. The question of whether an issue is subject to judicial resolution is called "reviewability."

Fortunately, virtually all issues that might arise in an environmental law case are subject to judicial review. This was made clear by the Supreme Court's decision in Citizens to Preserve Overton Park, Inc. v. Volpe, 401 U.S. 402 (1971). *Overton Park* involved a dispute over the use of federal highway funds to finance the construction of an interstate highway through Overton Park, a 342-acre city park in Memphis. The applicable statute prohibited the Secretary of Transportation from authorizing the use of federal funds to finance the construction of highways through public parks if a "feasible and prudent" alternative route existed. The plaintiffs contended that the Secretary had violated this restriction. The Supreme Court held that the plaintiffs were entitled to judicial review on this issue. The Court found the key to the reviewability problem in section 701 of the Administrative Procedure Act, 5 U.S.C.A. § 701. Section 701 provides that the action of every administrative agency is subject to judicial review except (1) where there is a statutory prohibition on review or (2) where "agency action is committed to agency discretion by law." In order to find the first exception applicable, a court must find "clear and convincing evidence" that Congress intended to restrict access to judicial review. Such evidence is rarely available. The second exception, action "committed to agency discretion", is not easy to understand, inasmuch as even discretionary agency actions can be

[*11*]

reviewed by a court to determine if the agency has abused its discretion. In *Overton Park*, the Court concluded that the "committed to agency discretion" exception is very narrow and applies only where statutes are drawn in such broad terms that in a given case "there is no law to apply." Thus, this exception really applies only in cases in which a statute gives an agency such broad powers, subject to so few restrictions, that a court could not reasonably conclude in any given case that the agency had exceeded its powers. This seems to be another way of saying that judicial review is pointless because we can conclude without considering the specific facts of the case that the agency could not possibly have acted illegally. Thus, holding that a question is "committed to agency discretion" comes very close to a holding on the merits that whatever the agency has done is necessarily lawful. In the specific case before it, the *Overton Park* Court concluded that the decision was not committed to agency discretion because the statute provided specific criteria which the Secretary of Transportation was supposed to apply.

In a few exceptional cases, the issue of reviewability has proved to be troublesome. Generally, these cases have involved statutes which provide either no limitations on administrative action or limitations which are so broad as to be almost nonexistent. Occasionally, administrative action may be held to be unreviewable because it involves some special area in which courts are hesitant to become involved, such as foreign affairs or military decisions. In the typical environmental law case, however, reviewability is unlikely to be a serious issue.

3. STANDARD OF REVIEW

We have seen that the plaintiff in an environmental law case must establish that he has standing and that the issues involved in the case are reviewable. Making this showing gets the plaintiff through the courtroom door. Of course, getting into the courtroom is not an end in itself; it is merely a means of getting a decision on the merits of the case. Thus, for many plaintiffs the important question is not whether a court will be willing to hear the case, but rather what kind of hearing the court will give. In particular, a great deal turns on the degree to which the court is willing to second-guess the administrative agency as opposed to deferring to that agency on the basis of its expertise. The extent of judicial review a plaintiff will obtain generally depends on the kind of issues involved in the case. In particular, it is useful to distinguish between issues relating to pure questions of law, issues relating to the factual basis for the agency's action, and issues relating to the agency's procedures. Courts apply a different level of scrutiny to each of these three kinds of issues.

The first kind of issue involves only questions of law. One of the primary functions of courts is obviously to decide legal issues. In general, courts have at least as much expertise in making these determinations as administrative agencies. Consequently, courts do not feel bound by an administrative agency's interpretation of the law. In deciding the meaning of a statute, courts will consider several factors. The most important factor is the language of the statute. Other evidence of what Congress intended, such as reports of the Congressional committees that considered a bill, are also given a great deal of weight. Courts are also mindful of the need to construe a statute in line with its purposes and with broader considerations of public policies. Finally, although courts by no means feel bound by the views of the administrative agency, those views do receive a respectful hearing.

Several reasons exist for giving some degree of deference to the administrative agency's view of the law. First, in a highly technical area, the agency has had more experience than any particular judge in applying the statute. Second, Congress has given the agency, rather than the court, primary responsibility for carrying out the law. Third, it is often important that private individuals or local governments be able to respond immediately in reliance on an administrative agency's view of the statute. If the agency's view of the statute were given no credence at all by the courts, it would be unsafe to rely on the agency's position until the issue had been litigated all the way to the Supreme Court. Thus, giving deference to the agency's view serves the purpose of expediting compliance with the law. Because of all these factors, courts will generally follow the agency's interpretation of a statute unless they are convinced that the interpretation is unreasonable. In other words, there is some presumption that the agency's view is correct.

The standard of review applied to purely legal issues does not depend on the form of the administrative action. In order to discuss the level of review for procedural or factual issues, however, it is necessary to understand the basics of administrative procedure. What follows is a brief sketch of the various forms of administrative procedure, which should help the reader understand the judicial review process more fully.

Under the Administrative Procedure Act, there are three important categories of administrative actions. The first category consists of adjudications. This form of procedure applies (with some exceptions) whenever the specific statute governing the agency requires an issue to be "determined on the record after opportunity for an agency hearing." The procedures required are essentially similar to those of a judicial trial. The second category of administrative action is rulemaking. With the limited exception of a few situations in which a "formal rulemaking" is required, the procedure is relatively simple. The first step is the publication of a notice in the Federal Register describing the proposed rule. The agency must then allow interested parties an "opportunity to comment" for at least thirty days. Then, the agency must issue, in conjunction with its promulgation of the rule, a "concise general statement" of the rule's basis and purpose. There are a limited number of exceptions to these requirements. The final category of administrative action consists of a vast number of government decisions that neither impose sanctions on individuals, grant licenses to them, nor impose rules governing future conduct.

With respect to factual issues, the standard of review depends on the type of proceeding. In an adjudicative action, the standard for review of factual issues is the "substantial evidence" test. The agency's action must be upheld by the Court unless there is no substantial evidence in the record to support the agency ruling. With respect to other forms of administrative action, the leading authority on review of factual issues is the *Overton Park* decision. In that case, the Court held that the standard of review for non-adjudicative administrative decisions was the "arbitrary and capricious" test. In applying this test, a court must examine the record considered by the administrative agency. On the basis of that record, the court must decide whether the agency considered all of the relevant factors and whether the agency made a clear error of judgment. In practice, this standard of review may involve either a very cursory examination of the administrative action or an intense scrutiny of the reasons given for the administrative decision to determine whether adequate actual support exists in the record. There has been a growing tendency in environmental cases for courts to apply the "arbitrary and capricious" test in a way that closely resembles the application of the "substantial evidence" test. This has become known as the "hard look" approach. Thus, agencies are likely to face intensive judicial scrutiny of their factual determinations. At the same time, of course, courts have not forgotten that many of these determinations involve highly technical matters with which judges have little familiarity. Hence, some tendency still exists toward deference to the agency, but less than one might expect from the phrase "arbitrary and capricious".

Some judges have felt uncomfortable about attempting to assess an agency's technical judgment on factual issues. Feeling more comfortable in assessing procedural issues, some of these judges, led by Judge Bazelon of the D.C. Circuit, imposed procedural requirements on some administrative agencies beyond those contained in the APA. While this approach has some arguable merit, it was rejected by the Supreme Court in Vermont Yankee Nuclear Power Corp. v. NRDC, 435 U.S. 519 (1978), a case involving a rulemaking about nuclear waste disposal. In *Vermont Yankee* the court held that judges lack the authority to impose any additional procedures on agencies beyond those required by statute, the Constitution, or the agency's own rules. The decision leaves open the possibility that in extremely compelling circumstances some additional procedures might be imposed. Fundamentally, the Court's rationale was that the agency itself is in the best position to decide on procedures.

Vermont Yankee has been subject to some sharp criticism. Some scholars such as Professor Nathanson have argued persuasively that the Court misconstrued the original intent of the Administrative Procedure Act. Other scholars such as Professor Davis argue that the lower courts were correct in constructing a "common law" of agency procedure. Whatever criticisms may be made of the Court's opinion, it is clear that *Vermont Yankee* represents the current law on the subject.

Lower courts have found, however, that *Vermont Yankee* does leave them some room for maneuver. One exception to the *Vermont Yan-*

kee rule is that courts may reverse agency actions when the agency has violated statutory procedural requirements. Some lower courts have responded to *Vermont Yankee* by giving an expansive reading to statutes relating to agency procedures. For example, the APA on its face requires only a brief explanation of the agency's rule and an opportunity to comment by outsiders. Several lower courts have held that the opportunity to comment is not "adequate" unless the agency has fully disclosed in advance the technical data which it is considering. In effect, these courts have required an additional procedure on the part of agencies. Although courts applying this rationale have stopped short of requiring agencies to allow oral presentation of testimony or cross-examination, they have required procedures which have been aptly described as involving a "paper hearing." It remains to be seen whether the Supreme Court will approve of these decisions. (In addition, it should be remembered that many individual statutes such as the Clean Air Act contain detailed provisions concerning agency procedures in certain kinds of cases. These provisions often go far beyond the minimum requirements of the APA.)

4. REMEDIES

Once the plaintiff obtains a decision from the court that an agency has violated the law, the

[*19*]

plaintiff is plainly entitled to some form of relief, if only an order directing the agency to give further consideration to the issue before acting. It has sometimes been argued that a court should withhold any remedy from the plaintiff if granting relief would be unreasonable. The Supreme Court has clearly rejected that position. In TVA v. Hill, 437 U.S. 153 (1978) the Court authorized an injunction against the completion of a multi-million dollar dam because the dam would threaten an endangered species of fish known as the snail darter. The Court found that completion of the dam would violate the Endangered Species Act. Having reached this conclusion, the Court held that it had no choice but to issue an injunction against completion of the dam. An enormous amount of money had already been spent on the dam and little work remained to be done, but the Court held that these factors were simply irrelevant. In passing the statute, Congress had weighed the importance of saving an endangered species against other government policies, and had found the policy of saving the endangered species to be paramount. The Court held that it was not its function to reassess a Congressional balancing of these policies.

In a more recent case, Weinberger v. Romero-Barcelo, 102 S.Ct. 1798 (1982), the Court held that a statutory violation need not result in an injunction. The violation in question was the Navy's failure to get a permit under the Clean Water Act before a training exercise. The permit was technically required because ordnance was dropped in the water, but the lower court found that no harm to the coastal waters would in fact result. Under the circumstances, the Court held that ordering the Navy to apply for a permit was a sufficient remedy. *Weinberger* does not seem to change the TVA v. Hill rule that the plaintiff in an environmental case is entitled to *some* remedy, having shown that the agency's action was illegal.

All of the issues we have been discussing are considered in far more depth in an administrative procedure class. The discussion given here, however, should be enough to enable the reader to understand how courts function in environmental law cases.

One restriction on agency action takes the form of judicial review. Each agency is also restricted by the particular statutes governing its activities. In addition, all federal agencies are restricted by a statute known as the National Environmental Policy Act or NEPA. The next section will consider this environmental statute in detail.

B. THE NATIONAL ENVIRONMENTAL POLICY ACT

NEPA imposes environmental responsibilities on all agencies of the federal government. Most of our discussion of NEPA will relate to section 102(2)(c), which concerns the environmental impact statement (EIS). Before turning to the EIS requirement, however, it is worth reviewing some of the other provisions of NEPA.

Section 101 of NEPA makes it the policy of the federal government to use all practicable means to administer federal programs in the most environmentally sound fashion. (Of course, such means must be consistent with other important national policies as well; NEPA does not give the environment greater priority than other national goals.) In furtherance of this purpose, section 102(1) requires that the laws and regulations of the United States be "administered in accordance with the policies set forth in this chapter." Prior to the passage of NEPA, some agencies contended that they lacked the statutory authority to consider environmental issues even if they wanted to do so. For example, the AEC contended that the thermal pollution caused by nuclear power plants was a matter beyond its jurisdiction. One important result of NEPA is to ensure that every agency has the authority to consider the environmental consequences of its actions. Of course, granting agencies the authority to consider the environment does not guarantee that they will actually do so, but it does open the door for those agencies which are willing to take this step.

Section 102(2) contains several provisions that are intended to force agencies to take this step. Subsections (a) and (b) require new agency procedures to ensure that the decisionmaking process takes into account environmental factors. When a proposal involves conflicts between alternative uses of available resources—which is likely to be true of any important government decision—subsection (e) requires the agency to develop alternatives to recommended courses of action. Subsection (f) requires agencies to recognize the worldwide and long-range character of environmental problems. These provisions are an important supplement to the EIS requirement and may provide a basis for judicial intervention where the EIS requirement does not apply. Another important aspect of NEPA was the establishment of the Council on Environmental Quality (CEQ), an advisory group primarily charged with advising the President about environmental matters.

Despite the importance of these other provisions of NEPA, the most significant provision of the statute is undoubtedly section 102(2)(c). The primary purpose of this provision is to force agencies to take environmental factors into consideration when making significant decisions. The crucial language of this subsection reads as follows:

The Congress authorizes and directs that, to the fullest extent possible: . . . (2) all agencies of the federal government shall—

. . .

(c) include in every recommendation or report on proposals for legislation and other major Federal actions significantly affecting the quality of the human environment, a detailed statement by the responsible official on—

(i) the environmental impact of the proposed action,

(ii) any adverse environmental effects which cannot be avoided should the proposal be implemented,

(iii) alternatives to the proposed action,

(iv) the relationship between local short-term uses of man's environment and the maintenance and enhancement of long-term productivity, and

(v) any irreversible and irretrievable commitments of resources which would be involved in the proposed action should it be implemented.

The subsection goes on to require the federal agency to consult other agencies with jurisdiction over or special expertise concerning the environmental problem involved. Copies of the EIS are to be circulated among federal, state and local agencies, to the President, to the CEQ, and to the public. The EIS is also supposed to "accompany the proposal through the existing agency review processes." In essence, the statute requires the agency to prepare a detailed explanation of the environmental consequences of its actions, and to make that report available to higher-level agency officials, other agencies, and the public.

The EIS provision in NEPA makes no reference to judicial enforcement. Indeed, the drafter of the provision apparently did not have such enforcement specifically in mind. Nevertheless, soon after the statute was passed, it became clear that courts would become actively involved in enforcing it. The crucial decision was written by Judge Skelly Wright in Calvert Cliffs' Coordinating Committee, Inc. v. AEC, 449 F.2d 1109 (D.C. Cir.1971). In that opinion Judge Wright made it clear that the statute establishes a "strict standard of compliance." NEPA "mandates a particular sort of careful and informed decisionmaking process and creates judicially enforceable duties. . . . [I]f the [agency] decision was reached procedurally without individualized consideration and balancing of environmental factors—conducted fully and in good faith—it is the responsibility of the courts to reverse." This remains the law today.

With this background in mind, we can turn to a detailed consideration of the EIS requirement. For convenience, we can divide our inquiry into two parts. The first issue to be considered is whether an agency needs to prepare any EIS at all. If the answer is affirmative, it is then necessary to consider the scope, timing and content of the EIS.

1. THRESHOLD REQUIREMENTS

We will begin by discussing the threshold question: is any EIS at all necessary? A reading of the statute indicates that three requirements must be met before an EIS is necessary. The proposed action must (1) be federal, (2) qualify as "major", and (3) have a significant environmental impact. There has been considerable litigation about these requirements.

We can begin our analysis with the first issue. In general, a proposed action is considered "federal" if some federal agency has the power to control the action. Thus, building a new nuclear reactor involves a federal major action because a federal license is required. Sometimes the federal control takes the form of licensing, sometimes of restrictions on funding, and sometimes of direct federal involvement, as in projects constructed by the Army Corp of Engineers. Occasionally, difficult problems arise when an attempt is made to structure a project so as to "defederalize" all or part of it. Nevertheless, in most cases the "federal" requirement poses little problem.

The second requirement, that the project be "major," has proved to pose little problem. Any substantial commitment of resources, whether monetary or otherwise, is enough to qualify a project as "major". Indeed, there is considerable dispute as to whether any project having a significant environmental impact could ever be considered "minor." In any event, neither of the first two requirements poses serious conceptual problems, although there are problems of line-drawing.

The final requirement, "significant environmental impact," is analytically more difficult. It poses two questions. First, what counts as an "environmental" impact? Second, when is such an impact "significant"? There is a temptation to assume that "environmental" refers only to the natural environment (wilderness areas, rivers, beaches, etc.). Nevertheless, the statute itself indicates that Congress had broader concerns. Section 101 of NEPA speaks of the need to assure all Americans "safe, healthful, productive, and esthetically and culturally pleasing surroundings." The same section speaks of the need to preserve the important historical and cultural aspects of our national heritage, to enhance the quality of renewable resources, and to achieve a balance between population and resource use. These goals are not limited to undisturbed natural areas. Judicial decisions confirm that NEPA is not limited to the natural environment. For example, in Hanly v. Mitchell, 460 F.2d 640 (2d Cir.1972), cert. denied, 409 U.S. 990, the Second Circuit held that the construction of a new jail in Manhattan potentially involved significant environmental impact. In addition to air pollution, among the impacts considered were the possibility of increased crime in the area, the esthetic impact of the building, and other socio-economic effects. Given this reading, the scope of NEPA could be virtually unlimited. Almost everything the federal government does has some effect on the quality of life. Yet, the drafters of NEPA presumably did not intend that the government issue an EIS for every foreign policy decision, even though foreign policy decisions presumably do affect the quality of human life.

The problem of defining the meaning of "environmental impact" reached the Supreme Court in *Metropolitan Edison Co. v. People Against Nuclear Energy*, ___ U.S. ___ (1983). The question before the Court was whether the NRC was required to prepare an EIS before allowing Metropolitan Edison to resume operation of one of the reactors at Three Mile Island. The D.C. Circuit held that an EIS was required because the psychological stress caused by reopening the plant would have a significant health effect on the residents of the surrounding communities. The Supreme Court apparently agreed with the lower

[*28*]

court that "effects on human health can be cognizable under NEPA, and that human health may include psychological health." Generally speaking, however, the Court believed that in NEPA "Congress was talking about the physical environment—the world around us, so to speak."

Under *Metropolitan Edison,* an effect qualifies as environmental only if it has a "reasonably close causal relation" to a change in the physical environment. NEPA requires consideration of the direct effects of present physical actions and of the possible effects should future risks materialize. It does not, however, require consideration of the psychological effects that the mere existence of a risk may have before that risk has materialized. Similarly, as the Court pointed out, in cases involving the construction of a new jail or other public facility, "the psychological health damage to neighboring residents resulting from unrealized risks of crime is too far removed from that event [the operation of the facility] to be covered by NEPA." In short, a psychological effect can only qualify as environmental if it is proximately caused by a physical event.

In addition to the problem of deciding what impacts count as being "environmental", there is also the problem of deciding when an environmental impact is sufficiently serious to be considered "significant". Courts have taken various approaches to this problem. The Second Circuit in

Hanly v. Kleindienst, 471 F.2d 823 (2d Cir.1972), cert. denied 412 U.S. 908 (1973), [*Hanly II*] adopted a two-part test involving the degree of change from current land use and the absolute quantity of the impact. Formulations adopted by other courts include "significant degradation of the environment", and "arguably adverse environmental impact", as well as other attempts to paraphrase the statute. In regulations prepared by the CEQ and implemented by President Carter, agencies are instructed to consider factors such as the impact on public health, unique features of the geographic area, the precedential effect of the action, and whether the action is highly controversial. Even after considering these factors, a decision obviously will have to be made about their magnitude. This is a "judgment call" about which very little can be said, except to observe that courts seem to have some tendency to resolve close cases in favor of requiring an impact statement.

Apart from *Metropolitan Edison*, the Supreme Court has made little contribution in this area. It has been confronted with issues relating to NEPA's threshold requirements on only two other occasions. Both involved rather atypical factual situations. The first case, Flint Ridge Development Co. v. Scenic Rivers Association, 426 U.S. 776 (1976), involved a statute requiring certain real estate developers to file a disclosure statement with HUD. The issue before the Court was whether HUD was required to file an EIS. The Court held that no EIS was required because the statutory 30-day deadline applying to HUD was too short to permit preparation of an EIS. Hence, requiring an EIS "would create an irreconcilable and fundamental conflict with the Secretary's duties under the Disclosure Act." The second case, Andrus v. Sierra Club, 442 U.S. 347 (1979), involved the question of whether appropriations requests are covered by NEPA. Although a federal agency's annual appropriation request might seem to be a "proposal for legislation," the Court held, in a decision having little precedential value beyond this particular issue, that no impact statement was required. The only aspect of *Andrus* that appears to have broader significance is the Court's reliance on CEQ regulations. The Court held that these regulations were entitled to "substantial deference". Because the CEQ regulations address the threshold requirements in some detail, *Andrus* may indirectly guide lower courts in resolving these issues by leading them to give more deference to the CEQ regulations. The Supreme Court has otherwise given little guidance in this area.

In close cases, agencies may tend to prepare an EIS, at least if litigation seems likely. The reason is that a decision *not* to prepare an EIS is reviewable under *Overton Park*. Thus, the agency must demonstrate that its decision was not arbitrary or capricious. To do so, it must prepare a detailed explanation of its decision showing why that decision was based on full consideration of all relevant factors. In the *Hanly* litigation, the case was repeatedly remanded for further explanations by the agency. Rather than go through this process, it is often simpler just to go ahead and prepare the EIS.

2.   SCOPE AND TIMING

This brings us to the most important set of issues relating to NEPA. Once an EIS is necessary, *what* must it contain and *when* must it be prepared? As we shall see, although the Supreme Court has not addressed the threshold issues to any significant extent, it has addressed repeatedly the issues relating to the scope and content of the EIS.

Before considering the EIS's *content*, it may be helpful to review briefly the procedure used in preparing an EIS. The CEQ regulations now contain detailed procedural requirements for the entire EIS process. The process begins with an "environmental assessment", which is a brief analysis of the need for an EIS. The environmental assessment must also consider alternatives to the proposed action, as required by section 102(2)(E) of NEPA. If the agency decides not to prepare an EIS, it must make a "finding of no significant impact" available to the public. If the agency does decide to prepare an EIS, the first step in the EIS process is called "scoping". Scoping is intended to obtain early participation by other agencies and the public in planning the EIS, to determine the scope of the EIS, and to determine the significant issues to be discussed in the EIS. The actual preparation of the EIS itself involves a draft EIS, a comment period, and a final EIS. Agencies with jurisdiction or special expertise relating to the project are required to comment. Major inter-agency disagreements are to be referred to CEQ for its recommendation. When an agency reaches a final decision on the project, it must prepare a "record of decision" summarizing its actions and explaining why it rejected environmentally preferable alternatives and mitigation measures.

As reflected by the CEQ regulations, one of the most important issues relating to the content of an EIS is its scope. This is the reason why CEQ included a special stage in the procedure focusing on this issue. Segmentation of a project is one means of evading NEPA. For example, suppose the Department of Transportation planned to fund construction of a highway through an environmentally sensitive area such as a wildlife preserve. If it did not wish to give full consideration to this environmental impact, it might proceed as follows: first, it could prepare an environmental impact statement on the highway segment terminating on one side of the preserve. Since this segment of the highway would not involve any environmentally sensitive areas, the agency would then conclude that that segment was environmentally sound. It could then do the same for the segment terminating near the other side of the preserve. Finally, when it got to the segment involving the preserve it would simply note the obvious fact that millions of dollars spent on the other segments would go to waste unless the segments were connected. Thus, by the time it got around to considering the environmental impact of the final segment, the decision would be a foregone conclusion. At no stage in the process would the agency have really given consideration to the overall environmental costs and countervailing benefits of the project. This would defeat the purpose of NEPA. In order to prevent such evasion of NEPA's purpose, courts must be prepared to determine the proper scope of an EIS. In this hypothetical, for example, a court must have some means of determining whether the scope of the EIS can be restricted to these individual segments, considered one by one, or whether a single EIS must be prepared covering the entire project.

The answer to the scope question posed in the previous paragraph is an obvious one. In many

[*34*]

cases, however, the issue is not nearly so clear-cut. A good example of the kind of problem faced by courts and agencies is provided by the D.C. Circuit decision in Scientists' Institute for Public Information, Inc. v. AEC, 481 F.2d 1079 (D.C.Cir.1973). That case, commonly referred to as the *SIPI* decision, involved the AEC's breeder reactor program. A breeder reactor is a nuclear reactor which not only consumes nuclear fuel but also produces such fuel. In the early 1970s, the government announced a commitment to complete the successful demonstration of a breeder reactor by 1980 and to proceed toward a full-scale development of the program. The expected cost of the program was well over $2 billion. The AEC predicted that by the year 2000 breeder reactor capacity would equal the total generating capacity of the United States in 1973. The AEC conceded that before building any particular breeder reactor plant, it would have to prepare an EIS on that plant. It argued, however, that it was not required to prepare an EIS covering the breeder reactor program as a whole. In an opinion by Judge Skelly Wright, the D.C. Circuit held that an EIS covering the whole program was required. In deciding this issue, the Court looked to two factors. The first was the exent to which meaningful information was presently available on the proposed technology and its alternatives. This factor was relevant because without such meaningful information the EIS itself would be pointless. Second, the Court asked to what extent irretrievable commitments were being made, and other options were being precluded, as the program progressed. This factor was significant because, to the extent that irreversible decisions are being made, it is obviously important to consider their environmental impact now, rather than some years in the future when it is too late to change the decision anyway. Applying these factors to the case before it, the court concluded that the AEC "could have no rational basis for deciding that the time is not yet right for drafting an impact statement." The court noted that by the year 2000, some 600,000 cubic feet of high-level concentrated radioactive wastes would be generated, which would pose an admitted hazard to human health for thousands of years. This and related environmental impacts, according to the court, required "the most searching scrutiny under NEPA." Thus, the D.C. Circuit's approach was functional, looking to the purposes of the EIS rather than to a formalistic test. Because it found that the purposes of NEPA would be served by early preparation of an impact statement covering the entire program, the court ruled that such an impact statement was necessary.

The Supreme Court has taken quite a different approach to the issue of "programmatic" impact statements. The Court has considered two cases involving the scope and timing issues. The first case involved rather unusual facts and attracted little notice at the time. This case was Aberdeen & Rockfish Railroad Co. v. Students Challenging Regulatory Agency Procedures, 422 U.S. 289 (1975) [*Scrap II*], a continuation of the lawsuit which was discussed in connection with the doctrine of standing. After the Supreme Court's standing decision, the case was remanded to the District Court which held that the ICC had failed to comply with NEPA. On appeal, the Supreme Court reversed. In deciding both the scope and the timing of the EIS, the Court used a relatively mechanical test. According to the Court:

. . . under the statute, the time at which the agency must prepare the final "statement" is the time at which it makes a recommendation or report on a *proposal* for federal action. Where an agency initiates federal action by publishing a proposal and then holding hearings on the proposal, the statute would appear to require an impact statement to be included in the proposal and to be considered at the hearing. Here, however, until the October 4, 1972 report, the ICC had made no proposal, recommendation, or report. The only proposal was the proposed new rates filed by the railroads. Thus, the earliest time at which the *statute* required a statement was the time of the ICC's report . . . .

[*37*]

> In order to decide what kind of an environmental impact statement need be prepared, it is necessary first to describe accurately the "federal action" being taken.

> Having defined the scope of the "federal action" being taken . . . our decision of this case becomes easy.

Thus, in *SCRAP*, the Court used a fairly mechanistic test. Under *SCRAP*, the key to determining the scope and timing of the EIS is simply to identify carefully the "proposal" in question. The EIS is due at the same time, and not before, the proposal is issued. Moreover, the scope of the EIS is simply determined by the scope of the proposal itself. It is the scope, impact, and alternatives to *that* proposal that must be discussed, not some broader set of issues.

Despite this relatively clear language in *SCRAP*, it failed to receive careful attention from either federal agencies or the lower federal courts. The reason, is that much of the other language in the Court's opinion seemed more specifically related to the special characteristics of ICC law.

The Supreme Court's next decision on this issue made it clear that *SCRAP* was intended to have a broader effect. That decision, Kleppe v. Sierra Club, 427 U.S. 390 (1976), is the Court's definitive statement on the scope and timing issues

to date. *Kleppe* involved the leasing of coal
reserves on public lands to private mining companies. The Sierra Club alleged that individual
leasing proposals in an area identified as the
"Northern Great Plains region" involved such in-
terrelated environmental effects that a single EIS
was necessary for the entire region. Applying a
further development of the *SIPI* test, the D.C.
Circuit agreed. The Supreme Court made its own
disagreement with the lower court's approach un-
mistakeable. In an opinion by Justice Powell, the
Court faulted the lower court for creating a balancing test to decide the issue rather than looking to the language of the statute. Looking to
the language of the statute, the Supreme Court
found it clear that an EIS is required only if there
has been a report on a formal proposal for major
federal action. On examining the record, the
Court concluded that there was no proposal with
respect to the Northern Great Plains region; instead, there were only proposals for actions of either local or national scope. The Court noted
that an EIS was plainly required both for the local issuance of a lease and for the adoption of a
national coal-leasing program. But, according to
the Court, there was "no evidence in the record
of an action or a proposal for an action of regional scope." Hence, the Court applied the *SCRAP*
test and concluded that no regional EIS was necessary.

Having disposed of the argument adopted by the lower court, the Supreme Court then turned to an additional argument made by the Sierra Club. The Sierra Club had stressed, not the possibility that some proposal on this region was under contemplation, but rather the inter-related environmental impacts of individual mining operations in this region. The Court rejected this argument also. Justice Powell pointed out that this argument could be viewed in two different ways. First, it could be viewed as an attack on the sufficiency of the EISs already prepared by the government on those projects already approved. As such, the Court held that the issue was not properly before them since the case was not brought as a challenge to any particular EIS. Second, the argument could also be viewed as an attack on the decision not to prepare one comprehensive impact statement on all proposed projects in the region. The Court conceded that when several proposals are pending before an agency at the same time, and when those proposals have cumulative or synergistic environmental impacts, their environmental consequences must be considered together. This apparent concession was undermined by two serious qualifications. First, the Court indicated in *dicta* that this consideration could be made as part of the issuance of the individual EIS governing each site. That is, a discussion of the general project could be tacked on to the EIS about each specific mine. Second,

the Court held that judicial review of the syner-
gism issue would have to be based on the arbitrary and capricious standard. So long as the agency does not act arbitrarily in deciding on the
scope of the impact statement, the Court held
that judicial interference was inappropriate. The
Sierra Club was unable to meet this standard.

Two important criticisms can be made of the
Kleppe opinion. First, the opinion indicates little
sympathy with the purposes of NEPA. The
Court exhibits little concern over whether its test
will advance or frustrate the underlying statutory purpose—ensuring that agencies seriously consider environmental factors, not simply prepare
additional paperwork in the course of making a
decision. Under the *Kleppe* Court's view, the
statute seems to require only the preparation of
an additional report at the time a decision is announced, rather than serious consideration by the
agency of the environmental factors discussed in
the report. This seems to substantially under-
mine the purposes of NEPA. The Court's position can best be understood as reflecting a desire
to require the minimum change in agency decisionmaking processes in order to comply with the
statutory language. Thus, the Court seems to
view NEPA as merely a gloss on a general body
of federal administrative law, rather than as reflecting a congressional desire for any radically
new approach by agencies. In part, the Court

[*41*]

seems to have been motivated also by the desire to have a clear, predictable test rather than requiring the kind of case-by-case balancing adopted by the D.C. Circuit.

This brings us to the second major criticism of the Court's opinion. The Court seems to have believed that it was adopting a clear, almost mechanical test. In fact, however, there is no tallismatic significance to the word "proposal". The *SIPI* case is a good illustration. In the course of the development of the breeder reactor project, there were probably dozens and perhaps even hundreds of major memoranda prepared by various agency officials either sketching possible courses of action or attempting to evaluate those courses of action. Some reports are made at higher levels within the agency than others, and some seem to reflect a more definitive disposition of the issues than others. Nevertheless, no bright line divides those memoranda which are merely evaluations of possible courses of action from those which constitute "recommendations or reports on proposals for action," to use the statutory language. Of course, the breeder reactor program involved in *SIPI* is not a routine government program. But even in more ordinary contexts the existence of a "proposal" is often unclear. For example, in a rate case such as that involved in *SCRAP*, the ICC staff often participates in hearings and files briefs much like a party to the proceedings. These constitute recommendations or reports by the staff concerning a proposal, namely the staff's proposed disposition of the case. The Court gives little guidance as to whether these reports should be considered "reports on a proposal" as that phrase is used in the statute. Moreover, it is hard to see how this issue can be decided simply on the basis of labeling. Instead, a court considering this issue must clearly look, as the D.C. Circuit did in *SIPI*, to the functions of the EIS, to the extent to which a preparation of an EIS under these circumstances would be feasible, and to the extent to which such an EIS would be productive. The Supreme Court's attempt to replace this functional analysis with a mechanistic test must ultimately fail because the administrative process is simply too complex to lend itself to such simplistic treatment. This is not to say that the lower court's decision in the *Kleppe* case itself was correct. That opinion went far beyond the earlier decision in *SIPI* and may well have intruded too deeply into the administrative process. But the Supreme Court's cure in this case may have been as bad as the situation it was attempting to remedy.

The CEQ has attempted to clarify both the timing and scope issues. The current regulation defines the term "proposal" as follows:

"Proposal" exists at that stage in the development of an action when an agency subject to the Act has a goal and is actively preparing to make a decision on one or more alternative means of accomplishing that goal and the effects can be meaningfully evaluated.

This definition essentially captures the functional approach used in *SIPI* but restates that test in terms of the Supreme Court's emphasis on the determination of whether a "proposal" exists. Other CEQ regulations make it clear that the EIS should be "prepared early enough so that it can serve practically as an important contribution to the decisionmaking process," not simply "to rationalize or justify decisions already made." The CEQ regulations also require the EIS to consider (a) connected actions which are closely related, (b) actions which may have a cumulative effect with the proposed action under consideration, and (c) similar actions that should be considered together in view of other "reasonably foreseeable or proposed agency action." This seems to reflect an expansion on the *Kleppe* test by requiring agencies to consider other foreseeable actions even if there has been no formal proposal as to those actions. It remains to be seen whether the CEQ regulations, if they remain in effect, will be successful in liberalizing the *Kleppe* approach.

3. CONTENT OF THE EIS

Determining the scope of the EIS essentially decides what the precise subject-matter of the

EIS will be. The next important question, of course, is: what must be said about that subject-matter? In particular, what alternatives and environmental impacts must be discussed?

The leading case on the issue of what alternatives must be included in the EIS is NRDC v. Morton, 458 F.2d 827 (D.C.Cir.1972). This case involved the lease of 80 tracts of submerged land off Eastern Louisiana. These tracts included about 10% of the total leased area. The purpose of the suit was to enjoin sale of oil and gas leases pending compliance with NEPA. The sale was a part of President Nixon's energy program. The plaintiffs attacked the EIS for failing to consider a number of alternative approaches to the energy problem, such as relaxing oil quotas. The plaintiffs argued that the need to discuss such alternatives was especially acute in view of the impact of the project. (The lease area was adjacent to the greatest estuary and marsh area in the United States. It was agreed that if substantial oil pollution resulted from off-shore operations, the result could be serious damage to the biological community in the area.) The D.C. Circuit held that the test in determining which alternatives must be discussed in the EIS is the "rule of reason." The Court also rejected the argument that the Interior Department was only required to discuss alternatives that were within its own jurisdiction. The Court held that the Interior Department must discuss all reasonable alternatives within the jurisdiction of *any* part of the federal government. The court also held that EIS must discuss environmental effects of all the reasonable alternatives. On the other hand, the less likely an alternative is to be implemented, the less need there is to discuss it in detail. Alternatives which are extremely implausible need not be discussed at all. The test for deciding these issues is whether a reasonable person would think that an alternative was sufficiently significant to warrant extended discussion.

This test was endorsed by the Supreme Court in the *Vermont Yankee* case. In addition to the rule-making procedure which is reviewed in another part of the decision, *Vermont Yankee* also involved a challenge to the issuance of a particular license. In attacking the issuance of the license, the plaintiffs had argued that the AEC had failed to adequately discuss energy conservation as an alternative to building new nuclear plants. Applying the "rule of reason" approach, the Supreme Court rejected this argument for several reasons. First, energy conservation had not become an important subject of discussion at the time this particular license was issued. It was only shortly thereafter, with the advent of the energy crisis, that conservation became highlighted. Second, the plaintiffs involved in this aspect of the litigation had failed to participate adequately

[*46*]

in the proceedings before the agency. They had
filed a list of objections to the grant of the license, but only 17 out of 119 of these objections
related to the general topic of energy conservation. This group participated in none of the hearings in the final stage of the proceedings. The
Court stressed that the plaintiffs should have
structured their participation so that it would
alert the agency to their position. This was "especially true when [the plaintiffs] are requesting
the agency to embark upon an exploration of un-
charted territory, as was the question of energy
conservation in the late 60's and early 70's." The
Court also stressed that the deceptively simple
"energy conservation" involves a vast number of
possible actions that might in one way or another
ultimately reduce projected demands for electricity. The plaintiffs had done nothing to specify
which of these alternatives should be considered.
The Court stressed the need for a reasonable approach to the question of inclusion of alternatives:

> Common sense also teaches us that the "de-
> tailed statement of alternatives" cannot be
> found wanting simply because the agency
> failed to include every alternative device and
> thought conceivable by the mind of man. Time
> and resources are simply too limited to hold
> that an impact statement fails because the
> agency failed to ferret out every possible alter-

native, regardless of how uncommon or unknown that alternative may have been at the time the project was approved.

For this reason, the Court adopted the "rule of reason" test promulgated in NRDC v. Morton, supra.

Under the CEQ regulations, one alternative which must always be discussed is the alternative of doing nothing. The momentum of decisionmaking often creates a desire on the part of the agency to take action about a particular problem. Often, however, the most serious alternative to the agency's projected form of action is not some modification in the agency action, but rather a decision to take no action at all. Certainly, given the growing emphasis on deregulation which we have seen in the last few years, we should not presume that government intervention into every problem is always the ideal solution. For this reason, the regulations require that the agency explain why it has not chosen the alternative of "no action".

If the EIS is to be more than a checklist of alternative actions, the consequences of each alternative must be discussed in detail. One frequently litigated issue is whether the discussion of the environmental impact of the alternatives was adequate. In deciding which impacts must be discussed, the test once again is "rule of reason." Speculative impacts need not be discussed. Unfortunately, courts have not done well in deciding what impacts are too speculative to require discussion. For example, in Carolina Environmental Study Group v. United States, 510 F.2d 796 (D.C. Cir.1975), the D.C. Circuit held that the possibility of a Class Nine accident to a nuclear reactor was too unlikely to require discussion in an environmental impact statement. The NRC staff was later to classify the accident at Three Mile Island as a Class Nine accident.

The preceding discussion gives only the general issues likely to arise in an EIS case. Courts are often forced to engage in extensive factual inquiries concerning the agency's evaluation of the seriousness of the various impacts, and its explanations of the countervailing benefits of the project. Agencies often engage in extremely slipshod cost-benefit analysis of their proposals, frequently biasing their results in favor of their projected course of action. Courts have proved capable on a number of occasions of perceiving the unreliability of the agency's analysis and have not hesitated to require the agency to redo its work. Very little can be said in the way of general rules governing the disposition of these issues, because the issues are generally tied to the specific facts of each individual case.

4.   REVIEW ON THE MERITS

Thus far, we have been concerned with the contents and necessity for an EIS. The reader may well be asking a question which goes beyond the EIS itself: what happens if the EIS is perfect, the project is clearly an environmental disaster, and the agency decides to go ahead anyway? That is, is NEPA only a procedural requirement imposing additional paperwork on agencies, or does it also impose substantive limits on agency decisions? The courts of appeals are split on this issue. The majority view is apparently that NEPA does impose substantive limits on agencies and that agency action is subject to judicial review if it transgresses these limits. However, except for the Second Circuit's decision reversed by the Supreme Court in Strycker's Bay Neighborhood Council, Inc. v. Karlen, 444 U.S. 223 (1980), no court of appeals has actually overturned an agency for violating NEPA's substantive limits. *Strycker's Bay* involved construction of a housing project in a middle income area. The Second Circuit held that the agency's choice of site was unjustifiable. According to the Second Circuit, when the agency considers such projects, "environmental factors such as crowding low-income housing into a concentrated area, should be given determinative weight." The Supreme Court summarily reversed the Second Circuit decision. The Court stated that:

[I]n the present case there is no doubt that [the agency] considered the environmental consequences of its decision to redesignate the proposed site for low-income housing. NEPA requires no more.

This statement by the Court could well be read as a holding that NEPA imposes no substantive duties on agencies, or at least that violation of such duties is not subject to judicial review. In an important footnote, however, the Court made it clear that it was not going as far as the previous quotation might indicate:

If we could agree with the dissent that the Court of Appeals held [the agency] had acted "arbitrarily" . . . we might also agree that plenary review is warranted. But the District Court expressly concluded that [the agency] had not acted arbitrarily or capriciously and our reading of the opinion of the Court of Appeals satisfies us that it did not overturn that finding. Instead, the Appellate Court required [the agency] to elevate environmental concerns over other, admittedly legitimate, considerations. Neither NEPA nor the APA provides any support for such a reordering of priorities by review in court.

This footnote in the decision clearly suggests that review on the "arbitrary and capricious" standard is available in NEPA cases. This conclusion appears to be correct. The policy sections of NEPA do impose substantive duties on agencies and no apparent reason exists why violation of these duties should not be reviewable under *Overton Park.* Even though those duties may be vague, they do not appear to be so vague as to leave "no law to apply", which is the *Overton Park* test for reviewability. Thus, it appears that violation of NEPA's substantive policies would be subject to judicial review.

One reason why no court has ultimately found it necessary to reverse an agency on this basis (except for the Second Circuit's ill-fated decision in *Strycker's Bay*) is that courts can readily avoid making an express holding on this basis. If the court is convinced that an agency has seriously erred in its decision, rather than expressly reversing the agency on the merits of its decision, it is easier to simply hold the EIS inadequate. This course of action is less offensive to the agency and also less likely to draw a reversal from a higher court.

5.   EVALUATION OF NEPA

We have not yet dealt with one important question about NEPA, the question of whether NEPA has served a useful purpose. There seems to be no objective way of answering this question, and opinions by experts differ. Very few, if any, federal projects have actually been halted by permanent injunctions based on NEPA. A 1978 survey

by CEQ found that of 938 projects involved in
NEPA litigation, none was permanently halted by
a NEPA-related injunction. Roughly one-tenth of
the projects were delayed for periods of a year or
more. Roughly six percent of the projects were
halted at some point after initiation of the NEPA
litigation, most often because either a local agency or a federal agency decided to withdraw from
the project. It is unclear to what extent the decisions to withdraw from projects resulted from
the delays caused by the NEPA litigation. It is
also impossible to know the extent to which agencies have refrained from taking controversial actions because of the desire to avoid the expense
and delay of NEPA litigation. At least some environmentally unjustifiable projects surely have
either been abandoned or never begun because of
NEPA. In addition, a number of other projects
have been modified to reduce their environmental
impact. The unanswered question is whether the
benefits thus attained are sufficient to justify the
expense and delay created in all those instances
in which the project ultimately proceeds.

It may be useful at this point to summarize
briefly the discussion of NEPA. As we have
seen, NEPA requires an EIS when an agency has
made a report on a proposal for a major federal
action with a substantial environmental impact.
In deciding whether any EIS is required, the most
difficult question to answer has been whether

[*53*]

there will be a substantial environmental impact. Once it has been concluded that an EIS is required, the next question is the scope of the EIS. The Supreme Court has made it clear that the answer to this question is to be found by determining the precise scope of the agency "proposal" which is under consideration. The alternatives to that proposal and the environmental impact of the proposal must be discussed in detail. In deciding which alternatives and which environmental impacts must be discussed, the applicable test is the "rule of reason." Finally, although the Supreme Court has not decided the issue, it appears that agency action is reviewable under the "arbitrary and capricious" test to determine if the agency has abused its discretion in applying NEPA's substantive policies.

CHAPTER 2

POLLUTION CONTROL

In his classic article, "The Tragedy of the Commons," Garrett Hardin poses the problem of a common pasture open to all. Even as the numbers of cattle begin to exceed the carrying capacity of the land, each herdsman perceives that continuing to increase the size of his own herd is to his net benefit. To him, the marginal utility of adding one more animal always seems positive, since he receives all the sale proceeds or other benefits from the animal while most of the costs of overgrazing are borne by other herdsmen. Since they all act in the same way, freedom in the commons brings ruin to all. While land is protected as a source of food and minerals by allocating ownership among individuals as private property, protection of the remaining commons from waste discharges cannot be managed so handily: unlike land, the air and waters cannot readily be fenced.

The economic reason why society may not strike a proper balance between economic output and the quality of the environment is that the costs of many kinds of pollution are borne not by the polluters but by somebody else. As a result, these "externalized" costs will not, in general, be taken fully into account by those who cause pollution. Because there is not enough incentive to reduce the amount of pollution per unit of production of the goods and services responsible, insufficient resources and effort are devoted to this objective. Insofar as pollution costs are not borne by those who cause pollution, or by the purchasers of their products, some of the total welfare resulting from the economic activity of the community is redistributed away from the victims of pollution in favor of other groups in the society. Further, to the extent that the total costs of pollution exceed the benefits to producers and their customers, production is not "efficient", that is, total wealth (without regard for its distribution) is not maximized.

An example of economic activity which confers external *benefits* is the renovation of a deteriorated building, with resultant upgrading of aesthetic and property values for nearby landowners. Because the neighbors rarely pay for these benefits, they (the benefits), like external costs, usually are not reflected in the producer's profits or losses. Closely related to the concept of external benefits is that of collective or public goods, commodities which cannot readily be supplied to one person without also enabling many other persons to enjoy them. Examples are national defense and the clean air "produced" by installing emission control equipment at large power plants or on all motor vehicles. Consumption of such goods is collective, and within limits enjoyment by any one person does not diminish the enjoyment available to others. The nonexcludability which characterizes collective goods tends to cause them to be underproduced by the market system, even though their value to all consumers may substantially exceed the production costs.

Because the free market does not provide adequate incentives, government must intervene to limit external costs and facilitate production of external benefits and collective goods. The basic approaches available include the following:

Property Rights. In the case of pollution, the common law doctrine of nuisance offers the remedies of damages and injunctions to injured landowners. Implicitly applying principles of economic efficiency, courts often deny injunctions when the resulting losses to polluters would greatly exceed the benefits to their victims. Manipulating property rights to encourage production of collective goods other than a less polluted environment is less feasible because of the difficulty of excluding freeloaders from enjoying the same benefits as paying customers. In most cases, therefore, government resorts to the other approaches described below or provides the goods itself, using tax revenues.

Direct Regulation. Beyond the recognition of private property rights, the principal method adopted by government to control pollution has been to prohibit emissions beyond prescribed limits. When the method of enforcement is imposition of financial penalties, rather than injunctions or jail sentences, the boundary between direct regulation and the last method below becomes blurred.

Subsidies. Another approach, frequently used in combination with direct regulation, is for government to pay some or all of the costs of private activities which avoid external costs or produce collective goods. Examples are tax incentives—special deductions and credits—for installation of pollution control equipment, and federal grants to municipalities for construction of waste treatment facilities.

Charges. In lieu of or in addition to the foregoing approaches, government can require payment of penalties or fees for private activities which generate external costs or fail to provide collective goods. Relating the amounts of such charges to the estimated costs (to the producer) or benefits (to the public) of avoiding the undesired results can create a simulated market incentive for the producer to alter his activities.

The following sections discuss methods and problems of controlling pollution through application of nuisance law, by regulation under the federal Clean Air and Clean Water Acts, and through creation of economic incentives. Special emphasis is given to the consideration of economic and technological feasibility in a regulatory system.

A. COMMON LAW REMEDIES

The facts in Boomer v. Atlantic Cement Co., 26 N.Y.2d 219, 309 N.Y.S.2d 312, 257 N.E.2d 870 (1970), present a classic common law nuisance. Defendant operated a large cement plant, and neighboring landowners incurred property damages from dirt, smoke and vibration emanating from the plant. The neighbors sought an injunction against continuation of the polluting activities, and compensatory damages for injuries already suffered. The court found that the total damages to plaintiffs' properties were relatively small in comparison with the value of defendant's plant, and that to enjoin further pollution would have the effect of forcing closure of the plant, which already employed the best pollution abatement technology available. In this kind of situation it long has been common among most state courts to "balance the equities" and deny injunctions on the ground that the hardships which they would impose upon defendants are relatively greater than the hardships to be suffered by plaintiffs left to their damage remedies. In New York, however, there was a line of cases holding that where a nuisance was found and any substantial damage was shown by the plaintiff, an injunction would be granted notwithstanding any disparity in economic consequences between the effect of the injunction and the effect of the nuisance. In *Boomer* that rule finally was disavowed. The court considered granting the injunction but postponing its effect to a specified future date to give defendant an opportunity to develop new technical means to eliminate the nuisance. That course of action was rejected, however, because the court was uncertain of defendant's ability to achieve such advances and believed that, realistically, such advances were the responsibility not of one company but rather of the entire cement industry. More importantly, the New York court deviated from the usual path of awarding compensatory damages for past injuries and leaving plaintiffs free to sue again for future injuries. Instead, the court ordered that the injunction be issued unless defendant paid permanent damages to plaintiffs which would compensate them for the total economic loss to their properties, present and future, caused by defendant's operations. A dissenting judge said that the decision was, in effect, "licensing a continuing wrong [by] saying to the cement company, you may continue to do harm to your neighbors so long as you pay a fee for it." Once permanent damages were paid, the incentive to alleviate the wrong would be eliminated. The dissenter likened the result to conferring the power of eminent domain—the power to condemn an easement—upon a private corporation, to be used for private gain rather than for public use.

The courts' tendency to balance hardships and deny injunctions is not the only factor which has made nuisance law inadequate to control widespread pollution. Another is lack of "standing" to sue. The common law distinguished "public" and "private" nuisances. A public nuisance was one which damaged a large number of persons. Only the attorney general or local prosecutor was permitted to sue to abate a public nuisance, unless a private individual could show "special" damage, distinct from and more severe than that of the public generally. Elected officials frequently were hesitant to seek injunctions which might shut down major industries. Only if a private plaintiff could show special damage, or that damage was limited to him or a small number of persons (thus making the nuisance private rather than public), was he recognized by the courts as having "standing" to seek injunctive relief. While some states today have constitutional or statutory provisions which allow private citizens to sue to abate public nuisances, lack of standing remains a problem elsewhere. Still another difficulty, in all states, can be the burden of proving material harm attributable to unreasonable conduct of defendants. Frequently the receiving air or water receives effluents from many sources,

[*61*]

none of which by itself would produce the alleged damage. It may be impossible to prove any particular polluter responsible for the poor air or water quality. Also, attempts to join multiple defendants and to allocate damages among them can pose difficult procedural problems. Finally, nuisance law simply fails to provide a systematic mechanism for supervising pollutant discharges into the ambient air and water. Just as the common law has had to be supplemented in most communities by land use planning and zoning, so it has had to be supplemented by legislative intervention in the area of pollution control.

Nevertheless, in some situations—especially those in which there is a single polluter and the balance of hardships favors plaintiffs—nuisance law remains a useful tool. An interesting case is Spur Industries v. Del E. Webb Development Co., 108 Ariz. 178, 494 P.2d 700 (1972). In 1957 Del Webb had begun construction of a retirement community called Sun City, west of Phoenix. By 1967 the development had moved close to Spur's feedlot, which had been in operation for several years before Webb came into the area. Webb complained that the Spur feeding operation was a nuisance because of the flies and the odor which spilled over into parts of Sun City. Some residents were unable to enjoy the outdoor living which Webb had advertised, and Webb was faced with sales resistance from prospective purchas-

[*62*]

ers. The court found that as to citizens of Sun
City, Spur's feedlot was both a public and a private nuisance. Webb, having shown a special injury in the loss of sales, was found to have standing to bring suit to enjoin the nuisance. The
court stated that if Webb were the only party injured, it would feel justified in holding that the
doctrine of "coming to the nuisance" barred relief. In Arizona and some other states, the
courts have held that residential landowners
could not have relief after knowingly coming into
areas with industrial or agricultural uses which
caused conditions viewed as unpleasant by the
residents. In *Spur* the court found that Webb
was entitled to injunctive relief because of the
damage to people who had purchased homes in
Sun City. However, the court also concluded
that Webb should not be free of liability to Spur
because Webb was the cause of damage sustained by Spur. The court therefore required
that Webb, having brought people to the nuisance
to the foreseeable detriment of Spur, should in-
demnify Spur for a reasonable amount of the cost
of moving or shutting down, as a condition to obtaining the injunction.

A *federal* common law of nuisance has been developed and applied by federal courts in cases of
interstate air and water pollution. Thus, in Georgia v. Tennessee Copper Co., 206 U.S. 230 (1907),
the State of Georgia obtained an injunction

against a Tennessee company whose noxious gases were causing wholesale destruction of forests, orchards and crops in Georgia. However, in Milwaukee v. Illinois and Michigan, 451 U.S. 304 (1981), a case in which a Wisconsin city's discharges of untreated sewage into Lake Michigan were affecting recreation and water supplies in Illinois, the Supreme Court held that the comprehensive regulatory system established by the federal Clean Water Act had completely *preempted* federal common law applicable to interstate water pollution. If that is so, it seems likely that the Clean Air Act eventually will be held to have displaced the federal common law pertaining to interstate air pollution.

The decision in Milwaukee v. Illinois is open to serious question. The Clean Water Act expressly provides that it does not preempt more stringent state law, presumably including state common law. Therefore, Illinois may remain free to sue Milwaukee in the Illinois or federal courts for creating a nuisance under Illinois common law. That prospect seems less desirable than recognizing a federal common law of interstate pollution.

B. REGULATION UNDER THE CLEAN AIR ACT

Five main classes of pollutants are emitted into our air by a variety of sources. *Carbon monoxide* (CO) is a colorless, odorless, poisonous gas, slightly lighter than air, that is produced by the incomplete burning of carbon in fuels. The majority comes from internal combustion engines, mostly in motor vehicles. *Particulates* are particles of solid or liquid substances in a wide range of sizes, produced primarily by stationary fuel combustion and industrial processes. Techniques for controlling particulates include filtering, washing, centrifugal separation, and electrostatic precipitation. These work well for most of the particles, but complete removal, especially of the very finest particles, is technically and economically difficult. *Sulfur oxides* (SO_x) are acrid, corrosive, poisonous gases produced when fuel containing sulfur is burned. Electric utilities and industrial plants are its principal producers. *Nitrogen oxides* (NO_x) are produced when fuel is burned at very high temperatures. The principal sources are stationary combustion plants and transportation vehicles. Sulfur dioxide and nitric oxides, after being emitted into the atmosphere, can be chemically converted by oxidation into sulfates and nitrates, which may return to the earth as components of rain or snow, known as acid precipitation. *Hydrocarbons* (HC), like carbon monoxide, represent unburned and wasted fuel. Unlike carbon monoxide, gaseous hydrocarbons at concentrations normally found in the atmosphere are not toxic; but they are a major pollutant because under the influence of sunlight they combine with NO_x to form photochemical ox-

[*65*]

idants, or smog, a complex mixture of secondary pollutants including ozone (an unstable, toxic form of oxygen), nitrogen dioxide, peroxyacyl nitrates, aldehydes, and acrolein. In air they can cause eye and lung irritation, damage to vegetation, offensive odor, and thick haze.

The most important effect of air pollution is its threat to human health. Occasionally there are acute episodes marked by dramatic increases in death and illness rates, especially among the elderly and those with preexisting respiratory or cardiac conditions. However, of much greater significance for the total population are the subtle, long range effects on human health of exposure to low level, long-lasting pollution. Such pollution contributes to the incidence of such chronic diseases as emphysema, bronchitis and other respiratory ailments, and has been linked to higher mortality rates from other causes such as cancer and arteriosclerotic heart disease. Smokers living in polluted cities have a much higher rate of lung cancer than smokers in rural areas.

Public regulation is made more difficult by the fact that overall health effects of air pollution on diverse human populations are not known to possess meaningful "thresholds" or "safe" levels. For example, there is no scientific way to demonstrate that exposure to a pollutant in a concentration of one hundred parts per million for twenty-four hours is "safe" while exposures above that level are "dangerous." It is not even possible to establish that effects of exposure become rapidly more serious at or near some particular exposure level. At best, we may find an exposure level at which no experiments have yet demonstrated adverse effects, and slightly above which only slight effects have been observed.

1. STRUCTURE OF THE CLEAN AIR ACT

Beginning in 1955, Congress responded to the problem of air pollution by offering technical and financial assistance to states. Amendments in the 1960s authorized federal agencies to expand their research efforts, to intervene directly to abate *interstate* pollution in limited circumstances, to control emissions from new motor vehicles, and to exercise certain powers of supervision and enforcement of state controls. When by the end of the decade states had made little progress, Congress enacted the Clean Air Amendments of 1970. These amendments sharply increased federal authority and responsibility. For example, section 111 of the amended Act provided for uniform national standards of performance for "new" stationary sources of air pollution. ("New" sources included preexisting sources subsequently "modified" by any physical change, or change in the method of operation, which increased emissions of any pollutant.) Similarly section 112 provided for uniform national emission standards for "hazardous" air pollutants likely to cause an increase in mortality or in serious irreversible, or incapacitating reversible, illness. Nevertheless, section 107(a) still provided that each state "shall have the primary responsibility for assuring air quality within the entire geographic area comprising such state." But states no longer were given a choice as to whether they would meet this responsibility. For the first time they were required to attain air quality of specified standards, within a specified period of time.

The United States Environmental Protection Agency (EPA) also was created in 1970, by executive order of President Nixon combining preexisting units from various federal departments. Section 109 of the Clean Air Act directed the EPA Administrator to establish national ambient air quality standards (NAAQSs) for air polluants which endanger public health or welfare. For each pollutant there were to be two types of standards: "primary" standards which in the judgment of the Administrator, "allowing an adequate margin of safety, are requisite to protect the public health"; and "secondary" standards, those which in his judgment were "requisite to protect the public welfare [structures, crops, animals, fabrics, etc.] from any known or anticipated adverse effect associated with the presence of such air pollutant in the ambient air." Within nine months after promulgation of an NAAQS, each state was required to submit to EPA a plan designed to implement and maintain that standard within its boundaries. Section 110(a)(1). EPA, in turn, was required to approve a state implementation plan (SIP) if it had been adopted after public hearings and satisfied the conditions specified in section 110(a)(2). The most important condition was that the SIP provide for attainment of primary NAAQSs "as expeditiously as practicable but . . . in no case later than three years from the date of the approval of such plan." Secondary standards were to be achieved within "a reasonable time." A SIP had to include "emission limitations, schedules, and timetables for compliance with such limitations," as well as assurances that appropriate state agencies will have the necessary legal authority and resources to enforce the plan. Once a state plan was approved by the Administrator, it was enforceable not only as state law but also as federal law under section 113. If a proposed state SIP was found by EPA to be inadequate to attain any NAAQS in all or any region of the state, and if the state failed to make adequate amendments, section 110(c)(1) directed the Administrator himself to issue amendments which would be binding on the state.

The EPA Administrator established NAAQSs for carbon monoxide, particulates, sulfur dioxide, nitrogen dioxide, hydrocarbons, ozone, and lead.

Initially, the NAAQSs were the driving force behind EPA's control strategy, since all emissions contributing to violation of the standards were to be eliminated by 1975–1977. This did not happen, however, and the Act has been amended to extend the deadlines, thereby reducing the "absolute" nature of the standards. In 1982 EPA rescinded the hydrocarbon standard on the ground that it was unnecessary, but the remaining NAAQSs continue to play an important role in air pollution policy. Different abatement requirements apply with respect to construction of "major" new stationary sources and to mandatory periodic inspection and maintenance of motor vehicles, depending upon whether a region is an "attainment" (clean) or "nonattainment" (dirty) area. In some cases the EPA approved or promulgated SIP provisions which for economic or political reasons were unlikely to be enforced, such as an EPA-imposed requirement which would have reduced automobile traffic in Los Angeles by seventy to eighty percent in 1975. After various amendments to the Act, the states and EPA settled into a process of negotiations with individual sources regarding emission limitations and compliance schedules.

As the foregoing indicates, the basic approach of the 1970 Clean Air Act with respect to "existing" stationary sources and motor vehicles in use was that EPA would establish uniform

NAAQSs and the states would adopt emission standards necessary to attain the NAAQSs by the statutory deadlines. However, with respect to new vehicles, new stationary sources, and hazardous air pollutants from either new or existing stationary sources, EPA was required to establish nationally uniform emission standards. For new motor vehicles, the aim was to reduce 1970 emission levels by 90 percent by 1975; however, the Act was amended in 1974 and 1977, extending the deadline to 1983-model vehicles. New source performance standards (NSPSs) for stationary sources were to reflect best available control technology, taking into account the costs of compliance. Originally, the NSPSs specified how many pounds of a pollutant could be emitted per unit of plant input or output, leaving it to each source to decide what combination of technological measures and fuel changes to use. However, as amended in 1977, section 111 directs EPA to take a new approach to setting NSPSs for three pollutants from combustion of fossil fuels—sulfur dioxide, nitrogen dioxide, and particulates. Now emissions are to be reduced by a specified *percentage* below what they would be in the absence of technological control measures, *regardless* of the type of fuel burned. (The political intent of these amendments was not only to reduce total pollutant emissions but also to reduce the economic incentive for eastern industries to use low sulfur western coal instead of high sulfur

[*71*]

eastern coal.) With respect to hazardous air pollutants, section 112 requires that EPA establish
emission standards with "an ample margin of
safety to protect public health." There is no provision for consideration of the economic costs or
technological feasibility of such standards, except
that the President may exempt a source from
compliance for up to two years if he finds that
technology to implement the standards is not
available and that operation of the source is required for reasons of national security.

For geographic areas in which ambient pollutant levels are substantially below those prescribed by NAAQSs, the 1977 amendments asserted a congressional commitment to the
principle of prevention of significant deterioration
(PSD). Each region in the country which com-
plies with the NAAQSs is put into one of three
classes. Large national parks and wilderness areas are Class I areas, where very little deterioration of air quality (defined in terms of increments
in ambient concentrations) is allowed. All other
areas are Class II, where moderate increases in
ambient concentrations are allowed (but not to
exceed NAAQSs). A governor may reclassify a
Class II area in his state as Class I, or as Class
III (where larger increments are allowed, usually
to permit industrial development) so long as no
violation of any NAAQS will result. To establish
a "major" new source in any PSD area, the own-

[*72*]

er must apply for a permit. He must demonstrate that the emissions will not cause any violations of the ambient concentration increments allowed, and he must agree to apply "best available control technology" for *all* pollutants, whether or not that is necessary to avoid exceeding the allowable increments.

The problem of interstate transport of air pollutants is addressed by sections 110(a)(2)(E) and 126 of the Act. The former requires that each SIP contain provisions prohibiting any stationary source within the state from emitting pollutants in amounts which will (i) prevent attainment or maintenance of any NAAQS by another state or (ii) interfere with another state's PSD program. Section 126 sets forth a procedure for a downwind state to obtain an EPA determination that a violation of section 110(a)(2)(E) exists or is threatened, and should be stopped or prevented.

The following section focuses on probably the most important factor, economically and politically, in implementing the Clean Air Act: the extent to which the feasibility of compliance is considered in establishing and enforcing limits on pollutant emissions by individual sources. Different categories of sources and pollutants recognized by the Act are discussed in separate subsections.

2.   CONSIDERATION OF ECONOMIC AND TECHNOLOGICAL FEASIBILITY

In establishing national ambient air quality standards, the EPA Administrator is not permitted to consider the feasibility of attaining them. Under section 109 of the Act, NAAQSs are to be fixed at levels necessary to protect the public health (with an "adequate margin of safety") and public welfare. If the Administrator bases primary standards upon evidence providing a rational basis for his determination that they are necessary to protect the health of substantial numbers of people (including the most sensitive segments of the population, such as the elderly and persons with respiratory diseases), the standards will not be overturned judicially. Lead Industries Association, Inc. v. EPA, 647 F.2d 1130 (D.C.Cir.1980), cert. denied 449 U.S. 1042.

However, in fixing emission standards and timetables applicable to various pollution sources and pollutants, the Administrator in some cases is required to consider economic and technological difficulties of compliance.

a.   New Motor Vehicles

Section 202(b) of the 1970 Clean Air Act provided that, beginning with the 1975 model year, exhaust emissions of hydrocarbons and carbon mon-

[74]

oxide from "light duty vehicles" must be reduced
at least ninety percent from the permissible emission levels in the 1970 model year. As noted by
Judge Leventhal in International Harvester Co. v.
Ruckelshaus, 478 F.2d 615 (D.C.Cir.1973), Congress was aware that these standards were
"drastic medicine," designed to "force the state
of the art." Because there was concern whether
manufacturers would be able to comply, Congress provided a "realistic escape hatch"; the
automakers could petition EPA for a one year
suspension of the 1975 requirements. The Administrator was authorized to grant the suspension only if he determined, among other things,
that the applicant had established that "effective
control technology, processes, operating methods,
or other alternatives are not available or have not
been available for a sufficient period of time" to
achieve timely compliance. In 1972, International
Harvester, Ford, Chrysler, General Motors and
Volvo applied for suspensions. The Administrator denied the applications on the ground that he
could not make the required finding that technology was unavailable. Although in actual tests no
car had conformed to the standard, the Administrator "adjusted" the auto companies' test data
by use of several critical assumptions and predicted that technology allowing compliance would be
available by the 1975 model year.

The court in *International Harvester* agreed
with EPA that the proper question was whether

technology would be available for 1975 models, not whether it was available in 1972 when the manufacturers applied for suspensions.   However- er, the court declined to affirm the Administra- tor's determination that technology would permit compliance without the one year suspension.   In support of its decision to remand the matter for further consideration, the court cited the "unex- plained assumptions" of the Administrator, the "absence of an indication of the statistical relia- bility" of his prediction that technology would be available by the 1975 model year, and the "eco- nomic and ecological risks inherent in a 'wrong decision'."   Rather than an enforced shutdown of one or more auto companies, the court saw the realistic risks of an erroneous prediction by the Administrator to be a last-minute Congressional or administrative forgiveness of noncompliance, with a resulting competitive disadvantage for companies able to comply because their vehicles would cost more and be less fuel efficient.   On the other hand, the court believed that the envi- ronmental risks of granting an unnecessary sus- pension were small, especially in light of the Ad- ministrator's authority to prescribe special interim emission standards for 1975 model vehi- cles.   Considering the entire record, including the risks of a mistaken denial of suspension, the court concluded that the Administrator had not sustained the burden of adducing a reasoned presentation supporting the reliability of his methodology for predicting the availability of technology. In so holding, the court seems to have ignored the statutory provision placing the burden of proof regarding technological availability on the industry rather than on EPA.

Following the court's decision, the Administrator granted the extension and imposed interim standards more lenient than the ninety percent reduction. In 1974 Congress amended the Act to postpone the final compliance deadline until 1977, with another "escape hatch" to 1978; in 1975 the Administrator granted the further suspension. The Act subsequently was amended again and presently provides for waivers of compliance, which the Administrator has granted, until model year 1983. 42 U.S.C.A. § 7521(b)(5)(A).

b. *Existing Stationary Sources*

Emission standards applicable to preexisting stationary sources appear in state implementation plans (SIPs). Usually the standards are set in administrative regulations adopted by state environmental agencies. For "nonattainment" areas, in which pollutant concentrations exceed NAAQSs, section 172 of the Act requires, at a minimum, that SIPs impose "reasonably available control technology" (RACT) on existing sources. If the EPA Administrator determines that the state standards are not sufficiently stringent to attain primary NAAQSs "as expeditiously as practicable" (but not later than three years after his approval of the SIP), or to attain secondary NAAQSs within a "reasonable time," under section 110 he is to issue amendments which will assure timely attainment. The fact that compliance may be difficult or even impossible for some sources does not excuse promulgation of such standards.

The Act does not preclude a state from adopting an implementation plan which will exceed national ambient standards, i.e., will produce ambient air even cleaner than that mandated by NAAQSs. In Union Electric Co. v. EPA, 427 U.S. 246 (1976), rehearing denied 429 U.S. 873, an electric utility company petitioned EPA to disapprove SO_2 emission limitations in Missouri's SIP on the ground that compliance by the company's coal-fired generating plants in St. Louis was economically and technologically infeasible. Union Electric argued that a state plan which proceeds more rapidly than economics and available technology appear to allow should be rejected under section 110 as not "practicable" or "reasonable." A state can not, the company argued, engage in technology forcing on its own. However, the Court upheld EPA's position, agreeing that Congress intended claims of economic and technological infeasibility to be wholly foreign to the Administrator's consideration and approval of a SIP.

[*78*]

Union Electric does not mean that claims of infeasibility are never relevant, or that all sources unable to comply with generally applicable emission limitations must be shut down. As the Court pointed out, the most important forum for consideration of claims of infeasibility is the state agency which initially formulates the SIP. So long as NAAQSs will be met, the state generally may select any mix of controls which it desires for existing stationary sources (subject, since 1977, to the RACT requirement in nonattainment areas), and industries with particular economic or technological problems may seek special treatment in the plan. Moreover, if an industry is not accommodated by the plan's emission limitations, individual plants within the industry may be able to obtain hardship variances. Further, if denied variances, the sources may be able to assert their claims of infeasibility in the state courts. In Illinois, for example, the courts have invalidated both statewide emission limitations and individual enforcement orders because the agency which establishes limitations and determines violations thereof failed to sufficiently "take into account" the "technical feasibility and economic reasonableness" of compliance, as required by the Illinois Environmental Protection Act. Commonwealth Edison Co. v. Pollution Control Board, 62 Ill.2d 494, 343 N.E.2d 459 (1976); Wells Manufacturing Co. v. Pollution Control

Board, 73 Ill.2d 226, 22 Ill.Dec. 672, 383 N.E.2d 148 (1978).

An exception to a state's usual freedom to select any mix of controls which will result in attainment of NAAQSs is the requirement that the ambient standards be met by "continuous" emission limitations where possible, and that "intermittent" and "dispersion" techniques be used only if continuous controls are not economically or technologically feasible. Section 110(a)(2)(B) requires that each SIP include "emission limitations, schedules, and timetables for compliance with such limitations, and such other measures as may be necessary to insure attainment and maintenance" of NAAQSs. In Kennecott Copper Corp. v. Train, 526 F.2d 1149 (9th Cir.1975), cert. denied 425 U.S. 935 (1976), Nevada's SIP required that Kennecott's smelter achieve a 60 percent reduction of SO_2 emissions by installation of a plant to convert SO_2 to sulfuric acid, i.e., by continuous controls. Further emission reductions, required when weather conditions threatened maintenance of the ambient standard, were to be achieved by reducing temporarily the level of production at the smelter, i.e., by intermittent controls. EPA rejected the Nevada plan on the ground that an 86 percent reduction of SO_2 emissions was required to achieve the NAAQS, and that noncontinuous controls (including also use of a tall stack, i.e., a dispersion technique) were accept-

[*80*]

able only after Kennecott employed continuous controls to the limit of economic and technological feasibility. Kennecott sought judicial review of the EPA ruling, contending that the agency was not authorized to require continuous emission reduction techniques in preference to intermittent controls or dispersion methods, and that EPA must approve a SIP that provided for attainment of the SO_2 NAAQS by any combination of controls. Citing both the policy of nondegradation, which courts had held was implied in the pre-1977 Clean Air Act, and certain actions of Congress in 1974 indicating approval of the EPA's position in *Kennecott*, the court held that the phrase "as may be necessary" in section 110(a)(2)(B) modified only "such other measures", and not "emission limitations." Thus, noncontinuous emission limitations were appropriate only when continuous controls were infeasible. The court said that the reliability and enforceability of intermittent control systems was questionable, since they may not be implemented when needed; and that dispersion techniques do not reduce emissions but only spread out the pollution, threatening other clean air areas.

Section 123 of the Act, the "tall stacks" provision added in 1977 after *Kennecott*, provides that the "degree of emission limitation required for control of any air pollutant" under a SIP "shall not be affected in any manner" by (1) so much of the stack height of any source "as exceeds good engineering practice (as determined under regulations promulgated by the Administrator)," or (2) any other dispersion technique. "Good engineering practice" means the height necessary to insure that emissions from the stack do not result in "excessive concentrations" of any pollutant in the "immediate vicinity" of the source. Ordinarily, such height may not exceed $2\frac{1}{2}$ times the height of the source.

State agency determinations of the limits of technological feasibility for continuous emission controls are not binding on the EPA, according to Bunker Hill Co. v. EPA, 572 F.2d 1286 (9th Cir. 1977). The Idaho agency had determined that a maximum of 72 percent of lead and zinc smelters' SO_2 emissions could be captured under currently available constant-control technology, and adopted a regulation to that effect. EPA refused to approve that part of the SIP and promulgated a substitute 82 percent limitation. Bunker Hill challenged EPA's action in court, contending that (a) EPA was bound by Idaho's determination on feasibility and (b) if not, EPA's determination was arbitrary and capricious. The court ruled in favor of EPA on the first issue, though not on the second.

Variances from SIP-prescribed emission standards are granted by state agencies, subject to approval by EPA. Such variances are treated as "revisions" of the SIP. Under Section 110(a)(3) (A) the Administrator "shall" approve any revision if it will not jeopardize timely attainment and susequent maintenance of NAAQSs, if it requires continuous emission controls to the maximum extent feasible, and if it satisfies the other requirements of section 110(a)(2). Train v. NRDC, 421 U.S. 60 (1975).

In 1977 the Clean Air Act was amended by the addition of several relief provisions for stationary sources unable to meet statutory deadlines for compliance with emission limitations. The most important is section 113(d). Besides a general provision for delayed compliance, it also contains specific provisions for sources unable to comply due to retirement of present facilities, due to investment in innovative facilities with the promise of greater pollution reduction in the future, or due to government orders to convert from cleaner fuels to coal. Section 113(d) authorizes a state (or, after 30 days notice to the state, the Administrator) to issue to any stationary source which is "unable to comply" with any requirement of an applicable implementation plan an order which specifies a date for final compliance with such requirement later than the date for attainment of any NAAQS. Among other things, the order must provide for final compliance "as expeditiously as practicable" but in no event later than three years after the date for final compliance with such requirements specified in the plan. A delayed compliance order (DCO) under this section may be issued only after notice to the public and opportunity for public hearing, and must contain "a schedule and timetable for compliance" as well as interim requirements for monitoring, reporting, and control, including measures to avoid "imminent and substantial endangerment to health of persons." A DCO must warn any "major" source (one which emits or has the potential to emit more than 100 tons per year of any air pollutant) that a "noncompliance penalty" (discussed in section D–1 below) will be assessed if the new deadline is not met. No state may grant a DCO to a major source unless the Administrator affirmatively finds that the order was issued "in accordance with the requirements" of the Act. Such a state order becomes "a part of the applicable implementation plan" and is a defense to any federal or private effort to compel earlier compliance. If a discharger violates a DCO, the Administrator "shall" enforce it by suit or order.

Can the DCO prerequisite that a source be "unable to comply" with statutory deadlines be satisfied by a firm which previously has failed to make good faith efforts to comply, or for which compliance is technologically feasible but only at an unreasonable cost? Because section 113(d) makes no reference to good faith efforts, EPA

[*84*]

has taken the position that a source is eligible for a DCO "regardless of its past history" so long as it is unable to comply. (However, "bad faith" inability does not excuse payment of a noncompliance penalty, as shown in section D–1 below). The requirement that a DCO provide for final compliance "as expeditiously as practicable" indicates that cost is to be considered at least in determining the duration of an extension, and it is likely that "unable to comply" does encompass economic as well as technological infeasibility.

Other specific relief provisions adopted in 1977 include section 119, authorizing a special DCO applicable only to nonferrous smelters, and section 110(f) and (g) permitting temporary suspensions of SIP requirements in cases of economic and energy emergencies.

The foregoing paragraphs have focused on the feasibility of individual sources complying with emission limitations. But what if a *state* is unable to achieve timely attainment of an NAAQS in one of its air quality control regions? Section 172 of the Clean Air Act, as amended in 1977, authorizes postponement of the date for compliance with primary standards until 1982, or 1987 for oxidants and carbon monoxide, if that is "as expeditiously as practicable." Under sections 110(a)(2)(I), 172 and 173, the main sanction for nonattainment of primary NAAQSs by the statutory deadlines is a moratorium on construction

[*85*]

and operation of "new" or "modified" "major" stationary sources. Section 176 also contemplates denial of federal grants for highway construction and various other purposes. Early in 1983 EPA designated more than one hundred counties nationwide as "probable" noncompliance areas and announced procedures to be followed in making final determinations, prior to imposing sanctions.

c. New Stationary Sources

Section 111 of the Clean Air Act directs the Administrator to promulgate "standards of performance" governing emissions of air pollutants by "new" stationary sources, i.e., sources constructed or modified after the effective date of pertinent regulations. The term "modification" means any physical change in, or change in the method of operation of, a stationary source which increases the amount of any air pollutant emitted or results in emission of a pollutant not previously emitted. "Standard of performance" means an emission standard which "reflects the degree of emission reduction achievable through the application of the best system of continuous emission reduction which (taking into consideration the cost of achieving such emission reduction, and any nonair quality health and environmental impact and energy requirements) the Administrator

[86]

determines has been adequately demonstrated for that category of sources." In Portland Cement Association v. Ruckelshaus, 486 F.2d 375 (D.C. Cir.1973), cert. denied 417 U.S. 921 (1974), plaintiff association sought judicial review of EPA's standards of performance for new or modified Portland cement plants. The companies contended that the Administrator had not complied with his mandate to "take into consideration the cost" of achieving the prescribed emission reductions, because he had not prepared a quantified cost-benefit analysis showing the benefit to ambient air conditions as measured against the cost of the pollution control devices. What the Administrator had done was to estimate the total capital and operating costs for the necessary control equipment and conclude that such costs were affordable by the industry and could be passed on to customers without substantially affecting competition with manufacturers of construction substitutes such as steel, asphalt and aluminum. Noting that the kind of cost-benefit analysis urged by petitioners would conflict with specific time constraints imposed on the Administrator by the Act, and that it would be difficult if not impossible to quantify in dollars the benefit to ambient air conditions, the court held that the Administrator had given sufficient consideration to economic costs to satisfy the requirement of section 111.

Subsequently, in 1977, the Clean Air Act was amended by addition of section 317. It provides that before publishing notice of a proposal to adopt or revise any standard of performance under section 111, the Administrator shall prepare an "economic impact assessment respecting such standard or regulation." This assessment, which shall be available to the public, is to analyze costs of compliance, potential inflationary or recessionary effects, and effects on competition, consumer costs, and energy use. However, section 317 also states that nothing therein shall be construed to "alter the basis on which a standard or regulation is promulgated" or to "authorize or require any judicial review of any such standard or regulation."

Under section 172 of the Act, a SIP applicable to any "nonattainment" area, in which one or more NAAQSs have not been met, must "require permits for the construction and operation of new or modified major stationary sources." In order to qualify for a permit, a major source must, under section 173, comply with the "lowest achievable emission rate" (LAER) and satisfy certain pollution "offset" requirements (discussed in section 3 below). Section 171 defines LAER as "the most stringent emission limitation . . . contained in the implementation plan of any state" (unless shown "not achievable"), or "the most stringent emission limitation achieved in practice,

. . . whichever is more stringent." Since LAER may not be less stringent than standards of performance for new sources under section 111, LAER must be at least "the best system of continuous emission reduction . . . adequately demonstrated," considering cost.

As amended in 1977 by addition of sections 160–169, the Clean Air Act requires that SIPs include measures to "prevent the significant deterioration" of air quality in areas designated by the states under section 107 as having ambient air quality better than the applicable NAAQS, or for which there is insufficient data to make a determination of the air quality. Since classification of areas is pollutant-specific, the same geographic area may be a "clean air area" with respect to one pollutant but a "nonattainment" area with respect to another pollutant. Areas subject to PSD regulation are divided into three classes, and maximum allowable increases in ambient concentrations of air pollutants, above initial baseline concentrations, are defined for each class. Class I areas, for which very small increments apply, include international parks and large national parks and wilderness areas. The Act also establishes requirements for protection of visibility in Class I areas, even though allowable increments are not exceeded. Initially, all other areas were designated Class II, for which increments were set permitting moderate economic growth. However, some Class II areas have been or may be redesignated Class III, for which increases in pollutants are allowed up to the national ambient standards. No "major" stationary source may be constructed or "modified" in a PSD area without a permit setting forth emission limitations for such facility; and a permit shall not be issued unless (1) the applicant demonstrates that emissions from the facility will not cause or contribute to air pollution in excess of the allowable increment or concentration for any pollutant in the PSD area, and (2) the emission limitations applicable to such facility reflect "best available control technology" (BACT) for each pollutant subject to PSD regulation. Demonstrations that emissions will not violate applicable increments are to be based on both monitoring and diffusion modeling.

d. Hazardous Pollutants

Section 112 of the Clean Air Act defines "hazardous air pollutant" to mean a pollutant to which no NAAQS is applicable and which in the judgment of the Administrator causes, or contributes to, air pollution which may reasonably be anticipated to result in an increase in mortality or an increase in serious irreversible, or incapacitating reversible, illness. The section directs the Administrator to publish a list of hazardous air pollutants and, with respect to each listed pollutant, to prescribe a national emission standard at

[*90*]

the level which in his judgment provides an "ample margin of safety to protect the public health." The economic and technical feasibility of compliance is not to be considered by EPA in setting such standards. However, section 112 does provide that the President may exempt any source from compliance with a standard for a period of not more than two years if he finds that the technology to implement the standard is not available and that operation of the source is required for reasons of national security. Such an exemption may be extended for one or more additional periods, not exceeding two years each. If in the judgment of the Administrator it is not feasible to prescribe or enforce an emission standard for control of a specific hazardous air pollutant in some situations—e.g., for control of asbestos emissions resulting from demolition of an old building—he may instead promulgate a design, equipment, work practice, or operational standard, or combination thereof, which in his judgment is adequate to protect the public health with an ample margin of safety.

3. OFFSETS AND BUBBLES

As was mentioned in subsection 2–c above, section 173 of the Act requires permits for the construction and operation of "new or modified major stationary sources" in "nonattainment" areas. Such permits are to be issued only if "total allowable emissions" from existing and new or modified sources are "sufficiently less than total emissions from existing sources allowed under the applicable implementation plan" when the permit is sought "so as to represent . . . reasonable progress." Thus total "allowable" emissions of each pollutant must be *reduced* even though a new source is added. New or modified major sources receive credit only for reducing emissions which are "allowable" under the SIP, not for reductions already overdue.

How does the offset requirement work in practice? Suppose the owner of a steel mill presently satisfying SIP requirements wants to construct a new furnace on the same site. If the NAAQS for particulates is not being met in that region, the owner may obtain the necessary offset credit by shutting down older furnaces in the mill, or by retrofitting them with additional control equipment not required by the SIP, if the resulting reduction of emissions sufficiently exceeds the emissions from the new furnace to "represent reasonable further progress" toward attainment of the ambient standard.

If the owner can not practicably reduce existing emissions at his mill, he still may be able to satisfy the offset requirement, since section 173 does not require that the source reducing its emissions be owned or operated by the person proposing construction or operation of a new or

modified major source. Section 173 refers to "total allowable emissions from existing sources in
the region," and EPA guidelines allow offsets
based on reductions at sources owned by others.
As long as net emissions are reduced, it is imma-
terial who reduces them. Thus the mill owner
may be able to pay a nearby foundry to close
down a marginal furnace, to control it beyond
SIP requirements, or to move to another air quality control region.

The result is that section 173 creates a private
market in emission rights. Since 1979 the EPA
has allowed "banking" of unused emission reduction credits, for offset against future new
sources. For example, localities may bank reductions which result from firms going out of business. These clean air credits could later be transferred to new firms locating in the community.
But who owns offsets which are not used immediately, and how should they be allocated among
potential new sources? According to EPA, "the
State is free to govern ownership, use, sale, and
commercial transactions in banked emission offsets as it sees fit." The offsets might be considered the exclusive property of the parent source
which produced them; they might be treated as
public property, even though created by private
investments; or the offsets might be viewed as
rights which can be made available either to the
parent source or to other investors, subject to

terms and conditions set by the government. Serious problems of hoarding or monopolization arguably could arise from purely private ownership of the offsets, threatening nonattainment areas with economic stagnation. It should be remembered that the fundamental purpose of the offset policy is to allow industrial growth despite stringent air quality standards.

If a state or local government becomes the "banker" of emission rights, how should it allocate the rights among potential users? The offsets could be allocated on a first-come-first-served basis, but that would give little control to state or local officials in planning the economic development of the region. Allocation by auction, to the highest bidder, a more traditional free market approach, may suffer from the same disadvantage. Another alternative might be for the government to condition permit approval upon the satisfaction of specified social, employment or tax-base criteria. How such problems will be worked out remains to be seen.

The preceding paragraphs were concerned with *inter*-source offsets. The following paragraphs deal with *intra*-source offsets and the so-called "bubble" concept. The basic idea behind the bubble is to treat the various components of an industrial plant as a single source for regulatory purposes. Thus, emissions from all stacks are considered only in the aggregate. Offsetting increases and decreases in emissions from different components entail no additional regulatory consequences so long as the net effect is not to increase total emissions. For example, the bubble concept could be used to allow a plant operator to reduce his total pollution abatement costs by changing the mix of controls so as to maximize emission reduction for the processes which are least expensive to control, while decreasing controls for processes which cost the most to clean up.

The first application of the "bubble" involved 1975 EPA regulations providing that a change in an existing plant, which would increase emissions from some components, would not trigger application of section 111 standards of performance for "modified" sources if the increases were more than offset by reductions in emissions of the same pollutants elsewhere in the plant. The regulations defined a stationary "source" for NSPS purposes to include "any one *or a combination of* . . . facilities." The purpose was to allow an entire plant to be treated as a single source. However, in ASARCO, Inc. v. EPA, 578 F.2d 319 (D.C.Cir.1978), the court invalidated this definition as contrary to that in section 111 itself, which defined a stationary source "for purposes of this section" as "any building, structure, *facility,* or installation." The court stressed that the goal of section 111 was to assure that all new and modified sources would employ the best control technology "adequately demonstrated" as a means of *enhancing* air quality. Permitting use of the bubble concept to avoid meeting the technological standard would subvert the central statutory purpose of improving, rather than merely maintaining, ambient air quality.

The next "bubble" case arose in the context of PSD areas. Section 169 of the Act provides that "for purposes of [PSD]" the term "major emitting facility" means "any of [fourteen specified types of] *plants*." In Alabama Power Co. v. Costle, 636 F.2d 323 (D.C.Cir.1979), the court said this language indicates that "with regard to PSD . . . Congress clearly envisioned that entire plants could be considered to be single 'sources'." Although the statutory definition of "source" in section 111 ("any building, structure, facility, or installation") was held to govern all PSD provisions, the court ruled that EPA had discretion to define further, by regulation, the four components of the definition "to carry out the expressed purposes" of the program at issue. Thus, the court recognized that the EPA might adopt for one Clean Air Act program regulations defining "the component terms of 'source' that are different in scope from" regulations employed in another program, "due to differences in the purpose and structure of the two programs." Applying this analysis, the court declared the

[*96*]

bubble concept "precisely suited" to the goals of the PSD program, "preserv[ing] air quality within a framework that allows cost-efficient, flexible planning for industrial expansion and improvement." A point-specific definition of source would be "contrary to the expressed purposes of the PSD provisions of the Act." The court regarded its decision as entirely in harmony with that in *ASARCO*, which dealt with a "significantly different regulation and statutory purpose," i.e., the purpose of enhancing rather than merely maintaining ambient air quality.

After *Alabama Power*, EPA addressed the possibility of allowing use of the bubble in "nonattainment" areas. Initially, in 1980, the Agency promulgated regulations which defined as a "stationary source" for nonattainment purposes "any building, structure, facility, or installation." The regulations further defined "building, structure, [and] facility" to mean, essentially, an entire plant. "Installation", however, was defined as "an identifiable piece of process equipment." This so-called "dual definition" of "source" as both a plant and an individual piece of equipment at a plant (a "source" within a "source") was intended to *preclude* use of the bubble in nonattainment areas, in order to maximize the scope of review of new and "modified" sources and produce greater emission reductions. However, in 1981, under a different administration concerned with "regulatory relief," EPA issued new regulations which *repealed* the dual definition trigger for new source review in nonattainment areas and adopted solely a plantwide definition of "stationary source." The change was justified on the grounds that it reduced regulatory complexity, since the same definition of "source" would apply to both PSD and nonattainment programs; and that it would "allow states much greater flexibility" in developing their nonattainment programs.

Environmental groups promptly sought judicial review of the 1981 regulations. They argued that the definition of "source" would allow most modifications in nonattainment areas to avoid new source review, thereby causing emission increases. In NRDC v. Gorsuch, 685 F.2d 718 (D.C.Cir.1982), the court applied the *Alabama Power—ASARCO* test to the nonattainment provisions of the Act and concluded that the bubble concept could not be employed in that scheme because the purpose of the nonattainment program is to enhance, rather than merely to maintain, air quality. Hence allowing the states, within their SIPs, broad leeway to define the sources to which federal nonattainment requirements apply could not be reconciled with the Act's design. EPA was bitterly disappointed with the decision, claiming that it "effectively stripped" the agency of all discretion in defining the term "source" under different Clean Air Act programs. At the end of

1982 the court of appeals had denied a rehearing, and EPA was considering whether to seek review by the Supreme Court.

C. REGULATION UNDER THE CLEAN WATER ACT

The major sources of water pollution are industrial, municipal and agricultural. The types of pollutants entering streams, lakes and oceans from such sources include organic wastes, other nutrients, toxic chemicals and other hazardous substances, heated water, and sediments.

Organic wastes decompose by bacterial action. They are commonly measured in units of biochemical oxygen demand (BOD), or the amount of oxygen needed to decompose them. Fish and other aquatic life need oxygen, and the amount of dissolved oxygen in a water body therefore is one of the best measures of its ecological health. If too much of the oxygen is spent in decomposition of organic waste loads, certain types of fish no longer can live there and are replaced by pollution-resistant, lower orders of fish, such as carp. If all the dissolved oxygen is used, an anaerobic (without air) decomposition process occurs. Rather than releasing carbon dioxide, anaerobic decomposition releases methane or hydrogen sulfide, and the stream or lake turns dark and malodorous.

[*99*]

Discharges of heated water into lakes and rivers also can harm aquatic life. Higher temperatures accelerate biological and chemical processes, reducing the water's ability to retain dissolved oxygen and other gases. The growth of aquatic plants like algae is hastened, and fish reproduction may be disrupted.

Eutrophication, or the "dying of lakes," is a natural process resulting from the addition of nutrients and sediments. Over time, lakes become shallower and biologically more productive, eventually evolving into swamps and finally into land areas. Normally this takes thousands of years, but man greatly accelerates the process when he adds nutrients such as detergents, fertilizers, and human and animal wastes, and allows soil runoff from agricultural and other lands.

Discharges of toxic chemicals, heavy metals, and other hazardous substances can impair aquatic life and render both the receiving waters (even after treatment) and fish and shellfish therefrom unsafe for human consumption.

Most industrial wastes can be controlled by treatment and production process changes. Some types of wastes, like those from food processing, can be treated efficiently—after pretreatment in some cases—in municipal treatment systems. Such systems receive about half of their wastes from industrial sources and about half from homes and commercial establishments.

Three levels of treatment are employed in municipal treatment plants. Primary treatment is a simple gravity process which separates and settles solids. It provides BOD removal levels of 25 to 30 percent. Secondary treatment is a biological process that speeds up what nature does in natural water bodies. Good secondary treatment plants remove 90 percent of measured BOD. Advanced waste treatment involves a wide variety of processes tailored for specific treatment needs. They may remove up to 99 percent of measured BOD. Even after treatment, however, municipal wastes contribute large amounts of phosphate and nitrate nutrients to water bodies. Secondary treatment plants remove an average of 30 percent of the phosphorous and up to 20 percent of the nitrogenous materials, although with modifications higher levels are possible.

Another municipal waste problem is street runoff into storm sewers. Where storm sewers are separated from sanitary sewers, runoff enters receiving waters untreated and can carry a variety of wastes, including organic and toxic wastes. Where storm and sanitary sewers are combined, both runoff and raw sewage pass directly into receiving waters when treatment systems become overloaded during storms or thaws.

1. STRUCTURE OF THE CLEAN
WATER ACT

Prior to 1972, the Federal Water Pollution Control Act prescribed a regulatory system consisting mainly of state-developed ambient water quality standards applicable to interstate or navigable waters. The standards for any particular segment of a water body depended upon the uses (e.g., agriculture, industrial, recreational) which the state wanted to facilitate. Enforcement was possible only where a discharge reduced the quality of the receiving water below the specified ambient level. This system failed due to the lack, if not infeasibility, of enforcement. Multiple polluters discharging into the same stream or lake presented problems of proof similar to those encountered under nuisance law.

In 1972 Congress adopted a totally different approach. The FWPCA amendments of that year established a system of standards, permits and enforcement aimed at "goals" of "fishable and swimmable" waters by 1983 and total elimination of pollutant discharges into navigable waters by 1985. Ambient water quality standards were to be supplemented by discharge standards in the form of effluent limitations applicable to all "point sources" ("any discernible, confined and discrete conveyance . . . from which pollutants are or may be discharged"). Under section

Gov./US   Y 4.P 96/10 : S. PRT. 103-18

Gov./US   Y 4.P 96/10 : 97-9

Wisc. Documents

NAT. 9/4 : W 285/4/1999

Stacks

KF 3794.Z9   K44 1986

TD 223. A4663   1993

301 of the amended Act, effluent limitations for all point sources except publicly owned treatment works were required to reflect "best practicable control technology currently available" (BPT) by 1977, and "best available technology economically achievable" (BAT) by 1983. Public treatment works were required to adopt secondary treatment by 1977, and "best practicable waste treatment over the life of the works" by 1983. In addition, all point sources were required to comply with any more stringent limitations established pursuant to state or federal law, or pursuant to section 302 in order to achieve ambient water quality standards. Section 306 required that "new" sources in specified categories meet effluent limitations equivalent to the 1983 BAT standards. Section 307 required that EPA maintain a list of toxic substances and establish separate limitations for them. These limitations were to be based mainly on protection of public health and water quality, rather than on technological feasibility, and were to provide an "ample margin of safety." A substance was to be considered toxic if its effect on organisms would be to cause death, disease, cancer, mutations, physiological malfunction or deformation.

Amended section 402 created a permit system, the National Pollutant Discharge Elimination System (NPDES), under which discharge permits could be granted by EPA or by states with EPA-

approved programs. *Any* discharges by point
sources, except in compliance with the limitations
imposed in a permit, were declared unlawful.
Permits had to incorporate applicable effluent
limitations established under sections 301, 302,
306 and 307, including enforceable schedules of
compliance to meet the 1977 and 1983 deadlines.

The 1972 amendments contemplated that enforcement would be primarily by the states.
However, the federal government was not con-
strained, as it had been under the previous FWP-
CA, from acting to enforce state or federal standards. Provisions allowing for inspection, entry
and monitoring, federal enforcement (including
emergency action), and citizen suits were all designed to facilitate enforcement of the new standards. Under section 505, citizens could sue to
enforce effluent limitations in state or EPA permits, as well as orders issued by EPA. Citizens
also could sue EPA for failure to perform nondis-
cretionary regulatory duties.

Like the Clean Air Act, the FWPCA was
amended in 1977. It was denominated the Clean
Water Act. EPA was authorized to grant case-
by-case extensions of the 1977 BPT deadline to industrial dischargers which had attempted in good
faith to comply; however, full compliance was required by 1979. The agency also could extend
the 1977 deadline for secondary treatment by municipalities for up to six years, until 1983, where

[*104*]

delays in compliance were caused by lack of federal construction grant funds. Another provision, section 301(h), authorized the EPA Administrator to waive the secondary treatment requirement permanently with respect to discharges from publicly owned treatment works into "marine waters" (oceans and tidal rivers) if the partially treated (or raw) sewage will "not interfere with the attainment or maintenance of [receiving] water quality which assures protection of" public water supplies, aquatic life, and recreational activities.

With respect to the previously established 1983 deadline for industry compliance with BAT effluent limitations, the 1977 modifications of the Act were more complex. Different requirements were adopted for three categories of pollutants: (1) "toxic" pollutants, including initially a list of 129 specific chemicals; (2) "conventional" pollutants designated by EPA, including BOD, fecal coliform, suspended solids, and pH; and (3) "nonconventional" pollutants, those not classified by EPA as either toxic or conventional. Sections 301(b)(2), 304(a)(4) and (b)(4), and 307(a). For toxic pollutants, BAT now must be employed by July 1, 1984 (or, for pollutants not on the original list, within three years after EPA adoption of applicable effluent limitations); no exceptions are allowed. Under pre-1977 law the EPA still may establish even more strict toxic standards, including zero discharge, where necessary either to protect public health with an ample margin of safety or to attain applicable ambient water quality standards.

For conventional pollutants, a new standard, "best conventional pollutant control technology" (BCT), was established and is to be achieved by July 1, 1984. In establishing effluent limitations for conventional pollutants, EPA is to consider, among other things, "the reasonableness of the relationship between the costs of attaining a reduction in effluents and the effluent reduction benefits derived." This mitigating cost-benefit factor is not included among those to be considered in formulating BAT limitations for toxic and nonconventional pollutants. Compare subsections 304(b)(2)(B) and (b)(4)(B). In general, effluent limitations based on the BAT standard are to be achieved for nonconventional pollutants within three years after the limitations are established or by July 1, 1984, whichever is later. Under section 301(g) the EPA, with concurrence of the state, may modify such requirements for a period not extending beyond July 1, 1987, if modification will not interfere with attainment of water quality standards or pose an unacceptable health risk. The economic "reasonableness" test employed to convert the BAT standard into a BCT standard for conventional pollutants is not to be considered by EPA in determining whether to approve a section 301(g) modification of BAT limitations for a nonconventional pollutant.

In 1981, sections of the Act applicable to publicly owned waste treatment works were amended again. Now the deadline for provision of secondary treatment may be extended to 1988 in cases where reductions in federal financial assistance or other changed conditions beyond the control of the owner make it impossible to complete construction by 1983. Further, the definition of what constitutes acceptable secondary treatment was relaxed: "such biological treatment facilities as oxidation ponds, lagoons, and ditches," in which sunlight and algae cause decomposition of the wastes, "shall be deemed the equivalent of secondary treatment" so long as receiving water quality will not be "adversely affected." Section 304(d)(4). Clearly, this redefinition, together with the provisions of section 301(h) concerning discharges into marine waters, amounts to a partial retreat—with respect to publicly owned treatment works—from technology-based effluent standards, back toward the pre-1972 concern only with attainment of ambient water quality standards.

So far, technology-based effluent limitations continue to govern discharges by industrial point sources. Section 301(b), as noted above, requires that effluent limitations reflecting different levels of technology—BPT, BCT and BAT,

depending upon the type of pollutant and the
deadline for attainment—"shall be achieved" by
dischargers. However, the statute does not
state explicitly who is to set the limitations, or
how. In E.I. du Pont de Nemours & Co. v. Train,
430 U.S. 112 (1977), du Pont disputed that section 301(b) authorized EPA to establish effluent limitations applicable to *classes* of plants,
the class in question being organic chemical
plants. The company argued that section 301(b)
merely indicated the level of technology to
be incorporated in limitations specially fash-
ioned for each *individual* plant in NPDES permits granted under section 402. The critical
question was whether the EPA Administrator
could set effluent limitations by regulation, i.e.,
by quasi-legislative rulemaking, or whether such
limitations had to be established in individual ad-
judicative-type proceedings by the state officials
or regional EPA officials responsible for issuing
NPDES permits. After considering the legislative history of section 301, the "impossible burden" of giving individual consideration to the
unique circumstances of each of the more than
42,000 dischargers who had applied for permits,
and the judicial deference due to EPA's "reasonable" statutory interpretation, the Supreme Court
concluded that section 301 authorized both 1977
and 1983 limitations to be set by regulation, so
long as some allowance was made for variations
in individual plants, as EPA had done by includ-

ing a variance clause in the challenged 1977 BPT limitations.

2. CONSIDERATION OF ECONOMIC AND TECHNOLOGICAL FEASIBILITY

Section 301's and 304's definitions of BPT, BCT and BAT leave EPA with considerable discretion in establishing effluent limitations for different categories and classes of dischargers. However, both the statutory language and judicial interpretations of it impose significant constraints upon the abatement efforts which the Agency can demand of industry. We shall consider, in order, the feasibility factors to be considered in implementing BPT, BCT and BAT standards. We also shall review relevant provisions of section 306, concerning national standards of performance for *new* sources of water pollution.

a. BPT

American Meat Institute v. EPA, 526 F.2d 442 (7th Cir.1975), is illustrative of industry challenges to various EPA limitations. The BPT regulations there covered the red meat processing segment of the meat products point source category. Under sections 301(b)(1)(A) and 304(b)(1) (B), factors to be considered in determining best practicable control technology currently available include total cost of application of technology in relation to effluent reduction benefits, age of equipment and facilities, production process employed, engineering aspects of control techniques, process changes, non-water quality environmental impacts, and such other factors as the EPA Administrator deems appropriate. *Meat Institute* shows that in construing this mandate EPA has relied on legislative history indicating that BPT should reflect "the average of the best existing performance by plants of various sizes, ages, and unit processes within each industrial category," except where existing practices are uniformly inadequate. The court approved this interpretation and sustained the red meat processing effluent limitations because they had in fact been achieved by one or more existing processing plants.

The courts have upheld EPA's refusal to consider receiving water quality in setting BPT effluent limitations. In Weyerhaeuser Co v. Costle, 590 F.2d 1011 (D.C.Cir.1978), pulp and paper makers challenged the validity of the BPT regulations for their industry. Some of the mills discharged effluents into the Pacific Ocean. They urged that because the amounts of pollutants were small in comparison to the receiving water, they should not have to spend heavily on treatment equipment, or to increase their energy requirements and sludge levels, in order to treat wastes that the ocean could dilute or absorb. However,

[*110*]

the court agreed with EPA that, based on long experience, and aware of the limits of technological knowledge and administrative flexibility, Congress in 1972 made the deliberate decision to rule out arguments based on the assimilative capacity of receiving waters. This decision was based not only upon the lack of enforceability of pre-1972 ambient water quality standards, but also upon a desire to have nationwide uniformity in effluent regulation and to free states from the temptation of relaxing local limitations in order to woo or keep industrial facilities. Receiving water quality was to be considered only in setting *more* stringent standards than those reflected in technology-based effluent limitations.

The court in *Weyerhaeuser* also interpreted the requirement, in section 304(b), that in setting BPT limitations EPA consider "the total cost of application of technology in relation to the effluent reduction benefits to be achieved from such application" ("comparison factors"), and also "take into account" the age of equipment and facilities involved, the process employed, engineering aspects of control techniques, process changes, and non-water quality environmental impacts ("consideration factors"). The pulp and paper industry contended that EPA must carefully balance costs versus effluent reduction benefits of its regulations, and that it also should balance benefits against non-water quality environmental

impacts to arrive at a "net" environmental benefit conclusion. The court concluded that Congress had mandated only a "limited" balancing
test with respect to the "comparison factors,"
and had left EPA with discretion to decide how to
account for the "consideration factors." EPA
was not required, with respect to "comparison"
factors, to measure the costs and benefits of each
additional increment of waste treatment control,
from bare minimum up to complete pollution control. In assessing "consideration" factors, EPA
was not required to use any specific structure,
such as a balancing test, nor was it required to
give each factor any specific weight.

Although the Clean Water Act is silent on the
question of variances from BPT standards, the
Supreme Court held in E.I. du Pont de Nemours
& Co. v. Train, supra, that EPA's practice allowing such variances was not only permissible
but required. Since uniform, category-wide BPT
effluent limitations are employed, there must be
a procedure by which the limits can be adjusted
for plants that are "fundamentally different"
from the industry norm. Weyerhaeuser Co. v.
Costle, supra. A BPT variance must, at a minimum, allow a plant operator to seek a dispensa-
tion from any effluent limitation which, as a
whole, demands more of him than section 301 allows EPA to demand of the industry as a whole.
Referring to the "comparison" and "considera-

tion" factors discussed above, state agencies and the EPA should excuse operators from making more than the maximum use of technology *practicably* available to them.

EPA's approach to BPT variances has withstood two lines of industry challenge. The first concerned the Agency's refusal to allow variances for individual plants which lacked economic ability to meet the BPT limitations. In EPA v. National Crushed Stone Association, 449 U.S. 64 (1980), the industry argued that the BPT variance should be triggered by individual economic inability to comply, since the variance provision in section 301(c), with respect to the more stringent BAT standards, explicitly requires consideration of individual economic impact. However, the Supreme Court held that for BPT variances, the Clean Water Act requires consideration only of whether costs are reasonable in relation to benefits for the industry category as a whole. The BPT variance is limited to cases where an individual plant so differs from others in the category, in terms of technology and the relation of effluent reduction benefits to costs (but not in terms of the financial resources available to the owner), that it would be irrational to apply the category-wide standards to that plant.

The second line of challenge to EPA's BPT variance practice contended that consideration should be given to the impact of the individual

[*113*]

plant's discharges upon receiving water quality. The courts rejected the claim, holding that receiving water quality was not one of the "comparison" or "consideration" factors mentioned in section 304(b), and that to permit variances on that basis would be returning water pollution control to its ineffective pre-1972 status in defiance of Congress' desire "to restore and maintain the chemical, physical, and biological integrity of the nation's waters." Crown Simpson Pulp Co. v. Costle, 642 F.2d 323 (9th Cir.1981), cert. denied 454 U.S. 1053; Appalachian Power Co. v. EPA, 671 F.2d 801 (4th Cir.1982). It should be noted, however, that in 1982 Congress enacted legislation specifically *exempting* the two bleached kraft pulp mills involved in the *Crown Simpson* case (but not any other point sources) from *any* limitations on pH and BOD in the effluents which the mills discharge into the Pacific Ocean near Eureka, California. Recall that section 301(h), enacted in 1977, allows water quality-related waivers of effluent limitations applicable to publicly owned treatment works.

b. BCT

As amended in 1977, section 304(b)(4)(B) spells out the criteria to be used in establishing BCT effluent limitations. Concerning cost considerations, the statute provides that BCT "shall include consideration of the reasonableness of the

[*114*]

relationship between the costs of attaining a reduction in effluents and the effluent reduction
benefits derived, and the comparison of the cost
and level of reduction of such pollutants from the
discharge from publicly owned treatment works
to the cost and level of reduction of such pollutants from a class or category of industrial
sources." In 1979 EPA promulgated a BCT
methodology which reduced this cost-reasonableness analysis to a single test, a comparison of the
marginal cost of going from BPT to BCT with the
marginal cost of going from "secondary treatment" to "advanced secondary treatment" at
publicly owned treatment works (the POTW comparison test). EPA analyzed POTW costs and established a figure of $1.15 per pound as the ap-
propriate marginal cost of advanced secondary
treatment at a POTW. It then screened existing
BAT rules for 41 industry subcategories to determine which rules passed the POTW comparison
test. All BAT limitations for 22 subcategories,
and limitations for some pollutants for 6 additional subcategories, passed the test and were made
BCT. The portions of the standards for the 6
subcategories which partially failed, along with
the BAT limitations for the remaining 13 subcategories which failed the test in their entirety,
were withdrawn pending further analysis to develop BCT standards from scratch.

Industry groups challenged the new BCT standards in a series of actions consolidated under the name American Paper Institute v. EPA, 660 F.2d 954 (4th Cir.1981). They argued that section 304(b) called for a two-part cost-reasonableness test: an industry cost-effectiveness test, and a POTW comparison test. EPA, on the other hand, argued that Congress did not require it to evaluate industry cost effectiveness, but only mandated a POTW cost comparison standard. EPA read the seemingly dual statutory requirements as one, commanding only a consideration of reasonableness. The court rejected EPA's position and invalidated all the BCT regulations. EPA's interpretation of the statute was found to be contrary to the plain meaning of the words contained therein, ignoring the mandatory language ("shall") and disregarding the conjunctive ("and"). On the other hand, the court concluded that EPA had not acted arbitrarily or capriciously in choosing advanced secondary treatment as the increment beyond secondary treatment for the POTW comparison test. The court did not explain how EPA was to devise the industry cost-effectiveness portion of the test.

In the fall of 1982, EPA proposed new BCT effluent limitation guidelines for sixteen industrial categories. Under the proposal, BCT would be more stringent than BPT only if (a) the incremental cost per pound of conventional pollutant removed in going from BPT to BCT is less than 27 cents per pound in 1976 dollars (the POTW test), and (b) the same incremental cost per pound is less than 143 percent of the incremental cost per pound associated with achieving BPT (the industry cost-effectiveness test). If either test is failed, BCT for that industrial category would be equal to BPT.

It does not appear that variances will be available to individual plants unable to comply with BCT effluent limitations eventually to be issued. Section 301(c) expressly permits, but does not require, the Administrator to provide for variances from BAT requirements, but there is no mention of BCT requirements.

c. *BAT*

Section 301(b)(2) prescribes BAT effluent limitations for "nonconventional" and toxic pollutants. Section 304(b)(2)(B) directs that factors relating to the assessment of BAT "shall take into account" the age of equipment and facilities, the process employed, engineering aspects of control techniques, process changes, "the cost of achieving such effluent reduction," and non-water quality environmental impact (including energy requirements). There is no requirement of a balancing between the costs and benefits of effluent reduction. Because section 301 mandates compliance with BAT limitations by 1984 for toxic

[*117*]

pollutants, but fixes no deadline for non-conventional pollutants, EPA's BAT program now is focused on toxics. Regulation of toxic pollutants under the Clean Water Act is discussed in Chapter 3.

Section 301(c) authorizes the Administrator to grant a variance from BAT standards upon a showing that "such modified requirements (1) will represent the maximum use of technology within the economic capacity of the owner or operator; and (2) will result in reasonable further progress toward the elimination of the discharge of pollutants." Thus consideration of individual economic impact, as well as environmental impact, is required. However, section 301(*l*) prohibits variances with respect to pollutants which are on the toxic pollutant list established under section 307.

d. *Standards of Performance for New Sources*

Section 306 directs the Administrator to establish federal standards of performance for various industry categories of new sources. The term "new source" includes any source, the "construction" (but not "modification") of which is commenced after EPA *proposal* of a section 306 standard which will apply to such source. "Standards of performance" must reflect the "greatest degree of effluent reduction which the Administrator determines to be achievable through application of the best available demonstrated control technology, processes, operating methods, or other alternatives, including, where practicable, a standard permitting no discharge of pollutants." In establishing such standards, the Administrator "shall take into consideration the cost of achieving such effluent reduction, and any non-water quality environmental impact and energy requirements."

The ability of owners and operators of individual new sources to comply with industry-wide standards may not be considered. In E.I. du Pont de Nemours & Co. v. Train, supra, the Supreme Court noted that there was no statutory provision for variances, and concluded that variances would be inappropriate for a standard intended to insure national uniformity and "maximum feasible control" of new sources.

D.   ECONOMIC INCENTIVES FOR ENVIRONMENTAL PROTECTION

Preceding portions of this chapter dealt with abatement costs and lack of technology as *constraints* upon environmental protection. This section examines ways in which government can intervene in the market to *promote* environmental protection, primarily by increasing the cost of nonabatement to those causing environmental degradation.

Economists tend to view a competitive or free market as the preferred means of allocating scarce resources in an "efficient" manner, that is, so as to maximize the total value of production. The market mechanism functions correctly, however, only if prices fully reflect the costs and benefits of production to the entire society. As discussed earlier, two factors which tend to distort the market system are the related problems of "externalities" and "collective goods." Pollution is a common form of external cost, a spillover effect of production which uses up other resources by degrading them. Collective goods are commodities which can not readily be supplied to specific persons without enabling large numbers of other persons to enjoy them too because exclusion is not practicable. One example is the clean air "produced" by installation of emission control equipment at large power plants or on new motor vehicles.

Because of the free market's failure to provide adequate incentives, government must intervene to limit external costs and to facilitate production of collective goods. The basic approaches are (1) recognition of *property rights*, with damage and injunctive remedies being available to injured owners; (2) *direct regulation*, e.g., emission limitations under the Clean Air Act; (3) *subsidies*, i.e., government payment of some of the expenses of avoiding external costs or producing collective goods; and (4) *charges* for activities generating external costs or failing to provide collective goods.

As we have seen, control of pollution via nuisance actions and direct regulation is not without its problems. Nuisance law proved inadequate to control widespread pollution from multiple sources. Even if plaintiffs can satisfy "standing" requirements and sustain the burden of proving material harm attributable to defendants' unreasonable conduct, courts often refuse injunctive relief after "balancing the equities", that is, after considering the relative economic hardships to the parties (and perhaps to others in the community) of granting or denying such relief. In addition, nuisance law fails to provide a systematic mechanism for supervising emissions. Direct regulation, by contrast, is systematic. However, it can involve enormous administrative costs because of the need to conduct economic analyses of entire industries, mastering the technologies of production and pollution control and classifying industrial processes which are sufficiently different to merit different abatement standards. As we have seen, regulatory limits arrived at through such involved procedures often are challenged in court on the ground that they do not represent "best practicable control technology" or some other statutory standard. Under the regulatory approach, the benefits of delay may

[*121*]

be so great in comparison with the costs of voluntary compliance that regulatory agencies face the possibility of having to take enforcement measures against large segments of some industries.

Typical subsidies employed for environmental management have included tax breaks (accelerated depreciation and credits), low interest loans, and grants for installation of treatment equipment. However, such devices provide only part of the cost of the equipment. They reduce losses, but they do not make installation of abatement equipment profitable. In short, subsidies may "sweeten" a regulatory program, but they can never replace it. Furthermore, subsidies provide incentives only for investments in *equipment*. In many cases the most efficient way to reduce discharges is to alter production processes, recover materials, produce marketable goods from by-products, or change the nature or quality of raw materials.

Because of shortcomings in the first three types of public intervention enumerated above, economists and others have shown increasing interest in effluent charges and marketable discharge permits.

1. EFFLUENT CHARGES AND NONCOM-PLIANCE PENALTIES

A "pure" effluent charge system requires payment of a fee or tax on each unit of pollution released into the air or water. Reducing pollution by, say, 90 percent may be relatively inexpensive for some plants but very costly for others. It is arguable, therefore, that rather than a regulatory system with uniform effluent limitations, it would be preferable to have a variable standard which would concentrate pollution abatement where it costs the least. Each firm would reduce pollution to the point where the cost of removing an additional unit was the same as that for every other firm. With a fixed charge per unit of pollution, each discharger, if acting rationally, would choose to remove pollution up to the point where the cost of removing an additional unit was greater than the effluent charge. The larger the charge, the greater the percentage of pollutants any firm would be motivated to remove, though firms with low costs of control would remove larger percentages than would firms with high abatement costs.

Fixing the levels of effluent charges poses some severe problems. Ideally, the legislature or administrative agency should impose on an environmentally damaging activity all of the external or social costs which it produces. A polluter then

[*123*]

would pay for all the resources which he consumes. However, computing total social damages involves enormous difficulties and probably
is not practicable. Other formulas for setting the
charges therefore must be considered. One
which has been suggested is the average costs of
controlling pollution in various industries. Another is simply that charge which in practice, perhaps after some trial and error, provides sufficient incentive to cause polluters to reduce total
discharges to levels determined to be socially acceptable.

Much skepticism concerning the workability of
a system of effluent charges stems from concern
that measuring the effluents produced by every
source subject to charges would be too difficult
or expensive. While it is true that other methods
of pollution control, such as direct regulation, also require some monitoring of discharges from
individual sources, those systems do not require
continuous monitoring (or some other way of determining or estimating *all* discharges without
time limitation) for *all* polluters. Obviously the
design of charge systems would have to be influ-
enced to some extent by what it is technically and
economically feasible to measure, and this may
move such systems a considerable distance from
the ideal mentioned above.

Despite avowed allegiance to the free market
system, private businesses are among the strong-

est opponents of effluent charges because many believe they are better off under the present system (of property rights, direct regulation, and subsidies) than under an effective charge system. Even though a typical firm might have to pay less for society to reach a given ambient standard under a charge system than under a regulatory system requiring uniform percentage reductions in discharges, any realistic comparison between the two systems must take into consideration the probabilities of having to comply. Under a charge system, if the problem of monitoring discharges accurately can be solved, a firm is almost certain to have to pay the charge or to spend money to abate its pollution so as to reduce the charge. Under direct regulation, however, some firms decide that, because enforcement is cumbersome and ineffective, they either will never have to pay for expensive controls or can gain the financial advantages of years of delay beyond official deadlines.

Noncompliance penalties under the Clean Air Act are aimed precisely at denying polluters financial advantages from delay. Section 120 of the Act, added in 1977, provides that the Administrator or the state "shall" assess and collect a noncompliance penalty against "every" person who owns or operates (i) a "major" stationary source (other than certain primary nonferrous smelters) which is not in compliance with any applicable implementation plan, (ii) a stationary source which is not in compliance with an emission limitation, emission standard, standard of performance, or other requirement established under section 111 or 112, or (iii) a stationary source for which an extension, order, suspension, or consent decree is in effect, and which is not in compliance with any applicable interim control requirement or schedule of compliance. However the owner or operator is exempt from the penalty if he demonstrates that his failure to comply is "due solely" to "an inability to comply . . . , for which inability the source has received [a delayed compliance] order under Section 113(d) . . . [and] which inability results from reasons entirely beyond [his] control." (Note that in cases of "bad faith" inability to comply, sources may receive DCOs under section 113 but still have to pay penalties under section 120.) The amount of the penalty assessed under section 120 shall be equal to "no less than the economic value which a delay in compliance beyond July 1, 1979 may have for the owner of such source," including both capital and operating costs, minus the amount of any expenditures actually made for the purpose of bringing the source into and maintaining compliance. Orders and payments under section 120 are in addition to other civil or criminal sanctions which may be imposed under the Act or state or local law.

Like these noncompliance penalties, existing effluent charge systems in other countries involve fees on discharges in excess of fixed effluent standards. That is, rather than adopting "pure" effluent charge systems, governments have chosen a combination of direct regulation and charges. In Hungary, for example, charges are based on the estimated costs of attaining the regulatory standards, though the condition of receiving waters and other factors also are considered. The same is true in East Germany. Most charge systems in operation rely on self-monitoring by polluters, with random spot checks by the regulators; the Hungarian system, however, appears to rely solely on discharge sampling by the government.

It should be noted that under a pure effluent charge system there would be no requirement that a polluter limit his discharges at all. So long as he was willing to pay the charges, then he would be in compliance with the law. This is not true with a system involving charges only for discharges in excess of publicly established effluent limitations. Another aspect of the pure charge system is that a polluter *always* has some financial incentive to reduce his pollution further, down to zero. There is no continuing incentive under either a pure regulatory system or a system involving a combination of direct regulation plus effluent charges payable only on discharges in excess of the regulatory limits.

2. MARKETABLE DISCHARGE PERMITS

Another kind of economic incentive system which has attracted attention in recent years would allocate discharge rights by means of publicly issued permits, which could be sold to other present or prospective dischargers, or to nondischargers entering the market for speculative or environmentalist purposes. Most proposals would limit the duration of permits to some specified time, such as five or ten years.

There are several ways in which initial permittees could be chosen. Permits could be allocated among existing polluters (free or for a price), or among broader groups of applicants by auction or lottery. There could be a question about whether nondischargers should be allowed to participate in the initial distribution, since acceptable ambient pollution levels presumably could be maintained even with all permits being exercised.

Once the permits had been allocated initially, they would be transferable, and sale prices would function as free-market equivalents of officially established effluent charges. Like an effluent charge system, a system of marketable permits would provide a continuous incentive to reduce pollution, since retained permits would tie up funds which could be freed by sale of unneeded permits for the going price. However, the permit system would involve two distinct advantages

[*128*]

over a charge system. First, the permit system would avoid the problems, discussed in the preceding section, related to setting effluent charges at the proper level. The government would set the price of a permit, if at all, only at the time of its initial issuance. If the price were wrongly fixed in relation to market forces, there would be automatic adjustments as permits were resold. The second advantage would be that, even if prices were "wrongly" fixed by the government or the market, there nevertheless would be a fixed limit on total permissible discharges. Excessive discharges and damage to the environment would not be "legal", as they would be under an effluent charge system (assuming willingness to pay the effluent charges), but could occur only through outright violation of the regulatory limit set in the permit.

It should be noted that transfers of permits from one geographic area to another—e.g., from one stretch of a stream to another, or from one portion of an air quality control region to another—would have to be regulated by exchange rates so set by the issuing authority that trading could not cause water or air quality to fall below the prescribed ambient standard at any site. For example, if discharges of BOD into stream zone B would be twice as harmful to a critical reach as identical discharges into zone A further upstream, a permit might allow a polluter to discharge either one pound per day into zone B or two pounds per day into zone A. Very fine distinctions between zones and the amounts of discharges authorized would provide more assured protection for ambient water or air quality, but also would complicate transfers and perhaps impair the marketability of permits.

Although no marketable permit systems have been instituted formally in this country, the "offset" requirement for construction of new sources in "nonattainment" areas under the Clean Air Act has had the effect of creating a market in emission rights. As we gain experience from operation of this market, and from the establishment of more "banking" arrangements by state and local governments, we shall be in a better position to evaluate the future of true marketable discharge permit systems.

CHAPTER 3

REGULATION OF TOXIC SUBSTANCES

A decade ago most of the effort in the environmental area was directed toward reducing smog, preserving wilderness areas, and cleaning up the nation's water. These remain high priorities today. In the meantime, however, a major new area of concern has emerged. We are becoming increasingly aware of the threats posed by chemicals which are released into the environment in relatively small amounts but which may pose severe threats to human life or health. Toxic substances regulation is one of the fastest growing areas of environmental law. In the first part of this chapter, we will begin by briefly sketching the scope of the toxics problem and by considering some of the more important statutes dealing with this problem. Then, in the second part of the chapter, we will consider one of the most serious obstacles to effective regulation. That obstacle is our lack of reliable scientific knowledge about the extent of the threat posed by particular chemicals. The problem of scientific uncertainty is, in fact, the most distinctive attribute of this area of environmental law.

A. TOXICS PROBLEM AND THE REGULATORY SCHEME

Several incidents involving toxic chemicals have received widespread publicity. In one incident, a Virginia chemical company dumped over 1.5 million gallons of a highly toxic material known as Kepone into the James River. In another well-known incident, Love Canal (a residential area of Niagra Falls) was found to have been built over a chemical dump containing roughly 352 million pounds of industrial wastes. Ultimately, the President was forced to declare a state of emergency in this area. At least one thousand other hazardous waste sites pose serious hazards.

Synthetic chemicals have become a pervasive part of our environment. Over 9,000 synthetics are now in significant commercial use. Production of the top 50 chemicals totals over 400 billion pounds per year. Society reaps enormous benefits from these chemicals, but their use has greatly increased the risk of grave health problems. For example, polychlorinated biphenyls (PCBs) had been in use for 40 years and approximately 390,000 tons had been released into the environment before this chemical was recognized as an enduring environmental poison. In the meantime, approximately 440,000 pounds of PCBs were discharged into the Hudson River, posing a health threat to the many up-state New

Yorkers who drink the water. Another chemical, vinyl chloride, was the twenty-third most produced chemical when it was discovered to cause cancer.

No coherent statutory scheme exists for regulating toxic chemicals. Instead, the toxics problem is dealt with by numerous federal statutes, most of which were enacted largely to deal with quite different problems. The most important of these statutes are the federal pesticide law, the Clean Water Act, the Resource Conservation and Recovery Act (RCRA), the so-called "superfund" law, and the Toxic Substances Control Act (TSCA). We will discuss briefly the main features of each of these statutes as they relate to toxic chemicals.

1. PESTICIDE REGULATION

The earliest toxic chemical problem to receive widespread public attention was that of pesticides, thanks in large part to Rachael Carson's *Silent Spring*. The federal statute regulating pesticides is called FIFRA, which stands for the Federal Insecticide, Fungicide and Rodenticide Act. In its present form, the act contains two significant sections. Section 135 embodies the original legislative scheme. Under this section, "economic poisons" must be registered with the EPA before they may be distributed in interstate commerce. An economic poison may lawfully be registered only if it is properly labeled. Proper labeling in turn requires that the label contain a warning or cautionary statement to prevent injury to human beings and to the environment. If no such label is possible because the substance is inherently unsafe, then the substance cannot be registered. If a substance is registered and later information indicates possible hazards, EPA can cancel the registration after a hearing. If the hazard is imminent, the EPA can suspend the substance's registration pending completion of the cancellation proceeding.

Section 136 now deals particularly with pesticides. This section resembles section 135 but contains a number of new provisions. First, the criterion for cancellation is "unreasonable environmental risk", which requires a weighing of harm and benefits. Second, the statute requires automatic review of each registration every five years. Third, it contains more detailed procedural requirements relating to suspension. Under section 136c(c), a suspension hearing must be held at the defendant's request within five days. If even a five-day delay would present a hazard, EPA may issue an emergency suspension. Fourth, EPA is required to consider restrictions on types or methods of use as an alternative to cancellation, and also to consider the effect of cancellation on the agricultural economy.

In a series of opinions arising out of disputes between EPA and the Environmental Defense Fund, the D.C. Circuit has created an extensive case law applying FIFRA. These opinions have established a number of rules concerning the burden of proof in suspension and cancellation proceedings. Once EPA decides to issue a notice of cancellation, a presumption arises in favor of suspension. The suspension decision is analogous to the issuance of a preliminary injunction and calls for the balancing of the equities. Issuance of a notice of cancellation shows that a substantial question of safety exists and, in the absence of countervailing benefits, requires suspension. (Conceivably, EPA could find that the evidence of risk was just strong enough to justify cancellation proceedings but that the danger was not quite immediate enough to justify suspension.) When EPA does suspend registration, a presumption will arise in favor of cancellation if (a) no benefit is shown, or (b) animal tests show that the chemical causes cancer. Moreover, if evidence shows that one mode of exposure is hazardous, a presumption arises that all modes are hazardous until proven otherwise. Thus, for example, if inhalation of a chemical is dangerous, there is a presumption that ingestion of the chemical would also be dangerous. Although these presumptions were developed on a somewhat *ad hoc* basis in a series of cases, the cases do have a unifying rationale when viewed as a group. In each case,

the court has held that the burden of proof is on
the manufacturer once substantial evidence of a
health hazard has been shown. Essentially, once
EPA has found sufficient evidence of risk to justify initiation of cancellation proceedings, the burden is on the proponent of continued registration
to demonstrate that the risk is minimal or that
the benefits of use outweigh the risks.

2. TOXIC CHEMICALS UNDER THE GEN-
ERAL POLLUTION STATUTES

Both the Clean Air Act and the Clean Water
Act contain specific provisions relating to toxics.
The provisions of the Clean Air Act are relatively
straightforward. Section 112 of the Act provides
for national emission standards for hazardous air
pollutants. The definition of a hazardous air pollutant has two elements. First, the pollutant
must not be covered by an ambient air quality
standard. Second, it must cause or contribute to
air pollution which "may reasonably be anticipated to result in an increase in mortality or an increase in serious irreversible, or incapacitating reversible, illness." Standards governing such
pollutants are to provide "an ample margin of
safety to protect the public health from such hazardous air pollutants." After promulgation of
such a standard, no new source may be constructed which will violate the standard. Existing
sources are given 90 days to meet the standard

unless they obtain a waiver from the EPA for a period of up to two years. If it is not feasible to enforce an emission standard, EPA may instead issue regulations controlling design, equipment, work practices, or operations.

Regulation under the Clean Water Act is more complex. As originally enacted in 1972, the Clean Water Act contained a section somewhat similar to section 112 of the Clean Air Act. This section required EPA to publish a list of toxic pollutants and to implement standards for these pollutants providing an "ample margin of safety." For various reasons, implementation of this section proved impractical. The agency lacked sufficient information about toxic pollutants and was not given sufficient time to develop such information under the statutory timetable. Furthermore, because of the "ample margin of safety" requirement, the agency had no leeway to consider feasibility. As a result, implementation of the statutory scheme would have required extensive plant closures and would have caused severe economic injury to some major industries.

The 1977 amendments to the Clean Water Act were an outgrowth of these problems. Because of the difficulty of implementing the original section, EPA had entered into a consent decree with the NRDC governing toxic pollutants. The decree required EPA to issue effluent limitations and new source performance standards for 21 major industries requiring the use of best available technology (BAT). The 1977 amendments essentially codified this consent decree. Under the present statute, a list of toxic pollutants is specified in section 307(a)(1). Each pollutant on the list is subject to effluent limitations based on the BAT standard. This requirement is contained in section 307(2) and is also incorporated in section 301(b)(2)(A). EPA in its discretion may impose more stringent limitations based on the "ample margin of safety" standard. Section 307 also provides for pretreatment standards for wastes that are to be introduced into municipal treatment systems rather than being discharged directly into the nation's waterways. These pretreatment standards are intended to prevent introduction of substances that cannot be adequately treated by public facilities or that might damage those facilities.

Two of the cases involving toxic water pollution are particularly interesting. In Hercules, Inc. v. EPA, 598 F.2d 91 (D.C.Cir.1978), the D.C. Circuit held that toxic substances covered by pre-1977 health-based standards remain subject to those standards after the 1977 amendments. The court emphasized that Congress was impatient with EPA's slow progress in regulating toxic water pollution. The new amendments were intended to allow more vigorous regulation, rather than representing a retreat by Congress from the protection of the public health. The court also held that section 307(a)(4) standards do not require consideration of economic or technological feasibility. In implementing such health-based standards, section 307(a)(2) requires EPA to "take into account" six factors. None of the six factors relates to feasibility, and the court held that this list of six factors was exclusive. Thus, when the agency acts under section 307(a)(4) (which requires use of an "ample margin of safety"), feasibility is not relevant. In another significant case, the Fourth Circuit held that the 1977 standards for toxic pollutants are subject to variances, despite section 301(1), which states that EPA "may not modify any requirement" of the section as it applies to any toxic pollutant. Appalachian Power Co. v. Train, 620 F.2d 1040 (4th Cir.1980). The Fourth Circuit held that a variance from the 1977 standards is not a "true variance", but is rather a tailoring of the general statutory standards to the specific situation of the individual source. (For further discussion of the nature of variances in relation to the 1977 standards the reader should consult Chapter 2–C–2.)

3. THE RESOURCE CONSERVATION AND RECOVERY ACT (RCRA)

RCRA was a response to growing public awareness of serious problems relating to the disposal of hazardous wastes. According to EPA estimates, 51 million tons of hazardous wastes are produced each year, and only 10 percent are properly handled. Of the 30,000 to 50,000 hazardous waste sites, at least 1,000 are thought to pose serious hazards. One of the primary risks is that toxic chemicals will enter groundwater and contaminate public drinking supplies. The primary basis for regulation of this problem is RCRA.

The hazardous waste provisions of the Act are contained in subtitle C of RCRA. Section 3001 requires EPA to promulgate criteria for identifying hazardous waste "taking into account toxicity, persistence, and degradability in nature, potential for accumulation in tissues," and other hazardous traits such as corrosiveness and flammability. These criteria are to be used as the basis for issuing a list of hazardous wastes. The remaining provisions of subtitle C relate to standards and enforcement.

Three sets of standards are required, covering generators, transporters, and disposal sites. EPA is given broad authority to prescribe such standards "as may be required to protect human health and environment". Certain specific types of standards are also required. Section 3002 requires standards for generators of hazardous wastes covering record-keeping, reporting, labeling, and use of appropriate containers. Section 3002(5) requires use of a manifest system to en-

[*140*]

sure that the hazardous waste generated by the source is ultimately processed onsite or at a facility with a section 3005 permit. The manifest system is incorporated into section 3003, which requires standards for transporters. (Transporters are also subject to recordkeeping and labeling requirements.) As the last phase of this "cradle to grave" system for hazardous wastes, section 3004 requires standards covering storage and disposal facilities. These standards cover compliance with the manifest system and other recordkeeping requirements. More importantly, they also cover treatment and disposal methods, as well as location, construction, and operation of disposal sites.

A permit system established under section 3005 is the key enforcement provision for disposal sites. EPA is given broad inspection powers (section 3007) and the power to issue compliance orders (with violators subject to a civil penalty) or bring a civil action against violators of any requirement (section 3008). Criminal penalties are also available for violation of the permit requirements or falsification of documents (section 3008(d)). Finally, RCRA makes careful provision for state regulation. Under a provision modeled on the Clean Water Act, states may assume responsibility for hazardous waste control (section 3006). State laws less stringent than federal requirements are preempted when the federal requirements become effective (section 3009). There are over 50,000 firms handling toxic wastes and subject to RCRA.

In addition to EPA's regulatory powers, RCRA also gives EPA authority to seek injunctive relief under certain circumstances. Section 7003 provides:

> Notwithstanding any other provision of this chapter, upon receipt of evidence that the handling, storage, treatment, transportation or disposal of any solid waste or hazardous waste is presenting an imminent and substantial endangerment to health or the environment, the Administrator may bring suit on behalf of the United States in the appropriate district court to immediately restrain any person contributing to the alleged disposal to stop such handling, storage, treatment, transportation, or disposal, or to take such other action as may be necessary. The Administrator shall provide notice to the affected State of any such suit.

The district courts have generally required only a relatively low level of danger to trigger the provision. On the other hand, in imposing remedies, they have balanced the hardship to the defendant against the public interest. A recent Court of Appeals decision, United States v. Price, 688 F.2d 204 (3d Cir.1982), cautions against undermining

RCRA by "either withholding relief or granting it grudgingly."

Another response to situations like Love Canal was passage of the so-called superfund legislation. This statute is more officially known as the Comprehensive Environmental Response, Compensation, and Liability Act of 1980 (CERCLA). The Act contains three major provisions. First, it authorizes the President to require clean-up of releases of toxic materials in accordance with a Presidentially implemented "national contingency plan." This authority can be delegated to the states. Second, the Act makes owners of facilities liable for government clean-up costs, and for destruction of natural resources owned by governmental units. The Act does not provide for liability for injuries to private individuals. Third, the Act establishes a fund, financed by a tax on the production of toxic chemicals, to be used for payment of "response costs." These response costs include the expenses of the national contingency plan, and the government's costs of restoring natural resources which have been injured by toxic chemicals. As yet, the Act has not been fully implemented.

4. THE TOXIC SUBSTANCES CONTROL ACT (TSCA)

Prior to 1976, as we have seen, federal regulation of toxics consisted of an assortment of specialized provisions, most of them contained in statutes whose main focus was elsewhere. The potential for regulatory gaps was obvious. In 1976, Congress moved to fill these gaps by passing the first comprehensive legislation governing toxic substances. The statute is hardly a masterpiece of insightful policymaking or incisive drafting. In part, its flaws are due to the existence of serious conflicts between the House and Senate versions, which were resolved with last-minute compromises. If experience with other environmental statutes is any guide, major amendments can be expected in the early years of implementation. Yet, the present statute is an important first step.

The Act as a whole must be read in light of the policy section (section 2(b)). Three policies are set forth. First, data should be developed on the environmental effects of chemicals; primary responsibility for the development of this data is placed on industry. Second, the government should have adequate authority to prevent unreasonable risks of injury to health or the environment, particularly imminent hazards. Finally, this authority should be exercised so as "not to impede unduly or create unnecessary economic barriers to technological innovation while fulfilling the primary purpose of this Act to assure that . . . such chemical substances . . . do not present an unreasonable risk of injury

. . . ." Obviously, much will depend on the relative weights given to these conflicting goals of protecting technological development and assuring environmental safety.

The most important substantive provisions of the Act are found in sections 4, 5, and 6. These sections concern testing, premanufacturing clearance, and regulation of manufacturing and distribution. We will consider only the main outlines of these provisions, without too much attention to the innumerable exemptions, exceptions, qualifications and procedural details.

Section 4 relates to testing. It empowers the EPA to adopt rules requiring testing by manufacturers of substances. Such rules must be based on a finding that insufficient data are currently available concerning the substance, and that the substance may "present an unreasonable risk," "enter the environment in substantial quantities," or present a likelihood of "substantial human exposure." There are, naturally, a variety of complicated procedural devices set out in exhaustive detail in the remainder of the section. In addition to section 4, the statute contains several other provisions aimed at collection of information.

Section 5 requires a manufacturer to give notice to the EPA before manufacturing a new chemical substance. If the substance is covered by a section 4 rule, the section 4 test results must be submitted along with the section 5 notice. For

substances not covered by section 4, but listed by
EPA as possibly hazardous, the manufacturer is
to submit data it believes show the absence of
any unreasonable risk of injury. Normally, the
next step would be a section 6 proceeding. But if
EPA finds that an unreasonable risk may be presented before a section 6 rule can be promulgated, it can issue a "proposed section 6 rule" which
will be immediately effective, issue an administrative order prohibiting manufacture, or seek an injunction (section 5(f)). Often, of course, EPA will
not have sufficient information to make a definite
finding about safety. EPA can then make findings similar to those triggering the section 4 testing rules and issue an administrative order
prohibiting manufacture or use. (If a timely objection to the order is filed, however, EPA must
seek injunctive relief (section 5(e)).

Section 6, unlike section 5, applies to all chemicals not just to new chemicals or new uses. The
finding necessary to trigger section 6 is that
"there is a reasonable basis to conclude" that the
substance "presents or will present an unreasonable risk of injury to health or the environment
. . . ." Having made such a finding, EPA may
by rule apply any of a number of restrictions "to
the extent necessary to protect adequately
against such risk using the least burdensome requirements" (section 6(a)). Obviously, much will
depend on whether more weight is given to the

[*146*]

"protect adequately" standard or to the "least burdensome" standard. In general, EPA is directed to use its powers under other statutes in preference to section 6 (section 6(c)). The effective date of a proposed rule may be accelerated if the EPA finds a likelihood of "an unreasonable risk of serious or widespread injury to health or the environment" before the effective date of the final rule. The requirements for acceleration under section 6(d), it should be noted, are somewhat different from those applicable to new chemicals under section 5(f). Finally, section 6 contains a special provision for the phasing out of polychlorinated biphenyls (PCBs).

One other provision which deserves mention is section 7, which allows EPA to obtain emergency judicial relief in case of "imminent hazards". The Act also contains the usual panoply of provisions on civil and criminal penalties, judicial enforcement, judicial review, hybrid rulemaking, and preemption.

After three years, EPA had only begun to put the statutory scheme into operation. It had compiled an initial inventory of 43,000 "old" chemicals, which it planned to revise. Its efforts to select chemicals for further testing were stalled by problems in developing the testing rules. By June 1979, EPA had managed to complete at least preliminary assessments of 74 chemicals, and it had promulgated a rule banning all non-essential uses of chlorofluorcarbons for aerosol sprays. Most of EPA's attention, however, has been focused on rulemaking efforts for new chemicals, on the theory that it is more efficient to prevent the introduction of new chemicals before widespread use.

B. PROBLEM OF SCIENTIFIC UNCERTAINTY

Many of the issues involved in toxics regulation are common in other areas of environmental law. For instance, we have already examined issues relating to the scope of judicial review and the relevance of cost and feasibility to regulation. In the toxics area, these issues are made even more intractable because regulation often takes place at or beyond the edge of scientific knowledge. How does a court engage in judicial review when even the leading experts in a field are unable to reach firm conclusions? How can a cost-benefit analysis be conducted when the substance being regulated is possibly deadly, but no one knows the odds?

The federal courts have been confronted with this problem on several occasions. For several years the only judicial opinions were those of the courts of appeals. More recently, the Supreme Court has had occasion to address this issue in two cases. We will begin by discussing the lower court opinions and will then turn to the Supreme Court's decisions.

1. THE LOWER COURT DECISIONS

The leading case on the problem of scientific uncertainty is Reserve Mining Co. v. EPA, 514 F.2d 492 (8th Cir.1975). Reserve Mining disposed of great quantities of mining byproducts by discharging them into Lake Superior. These materials contained asbestos, which is known to be a cause of cancer when inhaled. The district court ordered an immediate halt to all further discharges, which would have required closing the facility. On appeal, the Eighth Circuit considered three issues: (1) whether the ingestion of fibers, as opposed to inhalation, poses any health hazard, (2) whether that hazard is sufficiently great to justify judicial intervention, and (3) what form the remedy should take.

In considering the question of risk the court was handicapped by a lack of scientific evidence. The district court had directed a study of the tissues of long-time Duluth residents to determine whether asbestos fibers were present. The plaintiffs' principal medical witness had testified that the study should disclose the presence of asbestos if indeed asbestos is absorbed by the body. He explained that the individuals in question had ingested Duluth water for at least 15 years and that the water, drawn from Lake Superior, con-

[*149*]

tained substantial amounts of fibers. Nevertheless, the study failed to indicate that Duluth residents had any greater amounts of asbestos in
their tissues than residents of Houston, where
the water is free of asbestos fibers. Moreover,
animal tests intended to determine whether ingested fibers penetrate into the body were incon-
clusive and produced conflicting results. On the
other hand, strong evidence did exist that workers exposed to asbestos dust suffered from a
moderately increased rate of gastrointestinal cancer. One possible explanation, according to expert witnesses, was that asbestos workers first
inhaled the asbestos dust and then coughed up
and swallowed the asbestos particles. Taking all
of this evidence together, the most the court
could conclude was that public exposure to asbestos fibers "creates some health risk." The court
was unable to conclude, however, that "the
probability of harm is more likely than not."

The next issue to confront the court was
whether this showing of harm was sufficient to
satisfy the requirements of the Clean Water Act.
The Act authorizes suit by the federal government to abate discharges in interstate waters
where the discharges "endanger . . . the
health or welfare of persons." After careful consideration of the statute, the court concluded that
the requirement of a danger to public health was
satisfied by the evidence before it.

The final question was the form of the relief. The district court had ordered an immediate halt to discharges. Because of the weakness of the evidence of harm, the cost both to industry and the public of closing the plant, and the company's willingness to spend $243 million to dispose of the materials more safely, the court held that closing the plant was unnecessary. Balancing the equities, the court ordered that Reserve be given a reasonable time to stop discharging its wastes into Lake Superior.

The *Reserve* decision received strong support from the D.C. Circuit's opinion in Ethyl Corp. v. EPA, 541 F.2d 1 (D.C.Cir.1976) (en banc). That case involved section 211(c)(1)(A) of the Clean Air Act. This section authorizes EPA to regulate gasoline additives whose emission products "will endanger the public health or welfare." Acting pursuant to this power, EPA determined that lead additives in gasoline present "a significant risk of harm" to the public health and issued orders limiting the use of such additives. As in *Reserve Mining*, the court was faced with a high degree of scientific uncertainty. In this case, however, the uncertainty was not as to the harmfulness of the material. Lead is well known to be toxic and clearly can be absorbed into the body from ambient air. Nevertheless, because human beings are exposed to multiple sources of lead, it was difficult to determine whether the in-

[*151*]

cremental increase in the amount of lead in the environment due to gasoline additives had serious health effects. In upholding the EPA, the court stressed that assessment of risks involves policy judgments rather than simply factual determinations. Thus, the court accorded substantial deference to the EPA's conclusion. As the court explained:

Questions involving the environment are particularly prone to uncertainty. Technological man has altered his world in ways never before experienced or anticipated. The health effects of such alterations are often unknown, sometimes unknowable. While a concerned Congress has passed legislation providing for protection of the public health against gross environmental modifications, the regulators entrusted with the enforcement of such laws have not thereby been endowed with a prescience that removes all doubt from their decision making. Rather, speculation, conflicts, and theoretical extrapolation typify their every action. How else can they act, given a mandate to protect the public health but only a slight or nonexistent data base upon which to draw? . . .

Undoubtedly, certainty is a scientific ideal—to the extent that even science can be certain of its truth. But certainty in the complexities of environmental medicine may be achievable only after the fact, when scientists

[*152*]

have the opportunity for leisurely and isolated scrutiny of an entire mechanism. Awaiting certainty will often allow for only reactive, not preventive regulation. Petitioners suggest that anything less than certainty, that any speculation, is irresponsible. But when statutes seek to avoid environmental catastrophe, can preventive, albeit uncertain, decisions legitimately be so labeled?

Thus, the court concluded that a rigorous step-by-step proof of cause and effect should not be demanded where a statute is precautionary in nature, the evidence is on the frontiers of scientific knowledge, and regulations are designed to protect the public health. Hence, EPA may apply its expertise to draw conclusions from "suspected, but not completely substantiated" relationships between facts, from trends among facts, from theoretical projections and so forth.

This approach has been followed in numerous lower court opinions. For example, in Lead Industries Association, Inc. v. EPA, 647 F.2d 1130 (D.C.Cir.1980), the D.C. Circuit upheld a primary air quality standard for lead which incorporated an "adequate margin of safety." In setting the margin of safety, EPA had given no consideration to feasibility or cost. Moreover, the evidence of harm was unclear. Nevertheless, the court held that feasibility and cost were irrelevant and that EPA had acted properly in setting the mar-

[*153*]

gin of safety. As the court explained, use of a margin of safety is an important method of protecting against effects which have not yet been uncovered by research and effects whose medical significance is a matter of disagreement. As the court also explained, "Congress has recently acknowledged that more often than not the 'margins of safety' that are incorporated into air quality standards turn out to be very modest or nonexistent, as new information reveals adverse health effects at pollution levels once thought to be harmless." The court also reiterated the need for deference to EPA's expert judgments on these issues. Finally, the court held that the margin of safety requirement could be fulfilled by making conservative decisions at various points in the regulatory process, rather than by determining a safe level and adding a percentage to that as the "margin of safety."

In general, these lower court decisions demonstrated a high degree of deference to EPA's expert judgment. The lower courts, by and large, gave little weight to questions of cost and feasibility when dealing with toxic chemicals. Finally, these courts recognized that administrative action was justified without a showing that harmful effects were more likely than not. Instead, these courts concluded that regulatory intervention was justified whenever a reasonable likelihood of danger could be found.

[*154*]

Against this background of lower court decisions, we now turn to the two Supreme Court opinions in this area.

2. SUPREME COURT DECISIONS

The Supreme Court did not have occasion to consider the problem of toxic chemicals until 1980. It has now decided two cases in the area. Before proceeding to consider these cases, it should be noted that they arise in a somewhat different context from most environmental issues. Both of the Supreme Court cases involve protection of workers by the Occupational Safety and Health Administration (OSHA). These cases thus involve a rather special kind of environmental problem, since the environment in question is not one used by the general public.

The policy issues presented in OSHA cases are somewhat different from those in normal environmental cases. First, exposure to the risk is somewhat more voluntary than is exposure to, say, ambient air pollution. Second, negotiations between the source of the hazard and the possible victims are feasible to a much greater extent than in the normal pollution case. This is especially true when the victims of the hazard, the employees, are represented by a union. Thus, the transaction costs of private settlements are sometimes much smaller here. Third, the possible victims of the hazard have a much greater

[*155*]

stake in the economic health of the enterprise creating the hazard than is the case generally in environmental disputes. The option of closing the plant down in order to end the hazard is generally not acceptable to the workers, nor are actions which would seriously jeopardize the prospects for continued employment. For all of these reasons, the balance between protection from risks versus economic cost may be somewhat different than in the normal environmental case.

Moreover, the statutory scheme is primarily concerned with quite different problems of worker protection. The only provision dealing expressly with toxic chemicals is section 6(b)(5) of the Act, 29 U.S.C.A. § 655(d)(5). This provision requires the agency to set a standard for any toxic material "which most adequately assures, to the extent feasible, that no employee will suffer material impairment of health or functional capacity . . . ." Another section of the Act, section 3(a), 29 U.S.C.A. § 652(a), has been thought to be relevant by at least some members of the Court. This section simply defines an occupational safety and health standard as a regulation setting any one of a variety of requirements "reasonably necessary or appropriate to provide safe or healthful places of employment." These provisions are vaguer and provide less guidance than most of the analogous provisions of the Clean Air Act or Clean Water Act. In short, both the statu-

[*156*]

tory context and the policy choices presented in this area are atypical. It is unfortunate therefore that the only guidance we have had from the Supreme Court has been in this rather abnormal setting.

The Supreme Court's first encounter with the problem of toxic chemicals was Industrial Union Department v. American Petroleum Institute, 448 U.S. 607 (1980). (This decision is generally known as the "benzene case.") The case involved an OSHA regulation governing benzene. Benzene is known to be a carcinogen, and no safe level of exposure is known. On this basis, the Secretary of Labor had set the permissible exposure level for workers at 1 ppm (part per million), which he considered the lowest feasible level. OSHA estimated the total cost of compliance as including $266 million in capital investments, $200 million in first-year start-up costs, and $34 million in annual costs. About 35,000 employees would benefit from the regulation. The Fifth Circuit had struck down the regulation on the theory that the statute implicitly required a cost-benefit analysis by the agency. On review, only one member of the Supreme Court reached this issue; another member of the Court went off on a constitutional ground; and the Court divided 4–4 on another statutory issue.

The primary opinion was written by Justice Stevens but was joined in its entirety by only two other justices. Justice Powell also joined parts of the opinion. This plurality opinion resolved the case on the basis of an interpretation of section 3(8) as a limitation on section 6(b). According to the plurality opinion, section 3(8) requires that OSHA make a threshold finding of a "significant risk of harm" before issuing any regulation. On close examination of the record, the plurality observed that the industry had argued that the regulation would save at most two lives every six years. According to the plurality, a risk of one in a billion is clearly insignificant, but a risk of one in a thousand "might well" be considered significant. The Court declined to determine whether the risk level alleged by industry would be considered significant, since the agency itself had made no finding on this issue, which the plurality thought to be a critical requirement of the Act.

The plurality opinion goes to some lengths to rebut the dissent's charge that its approach would prevent effective regulation until deaths had actually occurred. First, the plurality stated that what constitutes a "significant" risk was a judgment for the agency to make and plainly involved policy considerations. Second, the plurality noted that the agency's findings need not be supported by "anything approaching scientific certainty." The agency must be given "some leeway" when its findings are made on the frontiers of scientific knowledge. Thus, the plurality concluded:

[S]o long they are supported by a body of reputable scientific thought, the Agency is free to use conservative assumptions in interpreting the data with respect to carcinogens, risking error on the side of over-protection rather than under-protection.

In a concurring opinion Chief Justice Burger was careful to stress the limitations of the plurality opinion. According to the Chief Justice:

A holding that the Secretary must retrace his steps with greater care and consideration is not to be taken in derogation of the scope of legitimate Agency discretion. When the facts and arguments have been presented and duly considered, the Secretary must make a policy judgment as to whether a specific risk of health impairment is significant in terms of the policy objectives of the statute. When he acts in this capacity, pursuant to the legislative authority delegated by Congress, he exercises the prerogatives of the legislature—to focus on only one aspect of a larger problem, or to promulgate regulations that, to some, may appear as imprudent policy or inefficient allocation of resources. The judicial function does not extend to substantive revision of regulatory policy.

The Chief Justice noted however, that "[p]erfect safety is a chimera; regulation must not strangle human activity in the search for the impossible."

Justice Powell was the only member of the Court to reach the cost-benefit issue. He agreed with the plurality opinion's reading of the statute. He also concluded, however, that the Agency was required to give fuller consideration to cost than it had done.

These four justices all based their vote on statutory grounds. The decisive fifth vote was cast by Justice Rehnquist, who reached his decision on constitutional grounds. Justice Rehnquist concluded that Congress had in fact provided no standard at all concerning the threshold requirements for regulation. He believed that Congress was simply unwilling to decide the relative weights to be given to protection of human life versus economic cost. Because Congress had failed to make this basic policy decision, Justice Rehnquist argued that the statute was an unconstitutional delegation of legislative authority to the agency. This view is somewhat out of line with the Supreme Court's decisions over the last half century. Not since the Court's unsuccessful attempt to block the New Deal has the Court struck down a statute on this basis.

Justice Marshall wrote a stinging dissent, joined by Justices Brennan, White and Blackmun. Justice Marshall found it incredible that the plurality could read any substantive meaning into the statutory definition of a health standard as one "reasonably necessary" to provide safe employment. In his view, the relevant section of the statute was plainly section 6, and the meaning of that section was clear: in dealing with any toxic chemical, the Secretary was to set a standard which would *ensure* that no risk would be presented to any employee. Furthermore, Justice Marshall argued that the "plurality's discussion of the record in this case is both extraordinarily arrogant and extraordinarily unfair." In his view, the Court was usurping the agency's power to make factual findings and was mischaracterizing virtually every aspect of the agency's decision. He concluded by accusing the plurality of "an extreme reaction to a regulatory scheme that, as the members of the plurality perceived it, imposed an unduly harsh burden on regulated industries."

This decision clearly leaves the law in a state of confusion. Only four members of the Court believed that a "significant risk" finding was required by the statute. Four members disagreed, while a fifth member believed that the statute was completely silent on the problem. Moreover, to the extent that the plurality approach represents the law, its meaning is quite unclear. In particular, the test for a "significant risk" is not stated with clarity. Finally, the standard used by

the plurality seems to be set too high. Note that
the plurality says a one-in-a-thousand risk "might
well" be considered significant. As applied to the
general population, such a risk level would mean
approximately 240,000 deaths. How may additional deaths would be required before the plurality would find a risk clearly significant?

The Supreme Court's other decision in this area
does little to clarify this issue. That case, American Textile Manufacturers Institute, Inc. v. Dono-
van, 452 U.S. 490 (1981), was decided one year after the benzene case. *Textile Manufacturers*
involved a standard regulating cotton dust. Cotton dust is the cause of a disease called byssinosis, more commonly known as "brown lung"
disease. The primary issue before the Supreme
Court was whether the agency was required to
engage in a cost-benefit analysis when issuing its
regulation. In an opinion by Justice Brennan, the
Court held that no cost-benefit analysis was necessary. According to the Court, all that is necessary is a feasibility analysis, that is, an analysis
showing that performance is possible but not an
analysis comparing the cost of compliance with
the benefits of the regulation.

The benzene case is discussed only in a footnote in *Textile Manufacturers*. The Court's discussion is not very helpful because the risk issue
in *Textile Manufacturers* was easy to resolve.
OSHA had expressly found that "exposure to cot-

ton dust presents a significant health hazard to employees." Data relied on by the agency showed that 25% of all employees in the industry suffered at least low-grade byssinosis, and that even at the level required by the new standard, about half this many employees would suffer from the disease. Thus, the prevalence of the disease "should be significantly reduced" by the new regulation. As the Court said, "[i]t is difficult to imagine what else the Agency could do to comply with this Court's decision in [the benzene case]."

Justice Powell took no part in the decision of the case, while Justice Stewart dissented on a factual ground. Justice Rehnquist, now joined by Chief Justice Burger, continued to argue that the statute was an unconstitutional delegation of legislative responsibility. Thus, with the exception of Justice Powell, no member of the Court has at any time agreed with the argument that a cost-benefit analysis is required by the statute. Five members of the Court have clearly rejected that position in favor of requiring only a feasibility analysis. Another group of four justices believes that a threshold finding of "significant risk" is required, while an equal number disagree.

The implications of these OSHA decisions for toxic regulation in general remain unclear. The four dissenters in the benzene case have clearly endorsed the approach taken by lower courts in cases like *Reserve Mining*. The members of the plurality in the benzene case have taken a more cautious view, but apparently are not willing to squarely reject the prevailing approach in the lower courts. One member of the Court, Justice Rehnquist, has never spoken to the merits of any of these issues, while the newest member of the Court, Justice O'Connor, was not present for the decision of either of these cases. Thus, we can only speculate about the direction in which the Court is likely to go in the future. Certainly, however, it would be an exaggeration to see the Supreme Court opinions as a repudiation of the doctrines developed by the lower courts in this area. The extent to which the Court will modify these doctrines is, as yet, unclear. So far, the lower courts have not seemed to change significantly their approach in response to these Supreme Court opinions.

The area of toxic regulation will undoubtedly continue to be one of the fastest-growing areas of environmental law. Despite the decreased enthusiasm for government regulation in general, regulations protecting human health from hazards such as cancer are unlikely to be repudiated. We may well see, on the other hand, a greater attention paid to the costs of reducing health risks. It seems relatively unlikely, however, that radical changes in regulatory policy will be implemented.

CHAPTER 4

FEDERALISM AND THE ENVIRONMENT

Our nation is divided into fifty states along with the District of Columbia. Environmental problems pay no heed to these geographic lines. Frequently, an environmental problem in one state is caused by conduct in another. Hence, any one state may be effectively unable to protect its own environment. On the other hand, when a state does attempt to engage in environmental regulation, the activity that it regulates may well have repercussions elsewhere. The regulating state may fail to take into account the full costs imposed by its regulations on individuals in other jurisdictions. (The resemblance to the economic concept of "externalities" discussed earlier should not have escaped the reader.) Thus, problems inevitably result from our division of governmental power into units that do not correspond with sharp divisions in either the environment or the economy.

In partial compensation for these problems, however, we obtain the benefits of fuller local government. As a result, individual states in which the public is more strongly motivated to deal with environmental problems may take such action without being held back by the less interested citizens of other states. This allows the government to be more responsive to the desires of the population. Furthermore, states may act as laboratories, in which various forms of environmental regulation may be tried out before being used on a nationwide scale. In short, federalism is both a problem and a useful tool.

To a great extent, the idea of federalism has its impact through the political process. Congressmen may be reluctant to vote for legislation that infringes the traditional prerogatives of the states. The discussion in this chapter, however, will be limited to the constitutional dimensions of federalism. In the first part of the chapter we will consider the constitutional limits on environmental regulation by the federal government. In the second part of the chapter, we will consider the extent to which the constitution limits environmental regulation by the individual states.

A.   SCOPE OF FEDERAL POWER

One of the basic assumptions of American constitutional law is that the federal government does not have unlimited powers. It does not have, at least in theory, the power to take any action it deems in the public interest. Instead, it is a government of limited, delegated powers. Environmental regulation by the federal government must utilize one of a limited group of specif-

[*166*]

ic powers. For our present purposes, the most important of these specific powers are the power to regulate interstate commerce, the power to tax and spend, the power to enter into treaties, and the power to regulate the use of public lands. Together, these specific powers form an imposing arsenal of regulatory authority.

1. THE COMMERCE POWER

In practice, the most important of these federal powers is the power to regulate interstate commerce. The Supreme Court has recently reaffirmed the broad scope of this power in Hodel v. Virginia Surface Mining and Reclamation Association, Inc., 452 U.S. 264 (1981). The *Hodel* opinion involved the Surface Mining and Reclamation Act, 30 U.S.C.A. § 1201 et seq. The Act imposes a detailed series of regulatory restrictions on strip-mining. The most important of these restrictions require restoration of the land to approximately its original state. A mining association argued that the Act's principal goal was regulating the use of private lands rather than regulating the effects of coal mining on interstate commerce. Thus, the association contended, the ultimate issue was whether land as such was subject to regulation under the commerce clause. The Court rejected the attempt to frame

[*167*]

the question in this manner. According to the Court:

> The task of a court that is asked to determine whether a particular exercise of congressional power is valid under the Commerce Clause is relatively narrow. The court must defer to a congressional finding that a regulated activity affects interstate commerce, if there is any rational basis for such a finding . . . . .
>
> Judicial review in this area is influenced above all by the fact that the Commerce Clause is a grant of plenary authority to Congress. This power is "complete in itself, may be exercised to its utmost extent, and acknowledges no limitations other than prescribed in the constitution." Moreover, this Court has made clear that the commerce power not only extends to "the use of channels of interstate or foreign commerce" and to "protection of the instrumentalities of interstate commerce . . . or persons or things in commerce," but also to "activities affecting commerce." As we explained in Fry v. United States, 421 U.S. 542, 547 (1975), "[e]ven activity that is purely intrastate in character may be regulated by Congress, where the activity, combined with like conduct by others similarly situated, affects commerce among the States or with foreign nations." [citations omitted]

Applying this test to the Surface Mining Act, the Court found a rational basis for the congressional determination that surface mining affects interstate commerce. The effect of mining on water pollution was especially significant. The Court also noted that uniform national standards were necessary because of the difficulties encountered by attempts by individual states to regulate the problem.

The Court went on to hold that it was irrelevant whether land use is properly considered a "local" activity. So long as Congress rationally determines that regulation is necessary to protect interstate commerce from adverse effects, characterization of the activity as local is irrelevant. The Court also rejected the argument that the Act was unnecessary because various other federal standards already adequately addressed the federal interests in controlling the environmental effects of surface mining. According to the Court, the "short answer to this argument is that the effectiveness of existing laws in dealing with the problems identified by Congress is ordinarily a matter committed to legislative judgment."

In the companion case of Hodel v. Indiana, 452 U.S. 314 (1981), the Court rejected another attack on the same statute. The district court in this case had held unconstitutional the provisions of the Act which attempted to protect prime farm land. The district court found that only .006% of the total prime farm land in the nation was affected annually by mining and that the effect on interstate commerce was therefore "infinitessimal." The Supreme Court rejected this quantitative test. According to the Court, the "pertinent inquiry therefore is not how much commerce is involved but whether Congress could rationally conclude that the regulated activity affects interstate commerce." The Court found an ample basis for this conclusion. There was testimony before Congress about the effects of strip mining on agricultural productivity. The Court noted that even given the District Court's finding concerning the amount of land affected, the amount of grain production involved would still be in the neighborhood of $56 million per year, which as the Court observed "surely is not an insignificant amount of commerce."

The two *Hodel* opinions make it clear that congressional power under the commerce clause is broad indeed. So long as Congress can rationally conclude that a class of activities, taken together, has a substantial effect that crosses state lines, the Court will uphold the statute. In the last half century, no congressional statute has failed this test.

2.   THE TENTH AMENDMENT

There is, however, one important limitation on the commerce power. This limitation involves the

Tenth Amendment of the Constitution, which reads as follows:

> The powers not delegated to the United States Constitution nor prohibited by it to the States, are reserved to the States, respectively, or to the people.

For a long time, the Tenth Amendment was considered to be nothing more than a truism stating that "all is retained which has not been surrendered." United States v. Darby, 312 U.S. 100, 124 (1941). In 1976, the Court resurrected the Amendment in National League of Cities v. Usery, 426 U.S. 833 (1976). In that case, the Court held that Congress is prohibited by the Tenth Amendment from using its power under the commerce clause to impair "attributes of sovereignty attaching to every state government" and that these attributes extend to local government units. As a result, the Court held in *League of Cities* that Congress could not constitutionally extend the minimum wage to state employees.

The Tenth Amendment problem has arisen in connection with attempts by Congress to force states to engage in environmental regulation. For example, EPA regulations were issued under the Clean Air Act requiring states to adopt inspection and maintenance programs for automobiles. These programs were intended to enforce pollution control requirements for existing cars.

[*171*]

In District of Columbia v. Train, 521 F.2d 971 (1976), the D.C. Circuit held that Congress lacked the power to force states to become involved in "administering the details of the regulatory scheme promulgated by the Administrator."

This issue reached the Supreme Court in EPA v. Brown, 431 U.S. 99 (1977), but the Court did not decide the case on its merits. Instead the Court remanded the case for further consideration. The basis for the remand was the federal government's apparent concession that the EPA regulations exceeded its statutory authority, at least to the extent the EPA regulations required the states to submit their own legally adopted regulations.

Two recent lower court opinions discuss Tenth Amendment attacks on the Clean Air Act. In one of these decisions, United States v. Ohio Department of Highway Safety, 635 F.2d 1195 (6th Cir. 1980), cert. denied 451 U.S. 949 (1981), the Sixth Circuit upheld a modified version of the inspection-and-maintenance program. In another recent case, Friends of Earth v. Carey, 552 F.2d 25 (2d Cir.1977), cert. denied 434 U.S. 902, the Second Circuit held that New York City could not complain on Tenth Amendment grounds of federal enforcement of an implementation plan adopted by the state government.

The Supreme Court addressed the Tenth Amendment problem in its *Hodel* decisions. In
[*172*]

both cases, it was argued that even if the strip mining act was within Congress's power under the commerce clause, such regulation violated the Tenth Amendment. The argument was that Congress had invaded an area of traditional state regulation.

The Supreme Court rejected this argument. In doing so, it also clarified the limitations on *National League of Cities*. The Court held that there were three requirements that must be met before a statute can be challenged on this basis. First, the statute must regulate the "states as states." Thus, the regulation must not simply regulate private parties but must directly impose duties on state officials. Second, the regulation must address matters that are indisputably "attributes of state sovereignty". Third, it must be apparent that the state's compliance with the federal law would directly impair its ability to "structure integral operations in areas of traditional functions." These constitute threshold requirements but do not ensure that *League of Cities* will apply. According to the *Hodel* Court, there are "situations in which the nature of the federal interests advanced may be such that it justifies State submission." That is, satisfaction of the three threshold requirements results in a balancing test in which the Court will assess the importance of the federal interests as opposed to the seriousness of the impact on the states.

[*173*]

In a more recent case, FERC v. Mississippi, 102 S.Ct. 2126 (1982), the Court further limited *League of Cities.* The issue in that case was whether Congress could compel state public utility commissions to *consider* various energy conservation measures. In an opinion by Justice Blackmun, the Court held that Congress could "condition continued state involvement in a preemptible area on the consideration of federal proposals." Because states have the option of abandoning regulation of public utilities to the federal government, they apparently cannot complain that the federal government has coerced their actions. If this opinion is given a broad reading, it would restrict *League of Cities* only to those areas (if any) of state activity beyond the reach of federal preemption.

The Court has never held that *League of Cities* applies to any federal power other than the commerce clause. The lower courts have generally held that other congressional powers are immune from this restriction. For example, in NRDC v. Costle, 564 F.2d 573 (D.C.Cir.1977), the D.C. Circuit held that federal programs which condition the availability of federal funds on the agreement of states to engage in various activities are exempt from the Tenth Amendment. Thus, it is important to examine the scope of congressional power under other portions of the Constitution in order to avoid any possible application of the

[*174*]

League of Cities test. Furthermore, Congress
may have failed to make findings about the effect
of some activity on interstate commerce, making
it difficult to uphold the resulting statute under
the commerce clause. Hence despite the breadth
of congressional power under the commerce
clause, it is still important to consider its powers
under other sections of the Constitution.

3. OTHER FEDERAL POWERS

Perhaps the most important of these other federal powers arises from the property clause of
the Constitution. This clause provides that "Congress shall have Power to dispose of and make all
needful Rules and Regulations respecting the
Territory or other Property belonging to the United States." This clause is of great significance
because of the vast amount of land owned by the
federal government. In 1970, the public lands
were estimated at nearly 725 million acres, an
area nearly the size of India. About one half of
this land was located in Alaska; most of the remainder was in the western United States. Almost 180 million acres have been reserved for national forests and parks. These enormous tracts
of land contain much of the nation's remaining
wilderness. It is the property clause that gives
Congress the power to protect these lands.

Historically, the federal government's main
goal was to divest itself as quickly as possible of

[*175*]

its lands.   Indeed, at one time, it was argued to the Supreme Court that this was the only permissible purpose for which Congress can manage the public lands.   It is now clear, however, that Congress is entitled to retain ownership of public lands and to use those lands for whatever purpose Congress believes is in the public interest. When it chooses to do so, its power over the retained lands is extremely broad.

The leading case on congressional power under the property clause is Kleppe v. New Mexico, 426 U.S. 529 (1976).   *Kleppe* involved the Wild Free-Roaming Horses and Burros Act.   The Act protects all unbranded horses and burros on public lands from capture.   If the animals stray onto private land, the owner may require the government to retrieve them.   In *Kleppe*, state game officers entered public land to remove wild horses. The state argued that the statute could not be supported by the property clause.   According to the state, the clause grants Congress only the power to dispose of federal property and to protect federal property.   The first power was allegedly not broad enough to support legislation protecting wild animals that live on federal property, while the second power was not implicated because the Act allegedly was designed to protect only the animals, which are not themselves federal property.   The Court rejected the narrow reading of the property clause implicit in these argu-

[*176*]

ments. According to the Court, the clause is not limited to rules regarding disposal, use, and protection of federal property. Rather, Congress possesses both the powers of a proprietor and of a legislature over the public domain. With respect to public lands, Congress has the full regulatory power which the state has with respect to its own lands. Thus, Congress may regulate for any public purpose concerning activities on public lands.

It is less clear whether the property clause gives Congress regulatory power over private lands which adjoin public lands. In one early case, the Supreme Court held that Congress had the power to order the removal of a fence built on private land which limited access to public land. Camfield v. United States, 167 U.S. 518 (1897). The Court held that the fence constituted a nuisance and that Congress had the power to abate this nuisance. The Court remarked more generally that Congress has the power to protect the public lands without being required to seek the aid of state legislatures. Following the logic of these remarks, some recent lower court opinions have read the property clause quite broadly to allow Congress to prevent any activity on private lands that would interfere with Congress's goals respecting the public lands. See Minnesota v. Block, 660 F.2d 1240 (8th Cir.1981); United States v. Brown, 552 F.2d 817 (8th Cir.1977), cert. denied

431 U.S. 949. Thus, if Congress sets aside public lands for quiet, peaceful enjoyment, it may prevent activities on adjoining private lands that would produce excessive noise. This reading of the property clause seems to be correct. If the Constitution gives Congress the power to dedicate public lands to a particular purpose, it must surely give Congress the power to effectuate that decision by preventing interference from private parties.

Two other sources of congressional power deserve at least brief mention. One is the treaty power. Under Missouri v. Holland, 252 U.S. 416 (1920), Congress has broad powers to make treaties with foreign nations on matters of international concern. Thus, the Court in Missouri v. Holland upheld a treaty restricting hunting of migratory birds. Today, legislation on this subject would undoubtedly be upheld through the commerce clause. The Court in Missouri v. Holland held, however, that even if Congress' power under the commerce clause did not extend to the subject of migratory birds, a treaty on the subject was still a proper basis for congressional legislation on the subject.

A final source of congressional power is the spending clause. The Constitution authorizes Congress to spend money in pursuit of the public interest. The Supreme Court has generally held that Congress has free rein in determining where that public interest lies. This clause rarely gives rise to litigation but has vast importance to the economy. It has been used, for example, to authorize the spending of vast amounts of money to enable local governments to build municipal treatment works.

As we have seen, congressional power in the environmental area is virtually unlimited. The commerce clause reaches essentially any private activity that has significant environmental consequences. That power, broad as it is, is augmented by the other broad powers to protect public property, to deal with matters of international concern, and to spend money in the public interest. Essentially the only limitation on congressional power of practical significance at the present time is the *League of Cities* restriction on direct federal interference with the operations of state government. After *Hodel*, this is plainly a narrow exception to an otherwise virtually unlimited power.

The Constitution not only grants powers to the federal government but also limits the activities of state governments. In the next section we will consider those limitations as they are relevant in the environmental area.

B.   COMMERCE CLAUSE RESTRICTIONS ON STATE POWER

In a unified national economy, the existence of a multitude of differing state environmental laws can impede the flow of commerce. Yet, the states have often been in the lead in the environmental area because of pressing local problems. The conflict between the local interest in regulation and the economic interest of other states cannot be resolved effectively by the courts of any of the states involved.   Obviously, both the state which is engaging in regulation and the states which are affected by the regulation have interests which disable them from providing a completely neutral forum.   For this reason, the federal courts have emerged as the tribunals in which these conflicting interests can be assessed.

The basis for federal court involvement is the commerce clause of the Constitution.   The commerce clause, on its face, is a grant of power to Congress, not a grant of power to the federal courts or a restriction on state legislation.   Yet, since the early 19th century, the Supreme Court has always construed the commerce clause as preventing certain kinds of state legislation even when Congress has not spoken.   Various doctrinal explanations have been utilized in an effort to support judicial intervention.   Moreover, the restrictions have been subject to changing formula-

[*180*]

tions. For present purposes, however, we can ignore the rather tangled history of commerce clause theory and concentrate on the theory as it exists today.

At present, there are three strands to commerce clause theory. One test governs state legislation which discriminates against interstate commerce. Such legislation is virtually *per se* unconstitutional. A second test applies to the State's proprietary activities. Such legislation is virtually immune from restriction under the commerce clause. The third test applies to the remaining forms of state legislation. These forms of legislation are dealt with by a balancing test.

1.   DISCRIMINATORY LEGISLATION

The first test is illustrated by City of Philadelphia v. New Jersey, 437 U.S. 617 (1978). This case involved a New Jersey statute prohibiting the import of most waste originating outside the state. The Supreme Court struck down this restriction. The parties in the case disputed whether the purpose of the restriction was economic favoritism toward local industry or environmental protection of the state's resources from overuse. The Court found it unnecessary to resolve this dispute. According to the Court, "the evil of protectionism can reside in legislative means as well as legislative ends." Thus, "whatever New Jersey's ultimate purpose, it may not be accomplished by discriminating against articles of commerce coming from outside the State unless there is some reason, apart from their origin, to treat them differently." Having found that the statute was discriminatory, the Court found it easy to resolve the case:

> The New Jersey law at issue in this case falls squarely within the area that the Commerce Clause puts off-limits to state regulation. On its face, it imposes on out-of-state commercial interests the full burden of conserving the State's remaining landfill space. It is true in our previous cases the scarce natural resource was itself the article of commerce, whereas here the scarce resource and the article in the commerce are distinct. But that difference is without consequence. In both instances, the State has overtly moved to slow or freeze the flow of commerce for protectionist reasons. It does not matter that the State has shut the article of commerce inside the State in one case and outside the State in the other. What is crucial is the attempt by one State to isolate itself from a problem common to many by erecting a barrier against the movement of interstate trade.

The Court conceded that certain quarantine laws have not been considered forbidden by the commerce clause even though they were directed against out-of-state commerce. The Court distin-

guished those quarantine laws, however, on the
ground that in those cases the "very movement"
of the articles risked contagion and other evils.
According to the Court, "[t]hose laws thus did
not discriminate against interstate commerce as
such, but simply prevented traffic of noxious articles, whatever their origin." Subject to this very
narrow exception, legislation which on its face
distinguishes out-of-state items from domestic
items seems virtually certain to be held unconstitutional, at least in the absence of compelling jus-
tification.

2.   PROPRIETARY ACTIVITIES

The second class of state regulations involved
proprietary or quasi-proprietary activities by the
State. Here, the leading case is Hughes v. Alex-
andria Scrap Corp., 426 U.S. 794 (1976). This
case involved a Maryland bounty system for old,
abandoned cars ("hulks"). Prior to 1974, no title
certificate was needed by the scrap processor in
order to claim the bounty. After 1974, Maryland
processors needed only to submit an indemnity
agreement in which their suppliers certified their
own rights to the hulks. In contrast, out-of-state
processors were required to submit title certificates or police certificates. The legislation was
challenged by a Virginia processor. The Court
held that this statute was valid because the State
was not exercising a regulatory function but

rather had itself entered into the market in order to bid up prices. As Justice Stevens noted in his concurrence, the interstate commerce at issue would never have existed except for the state's bounty system. Because a failure to create that commerce would have been unobjectionable under the commerce clause, Justice Stevens believed that out-of-state processors had no grounds for complaint if they were excluded from this commerce. Justice Brennan filed a strong dissent. Because *Hughes* came down on the same day as *National League of Cities*, Justice Brennan apparently feared that the Court was creating tremendous loopholes in the commerce clause in the name of state sovereignty.

In a more recent decision, the Court extended the *Hughes* rationale by holding that South Dakota could refuse to sell cement from a state-owned plant to out-of-state buyers during a shortage. Reeves, Inc. v. Stake, 447 U.S. 429 (1980). This decision seems to be a recognition that quasi-proprietary state activities are not subject to normal commerce clause restriction.

3.   BALANCING TEST

Most state legislation is neither proprietary nor discriminatory, and thus falls into the third class. State legislation of this kind is not as suspect as legislation which is discriminatory on its face. Nevertheless, there is a real risk that the state

may pass legislation without adequately considering its impact elsewhere in the country. In addition, the risk also exists that a state will use what
appears to be nondiscriminatory legislation as
covert means of burdening out-of-state businesses. In order to guard against these risks, the
Court subjects nondiscriminatory state legislation
to a balancing test. Under this test, the impact
of a statute on interstate commerce is balanced
against the state's justifications for the statute.
The Seventh Circuit decision in Procter & Gamble
Co. v. Chicago, 509 F.2d 69 (7th Cir.1975), cert.
denied 421 U.S. 978, is a good illustration of the
balancing test. The case involved a Chicago ordinance banning the use of detergents containing
phosphates. The Seventh Circuit found that the
ordinance did place a burden on interstate commerce. Due to the warehousing methods used in
the industry, the Chicago ordinance would restrict sales of phosphate detergents in a wide
area including parts of Wisconsin, Indiana, and
Michigan. Nevertheless, the court found that the
possible contribution of the ordinance to controlling the growth of algae in the Illinois River and
in Lake Michigan was sufficiently great to justify
the burden placed on commerce.

Balancing tests are notoriously unpredictable
in their application. This one is no exception. On
the whole, however, environmental laws have
fared well in commerce clause litigation. For ex-

ample, in a recent case, the Supreme Court found that the burden on commerce created by a Minnesota container law was not "clearly excessive," even though the Minnesota Supreme Court had found the supposed benefits of the statute to be illusory. Minnesota v. Clover Leaf Creamery Co., 449 U.S. 456 (1981).

C. FEDERAL PREEMPTION

The preceding section dealt with the validity of state regulation in the absence of federal regulation. In this section we will be concerned with the validity of state regulations in areas where Congress has acted. It is clear, of course, that in cases of direct conflict, the state statute must give way. The Supremacy Clause of the Constitution provides:

> This Constitution, and the Laws of the United States which shall be made in Pursuance thereof; and all Treaties made, or which shall be made, under the authority of the United States, shall be the Supreme Law of the Land; and the Judges in every State shall be bound thereby, any Thing in the Constitution or Laws of any State to the Contrary not withstanding.

The presence of a conflict between federal and state law, however, is often less than obvious.

The Supreme Court has set forth various factors which are to be considered in preemption cases. First, the federal regulatory scheme may be so pervasive and detailed as to suggest that Congress left no room for the state to supplement it. Or the statute enacted by Congress may involve a field in which the federal interest is so dominant that enforcement of state laws is precluded. Other aspects of the regulatory scheme imposed by Congress may also support the inference that Congress has completely foreclosed state legislation in a particular area. Even where Congress has not completely foreclosed state regulation, a state statute is void to the extent that it actually conflicts with the valid federal statute. Such a conflict can be found where compliance with both the federal and state regulations is impossible, or more often, where the state law interferes with the accomplishment of the full objectives of Congress.

These factors are obviously rather vague and difficult to apply. The Supreme Court has done little to create any more rigorous framework for analysis. Therefore, the only way to get some degree of understanding of the field is to examine particular cases in order to see what kinds of situations have been found appropriate for application of the preemption doctrine.

Perhaps the area in which preemption is most likely to be found is interstate transportation. Many of the same arguments supporting federal power under the commerce clause also suggest that state regulation is inappropriate in this area. Such state regulation might well be struck down under the commerce clause even if Congress had not spoken, but where Congress has addressed a regulatory problem, the argument against state regulation is even stronger.

Many of these factors are illustrated by Ray v. Atlantic Richfield Co., 435 U.S. 151 (1978). This case involved a Washington statute regulating the design, size and movement of oil tankers in Puget Sound. The statute contained three important provisions. First, all but the smallest tankers were required to carry a Washington licensed pilot while operating in the Sound. Second, tankers were required either to meet certain design standards or to use a tug escort. Third, tankers over a certain size were banned. The Supreme Court made a detailed inquiry into whether this state law was preempted by a 1972 federal statute empowering the Secretary of Transportation to establish vessel regulations and design standards for tankers. As to the pilot requirement, the Court found that the statute was preempted by much older federal statutes regulating pilots on vessels engaged in domestic trade or fishing. The analysis of the other provisions of the statute, however, required a more intensive inquiry.

The Court found clear evidence of preemption as to the design standard. It concluded that the regulations imposed under the federal statute

[*188*]

were a comprehensive scheme for environmental protection. For this reason, the state regulation was invalid:

> The federal scheme thus aims precisely at the same ends as does . . . Washington Law. Furthermore, under [the federal statute], after considering the statutory standards and issuing all design requirements that in his design are necessary, the Secretary inspects and certifies each vessel as sufficiently safe to protect the marine environment and issues a permit or its equivalent to carry tank-vessel cargoes. Refusing to accept the federal judgment, however, the State now seeks to exclude from Puget Sound vessels certified by the Secretary as having acceptable design characteristics, unless they satisfy the different and higher design requirements imposed by state law. The Supremacy Clause dictates that the federal judgment that a vessel is safe to navigate United States waters prevails over the contrary state judgment.

Furthermore, the Court found that Congress anticipated a need for international agreement concerning tanker design standards. The foreign policy area is one in which the federal interest is especially dominant and the room for state interference is extremely small. This international aspect of the problem gave strong support to the preemption decision.

The Court concluded, however, that the statute did allow the state to regulate movement within Puget Sound by requiring tug escorts. As the Court read the federal statute, state regulation was allowed until such time as the federal government actually imposed a tug requirement of its own or decided that no such requirement should be imposed at all. It did not appear to the Court that the federal agency had taken either course. On the other hand, the Court concluded that the agency had made such a decision with respect to tanker size, so that the state's decision as to that issue was preempted.

The *Ray* decision illustrates the complexity of preemption issues. Another transportation-related area in which preemption problems have arisen with some frequency relates to airport noise. Because of the need for uniform, centralized regulation of aircraft flights, the Supreme Court held in City of Burbank v. Lockheed Air Terminal, Inc., 411 U.S. 624 (1973), that a local municipality may not impose a night curfew on jet flights at a privately owned airport. The *Burbank* Court concluded that the widespread imposition of such local restrictions would interfere with flight scheduling and navigational patterns nationwide, thus hindering federal management of the national air traffic network. The *Burbank* Court did not impose similar restrictions on the rights of a municipality which owns a local air-

port. The lower courts have generally held that
regulations by such a local authority are not necessarily forbidden by *Burbank*, but are subject to
a requirement of reasonableness. For example,
in extended litigation over the supersonic transport, the Second Circuit held that the New York
Port Authority could not prevent SST flights
from landing at Kennedy Airport because the
Port Authority was unable to present persuasive
evidence of significant harm. Another significant recent case involved the power of a state
court to impose nuisance liability on a local airport because of the impact of airport noise on its
neighbors. The California Supreme Court held
that such regulation was not preempted by federal law, relying in part on a series of U.S. Supreme
Court decisions holding that under some circumstances an airport must compensate its neighbors
under the Taking Clause of the Fifth Amendment
when excessive airport noise prevents the peaceful use of residential land. Greater Westchester
Homeowners Association v. Los Angeles, 26 Cal.
3d 86, 160 Cal.Rptr. 733, 603 P.2d 1329 (1979),
cert. denied 449 U.S. 820 (1980).

The most controversial preemption issue currently before the country involves nuclear energy. Proposals have been made in a number of
states to impose various restrictions on the construction of nuclear power plants because of
doubts about their safety. The question is

whether such legislation is preempted by the Atomic Energy Act. In a 1971 case, Northern States Power Co. v. Minnesota, 447 F.2d 1143 (8th Cir.1971), affirmed 405 U.S. 1035 (1972), the court held that the state lacked the authority to impose conditions on nuclear waste releases stricter than those imposed by the AEC. The court relied heavily on a provision of the federal statute which allows the federal government to delegate regulatory authority to the states with respect to certain categories of nuclear materials. Radioactive releases from nuclear power plants did not fall within any of these categories, which the court considered the exclusive areas in which states may regulate with respect to radiation hazards. The court concluded that state regulation would interfere with the Congressional objectives expressed in the 1954 Act:

Thus, through direction of the licensing scheme for nuclear reactors, Congress vested the AEC with the authority to resolve the proper balance between desired industrial progress and adequate health and safety standards. Only through the application and enforcements of uniform standards promulgated by a national agency will these dual objectives be assured. Were the states allowed to impose stricter standards on the level of radioactive waste releases discharged from nuclear power plants, they might conceivably be so overprotective in the

[*192*]

area of health and safety as to unnecessarily stultify the industrial development and use of atomic energy for the production of electric power.

In contrast, the Supreme Court recently upheld a California nuclear moratorium in a recent decision, Pacific Gas & Electric Co. v. State Energy Commission, ___ U.S. ___ (1983). In an opinion by Justice White, the Court upheld a California statute prohibiting nuclear plant operation until the federal government approves a permanent method of waste disposal. The Court concluded that the state statutes were aimed not at radiation hazards but instead at economic problems posed by the failure of the federal government to approve a permanent method of waste disposal. The Court concluded that Congress had not intended to promote nuclear power at all costs, but rather had decided to leave the choice as to the necessity or economic benefits of a nuclear plant to the state through its utility regulatory powers. Thus, it appears that if the state casts its legislation in the form of utility regulation, it may indirectly accomplish what federal law would not allow it to do directly—that is, impose its own views as to the safety of nuclear reactors under various circumstances. So long as it can be reasonably argued that a possible safety risk would have repercussions on the economic desirability of nuclear energy, the Supreme Court would apparently allow the state to regulate.

Every preemption case in a sense is unique. Apart from some vague and general maxims, little can be said about this area of law that is of much help in deciding individual cases. The question before the court is whether Congress in passing a particular statute would have been willing to allow the state to impose certain kinds of regulations in the same area. This is essentially an issue of statutory construction. It can only be resolved by close attention to the language of the federal statute, to its legislative history, and to its purposes. Thus, the best advice in analyzing preemption problems is to carefully analyze the legislative materials and the extent to which the state statute would have a practical effect on the implementation of the federal statute.

In this chapter, we have seen that federal regulatory power in the environmental area is virtually complete. Only where the federal government is attempting to regulate the activities of state officials themselves is there any question about federal power. When the federal government has acted, any state legislation which interferes with the accomplishment of the Congressional purpose or the operation of the regulatory scheme is unconstitutional under the supremacy clause. Even when Congress has not acted, a state statute may run afoul of the dominant federal interest in the free flow of interstate commerce. Thus, while federalism imposes few restraints today on the national government, it continues to severely circumscribe the actions of state governments.

CHAPTER 5

ENERGY POLICY AND THE ENVIRONMENT

In the late 1970s approximately 50 percent of the energy consumed in the United States was derived from petroleum (half of it imported), while natural gas supplied 25 percent and coal 18 percent. Nuclear power plants provided 4 percent and hydroelectric facilities 3 percent. This mix has varied over time: in 1900 coal provided about 90 percent of our energy, and in 1970 natural gas was dominant at 41 percent, followed by petroleum at 33 percent. Declining reserves and national security considerations probably require that the proportion of our needs presently met by oil (exclusive of shale) be reduced. Decisions concerning alternate sources should be based, at least in part, on environmental factors.

Materials in this chapter are grouped into three major categories of energy sources: nuclear power, fossil fuels (oil, coal and synthetic fuels), and renewable and conservation sources.

A. NUCLEAR ENERGY

The Atomic Energy Act of 1946 gave the federal government a monopoly on nuclear power, but it was amended in 1954 to allow licensing of private facilities. Such facilities were expected to

[*196*]

produce electricity more cheaply than oil-fired and even coal-fired plants. Since then the cost of electricity from all sources has increased greatly due to escalating construction costs, higher world oil prices, and more stringent environmental and safety regulations. The 1979 accident at the Three Mile Island nuclear plant in Pennsylvania intensified public concern over possible catastrophic reactor accidents, radiation leaks, and the lack of proven means for safely disposing of nuclear wastes.

In the early years of private nuclear power it was contemplated that the fuel cycle would be a closed system: the ore would be mined, processed, used in reactors, reprocessed, and reused in reactors. However, this has not occurred, with the result that the waste problem has become more serious. In 1977 President Carter decided that the United States should defer indefinitely the reprocessing of spent fuel and otherwise seek to prevent plutonium (separated from spent fuel in connection with reprocessing) from becoming an article of world trade, in order to suppress its availability for weapons manufacture. Congress thereafter passed the Nuclear Non-Proliferation Act of 1978, 42 U.S.C.A. § 2153, which provides that the U.S. shall have a veto over foreign reprocessing of fuel manufactured from uranium produced or enriched in this country. In 1981 President Reagan announced

[*197*]

his support for the reprocessing of commercial fuel in the United States, and the Nuclear Regulatory Commission has resumed its decisionmaking processes concerning recycling of spent fuel.

1.   PLANT SAFETY AND SITING

Protecting the public against emissions of radiation from nuclear power plants requires careful selection of plant sites and proper design, construction and operation of the plants themselves. Regulation of these activities is the subject of this section.

The legal basis for regulation of the nuclear fuel cycle is the Atomic Energy Act of 1954, 42 U.S. C.A. §§ 2011–2282. The primary purpose of regulation is to protect human life and the environment from excessive exposure to radiation. The Nuclear Regulatory Commission (NRC), formerly the Atomic Energy Commission (AEC), exercises broad regulatory and licensing authority over essentially all activities related to civilian nuclear materials and facilities. In Northern States Power Co. v. Minnesota, 447 F.2d 1143 (8th Cir.1971), affirmed 405 U.S. 1035 (1972), the court said that "the federal government has exclusive authority under the doctrine of preemption to regulate the construction and operation of nuclear power plants, which necessarily includes regulation of the levels of radioactive effluents discharged from the plant." Though substantial, federal preemption of state and local regulation is not complete, especially with respect to nonradiological hazards. Thus, under section 316 of the Clean Water Act states may regulate thermal pollution from nuclear power plants; and under sections 302(g), 122 and 116 of the Clean Air Act, as amended in 1977, states may regulate radioactive air pollutants. The Atomic Energy Act provides that it shall not be construed to "affect the authority or regulations" of any state or local agency "with respect to the generation, sale, or transmission" of electricity produced by nuclear plants. The Act authorizes NRC, pursuant to a "turn-over" agreement with the governor of a state, to "discontinue" its control over radiation hazards with regard to "by-product" and "source" materials, and to "special" nuclear materials in quantities not sufficient to form a critical mass. 42 U.S.C.A. §§ 2018, 2021. Special nuclear materials include plutonium, enriched uranium, and other materials capable of producing atomic energy. Source materials, such as uranium and thorium, are the ores and raw materials from which special nuclear materials are produced. By-product materials are those which are made radioactive during the production or utilization of special nuclear materials.

NRC safety review of proposed nuclear power plants is supplemented by environmental reviews of site suitability and possible water and air pollution problems. Environmental reviews are conducted not only by the NRC under NEPA but also by the EPA under the Clean Water and Clean Air Acts and by state and local environmental and land use agencies. Calvert Cliffs' Coordinating Committee v. AEC, 449 F.2d 1109 (D.C.Cir. 1971), established that under NEPA the AEC was required to consider adverse environmental effects in its licensing actions, utilizing "a rather finally tuned and 'systematic' balancing analysis in each instance." The court declared invalid AEC regulations limiting both the types of environmental factors to be considered and the procedural stages at which the consideration could occur. Environmental issues must be considered, said the court, at every important stage in the decisionmaking process, i.e., at every stage where an overall balancing of environmental and non-environmental factors is appropriate and where alterations might be made in the proposed action to minimize environmental costs.

One device utilized by NRC to avoid detailed consideration of some environmental questions in every licensing proceeding is the so-called "generic" EIS. In Carolina Environmental Study Group v. United States, 510 F.2d 796 (D.C.Cir.1975), opponents sought review of the issuance of a construction license to build two reactors seventeen miles from Charlotte, North Carolina. The AEC had classified hypothetical reactor accidents from

Class 1 (trivial incidents with high occurrence probability) to Class 9 (ultimate severity with occurrence highly unlikely). A Class 9 accident, known as a breach-of-reactor containment accident, would involve concurrent rupture of the three-foot thick concrete containment vessel and the several inches of steel surrounding the reactor core, resulting in the exposure of the radioactive core to the atmosphere. The Commission's EIS for the Charlotte plant did not discuss the likely impacts of a Class 9 accident at that specific site. Accepting the AEC's rationale that the probability of such accidents was "so small that their environmental risk is extremely low" and not worth discussing in individual impact statements, the court found the EIS to be adequate.

In 1971 the Department of the Interior had requested that the AEC include in its EIS for the then proposed Three Mile Island nuclear plant near Middletown, Pennslyvania, a detailed analysis of the impacts of a Class 9 accident on the adjacent Susquehanna River. The Commission declined, saying that the environmental risk of such an event was acceptably low so that "generic discussion" was adequate. The TMI plant was duly constructed. On March 28, 1979, a Class 9 accident occurred at TMI. The accident was initiated by mechanical malfunctions and made much worse by human errors in responding to it. Two weeks later President Carter established a special commission chaired by John Kemeny, President of Dartmouth College, to conduct a comprehensive investigation and study of the accident. On October 30, 1979 the Commission submitted its report, *The Need for Change: The Legacy of TMI.* The Commission's overall conclusion was that:

> To prevent nuclear accidents as serious as Three Mile Island, fundamental changes will be necessary in the organization, procedures, and practices—and above all—in the attitudes of the Nuclear Regulatory Commission and, to the extent that the institutions we investigated are typical, of the nuclear industry.

The Commission found that after many years of operation of nuclear power plants, with no evidence that any member of the general public had been hurt, the belief that nuclear power plants were sufficiently safe had grown into a conviction. The Commission concluded that the NRC had shown a preoccupation with regulations and equipment, and a disregard for human factors and "operator error." The training of TMI operators to deal with equipment malfunctions—especially serious malfunctions and simultaneous multiple malfunctions—was "greatly deficient." Operating procedures were confusing, and lessons from previous "minor" accidents at other plants had not been passed on. Fortunately the Commission was able to conclude that in spite of serious damage to the plant, most of the radiation was contained and the actual releases probably would have negligible effects on the physical health of individuals. The major health effect of the accident was found to be mental stress. The direct financial cost of the accident to the utility was very large, in excess of $1 billion even if the damaged reactor eventually can be put back into service.

The Kemeny Commission criticized NRC's implementation of its policy that reactors should be located in a "low population zone" (LPZ), an area in which appropriate action could be taken to protect residents in the event of an accident. Because of the method of calculation used by NRC, the LPZs around many nuclear power plants were very small, e.g., a radius of two miles in the case of TMI. The Kemeny Commission found that if a very serious accident were to occur, many people living beyond the LPZ would receive massive doses of radiation. That LPZ as applied had little relevance to protection of the public was shown by the fact that during the TMI accident NRC was considering evacuation distances of up to twenty miles, even though the accident was far less serious than that postulated to calculate the LPZ during licensing. The Kemeny group recommended a new procedure under which a variety of possible accidents would be considered, particularly smaller accidents with a higher probability of occurring. For each such accident, probable levels of radiation releases would be calculated at a variety of distances, to decide the kinds of protective action necessary and feasible. Only such analysis, it was thought, could predict the true consequences of a radiological incident and determine whether a particular site was suitable for a nuclear power plant.

The Kemeny Commission also found that because NRC's primary focus had been on licensing, there was insufficient attention to the ongoing process of assuring nuclear safety. It pointed, as an example, to the case of "generic" problems. Once an issue was labeled generic, an applicant no longer was responsible for resolving the issue prior to licensing. While that might be acceptable if there were a strict procedure within NRC to assure timely resolution of such problems, the evidence indicated that labeling problems "generic" may have provided a convenient way of postponing difficult decisions. The upshot is that the more widespread a problem is, the less likely it is to be resolved.

In 1980, NRC changed its position concerning generic treatment of Class 9 accidents under NEPA. The new "interim" policy provided that EISs for nuclear plants should include "a reasoned consideration of the environmental risks attributable to accidents at the particular facility or facilities within the scope of each such state-

[*204*]

ment." The policy was to apply only to future impact statements and was not to serve, "absent a showing of . . . special circumstances, as a basis for opening, reopening, or expanding any previous or ongoing proceeding." 45 Federal Register 40101.

Also in 1980, Congress enacted a new law in response to TMI, P.L. 96–295, 94 Stat. 780. It authorized funds to train additional federal inspectors to be stationed at nuclear power plants. NRC was directed to develop a plan for agency response to accidents at licensed facilities, and to issue new regulations establishing demographic requirements for facility siting, including maximum population density and distribution for surrounding zones. The maximum civil penalty for each violation of NRC regulations by a licensee was increased from $5,000 to $100,000. Most importantly, NRC was ordered to submit to Congress a plan for improving the technical capability of licensee personnel, including a study of the feasibility and value of licensing plant managers and senior licensee officials. Since 1981, NRC has licensed nuclear plant operators. 10 C.F.R. §§ 55.1–55.60.

As noted above, the major health effect of TMI was found to have been "mental stress." The TMI nuclear facility has two reactors. Unit 1 was not in operation during the 1979 accident, which occurred in Unit 2. Thereafter, during hearings concerning the proposed restart of Unit 1, NRC refused to consider claims that the renewed operation would cause severe psychological health damage to persons living in the vicinity. Some of the residents sought judicial review of that refusal. The Court of Appeals concluded that NEPA (but not the Atomic Energy Act) did require NRC to evaluate "post-traumatic anxieties . . . caused by fears of recurring catastrophe." In Metropolitan Edison Co. v. People Against Nuclear Energy, ___ U.S. ___ (1983), the Supreme Court reversed the lower court's NEPA ruling. Although apparently acknowledging that in some circumstances psychological health effects are cognizable under NEPA, the Court interpreted the statute to include "a requirement of a reasonably close causal relationship between a change in the physical environment and the effect at issue." A mere *risk* of another accident at TMI, said the Court, was not a change in the physical environment, and served to lengthen the causal chain (from renewed operation of Unit 1 to psychological health damage) beyond the reach of NEPA.

Under NEPA the issuance of a construction permit for a nuclear plant must be preceded by consideration not only of the likely environmental impacts of the plant at the proposed site but also of the comparative environmental effects of locating the facility at alternative sites. Meaningful

consideration of alternatives sites is made difficult by NRC's practice of allowing utility companies to engage in on-site development before the
Commission approves the site and plant design.
In New England Coalition On Nuclear Pollution
v. NRC, 582 F.2d 87 (1st Cir.1978), NRC had instructed its Licensing Board that in considering
alternatives to the proposed site for a power
plant at Seabrook, New Hampshire, "the test to
be employed in assessing whether a proposed site
is to be rejected in favor of any of the alternative
sites considered [is] whether an alternate site is
obviously superior."   In addition, the Commission
had directed that "in comparing construction
costs of the proposed site and at alternate sites,
actual completion costs should be used."   Opponents argued that these standards violated
NEPA, impermissibly skewing the comparison in
favor of the applicant's proposed site, not only by
insisting on clear superiority of alternatives but
also by giving effect to money already expended.
The court held that neither the "obviously superi-
or" nor the "completion cost" standard was in
and of itself violative of NEPA, but it warned
that the standards could not be used as a facade
for shirking NEPA duties.   With respect to the
"obviously superior" standard, the court noted
that NEPA does not require that a plant be built
on the single best site for environmental purposes.   Concerning the "completion cost" test,
the court acknowledged that money already sunk

into a proposed site, where construction has occurred before issuance of a construction permit, will weigh to the benefit of that site when alternatives are considered; the likelihood that an alternative site will be selected as obviously superior declines, and the pressure against denying the application increases. "At some point," said the court, "the Commission could well find itself seriously prejudiced in trying to carry out its NEPA mandate."

Another issue in the *New England Coalition* case related to the subject of nuclear waste disposal, discussed below. Plaintiffs challenged the adequacy of NRC's NEPA review of the effects of decommissioning the plant at the end of its projected thirty to forty year useful life. The court found that the Licensing Board had heard testimony on this issue and given it sufficient consideration to satisfy its NEPA obligation. Despite the court's decision, it is clear that NRC has not formulated concrete plans for dealing with the problem of worn-out nuclear power plants. Plant components themselves will constitute a form of dangerous radioactive waste for thousands of years. Options that have been discussed include dismantling the plants immediately, or sealing them for at least a hundred years until the radioactivity has cooled sufficiently to make dismantling easier and cheaper. In either case, the radioactive parts at some time must be disposed of permanently, but it is not settled who should conduct and pay for these activities, much less how they should be carried out. There is still doubt whether TMI's Unit 2 can be cleaned up and put back into operation. If not, NRC may have to focus on the problem of plant decommissioning sooner than it expected.

2. FUEL REPROCESSING AND WASTE DISPOSAL

The flow of materials in the nuclear fuel cycle, from uranium mining through fuel reprocessing and waste disposal, is shown on the following page. The "back end" of the cycle—disposal or management of highly radioactive spent fuel, with or without separation of uranium and plutonium for reprocessing and fabrication into new fuel—poses the most serious problems in terms of technology, economics, public health and safety, and national security. However, there also are problems with disposal of low level radioactive wastes and mill tailings. Low level wastes may be disposed of by transfer to a recipient licensed by NRC, by burial pursuant to NRC license, by incineration, or by deposit at sea pursuant to EPA permit under the Marine Protection, Research, and Sanctuaries Act of 1972, 33 U.S.C.A. § 1431(b), as amended in 1983. Disposal

U. S. ENERGY RESEARCH & DEVELOPMENT ADMINISTRATION, OFFICE OF INDUSTRY RELATIONS, THE NUCLEAR INDUSTRY: 1974, at 69 (Wash. 1174–74):

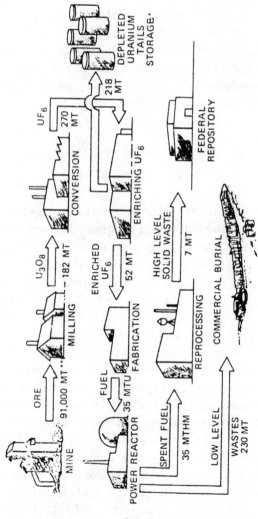

Figure 3–16. Average Annual Fuel Materials Requirements for a Typical 1000 Mwe Light Water Reactor

* Not required for reactor but must be stored safely. Has value for future breeder reactor blanket.
** Metric Ton

of mill tailings, residues from mining and milling, is regulated by NRC pursuant to the Uranium Mill Tailings Radiation Control Act of 1978, 42 U.S.C.A. §§ 7901–7942.

The kinds of problems posed by the back end of the fuel cycle depend in part upon whether spent fuel is recycled. The residue remaining after completion of the fission process contains elements of uranium and plutonium which, if separated, reprocessed, and fabricated into fuel rods containing plutonium and uranium oxides, could constitute a significant new energy source. Recycling necessarily involves transportation of the nuclear materials from reactors to separation and reprocessing facilities, to fabrication plants, and back to reactors. Whether or not spent fuel is recycled, there ultimately is the problem of how to dispose permanently of high level radioactive wastes. For the time being, such wastes are being stored, in most cases at the sites of the plants in which they were generated. Such interim storage requires an NRC permit.

In Vermont Yankee Nuclear Power Corp. v. NRDC, 435 U.S. 519 (1978), the court of appeals had invalidated NRC's "Table S–3 Rule," which (a) designated the environmental impact of fuel reprocessing and high-level waste disposal as a generic issue and (b) concluded that "the environmental effects of the uranium fuel cycle have been shown to be relatively insignificant" and need not be considered in individual plant licensing proceedings. The Supreme Court, after concluding that the appeals court had invalidated the rule because of inadequate procedures in the rulemaking proceedings, reversed on the ground that NRC's procedures met the minimum requirements of the Administrative Procedure Act. The case was remanded for a determination, on the merits, of whether NRC's rule was sufficiently supported by the administrative record.

In NRDC v. NRC, 685 F.2d 459 (D.C.Cir.1982), the court of appeals reviewed the rule again. Table S–3 contained a set of numerical values intended to quantify the radiological effluents associated with reprocessing, storage, and disposal of spent fuel and other wastes. It was to be included in the EIS for each proposed nuclear power reactor as a substitute for individualized consideration of the environmental effects of fuel cycle activities related to that reactor. The issues in the case concerned the adequacy of some of the numbers, in light of the fact that the table gave no explicit recognition to uncertainties underlying the projected releases, including those from permanently buried high level wastes expected to remain toxic for at least 250,000 years. Table S–3 indicated that buried wastes would have zero effect on the environment. A majority of the court concluded that the Table S–3 Rule was arbitrary and in violation of NEPA because it failed to reflect, or to allow individual licensing boards to consider, uncertainties underlying the assumption that no radiological effluents would be released into the biosphere after wastes were permanently buried.

The court considered the zero-release assumption both as a factual finding and, in the alternative, as a decisionmaking device by which NRC retained exclusive responsibility for considering uncertainties. The court determined that if NRC had made a factual finding that there would be no radiological releases from buried wastes, it represented a "clear error in judgment" under *Overton Park*, because the record and the Commission's own statements indicated the existence of substantial technological and institutional uncertainties. On the other hand, if the zero-release assumption was a decisionmaking device reserving to the Commission sole responsibility for considering the risk that long-lived wastes could not be disposed of with complete success, the question was whether the rule, together with the Commission's investigation, analysis and deliberation prior to promulgation, provided the type of consideration and disclosure of uncertainties which NEPA required. While agreeing that NRC was free to implement NEPA through generic rulemaking, two judges found that NRC had ruled that plant licensing decisions should be made on the basis of cost-benefit analyses which

omitted the *costs* represented by (1) the risk that
buried wastes from the plants eventually would
damage the environment by emitting radiation
from a faulty permanent repository and (2) the
risk that the wastes would have to remain temporarily in another type of repository, possibly on
site, and would emit radiation prior to permanent
disposal. Because NRC had not ruled that these
costs were insignificant, or that they were out-
weighed by generic benefits also excluded from
licensing boards' consideration, the court found
noncompliance with NEPA's requirement that environmental costs be considered "at every stage
where an overall balancing of environmental and
nonenvironmental factors is appropriate."   The
court also found the zero-release assumption to
be arbitrary and capricious.

One of the two prevailing judges wrote a separate opinion to the effect that Table S–3 also was
deficient because it failed to reflect consideration
of the dangers of "releases" of weapons-grade
plutonium, after separation for fuel reprocessing,
through theft by stealth or force while the material is being fabricated, stored and shipped all
over the nation.

In a strong dissent, Judge Wilkey asserted that
the majority had adopted an approach rejected by
the Supreme Court in *Vermont Yankee.* He said
there was an unequivocal mandate to limit action
in the case to review of the administrative record

to determine only whether NRC's rule was arbitrary and capricious within the meaning of the Administrative Procedure Act. He urged that NRC had given explicit consideration to uncertainties about long term waste storage and disposal; that its decision not to reflect the uncertainties in the table was a "quintessential *policy judgment*" entitled to greater judicial deference than a factual finding; that the Commission's decision to adopt the entire table, of which the zero-release figure was but one small part, was not arbitrary or capricious; and that NRC had not shirked whatever substantive obligations remained under NEPA after the Supreme Court's 1980 decision in the *Strycker's Bay* case.

The Supreme Court is reviewing the Table S–3 case during its October 1982 term.

If reprocessing of spent nuclear fuel poses a threat to national security, and if scientists have been unable to determine how to dispose of high level wastes safely, should NRC continue licensing more nuclear power plants? This question was raised in NRDC v. NRC, 582 F.2d 166 (2d Cir.1978). NRDC argued that the Commission, prior to granting new operating licenses, was required by the Atomic Energy Act's public health and safety requirement to make a determination (in a rulemaking proceeding) that high level radioactive wastes can be *permanently* disposed of safely. NRC defended its longstanding practice of issuing licenses with an *implied* finding of reasonable assurance that safe means of permanent disposal would be available when needed, on the ground that the practice was in accord with Congress' intent in enacting the Atomic Energy Act and the Energy Reorganization Act of 1974. After examining the acts' legislative history and Congress' prolonged failure to express disapproval of continued licensing, the court rejected NRDC's claims. It found that if there ever had been any doubt over the Congress' intent not to require NRC to declare a moratorium on reactor licensing pending an affirmative determination that high level wastes can be disposed of safely, the matter was laid to rest by adoption of the 1974 Act. That Act expressly recognized and impliedly approved NRC's regulatory scheme and practice under which the safety of interim storage of high level wastes at commercial reactor sites was determined separately from the safety of government owned permanent storage facilities not yet established.

The problem is that interim storage facilities are rapidly being filled. In Minnesota v. NRC, 602 F.2d 412 (D.C.Cir.1979), opponents of two nuclear power plants challenged an order of the Atomic Safety and Licensing Appeal Board (a unit of NRC) affirming licensing board decisions which granted the plant operators amendments to their operating licenses to permit expansion of

[*216*]

on-site capacity for the storage of spent nuclear fuel assemblies. The court recognized that when most of the nuclear power plants now in operation were licensed, it was anticipated that spent fuel would be stored at the reactor site only long enough to allow it to cool sufficiently to permit safe shipment off-site for reprocessing or permanent disposal. Hence spent fuel storage capacity at reactor sites is limited, though plans for off-site reprocessing, storage or disposal have not materialized. In the *Minnesota* case, two utility companies sought amendments to their licenses to permit expansion of their "spent fuel pools" to accomodate more assemblies, thereby permitting on-site storage through 1982 and 1987, respectively. Both companies proposed to accomplish the expansions by closer spacing of storage racks within the pools, rather than by increasing the physical dimensions of the pools. The opponents contended that uncertainty concerning permanent disposal of the wastes raised the possibility that the reactor sites might become long term storage sites. The Appeal Board had declined to consider the safety and environmental implications of indefinite storage on-site after decommissioning of the reactors. Defining its inquiry as whether it was "reasonably probable" that no off-site fuel repository would be available at expiration of the plant licenses, the Board held the question to be foreclosed by NRC's earlier decision (discussed in the preceding paragraph) not to suspend grants of further operating licenses pending a finding that nuclear wastes could be disposed of safely and permanently. Although the Appeal Board recognized that the NRC decision did not stem from a formal record developed in a rulemaking or adjudicatory proceeding, the Board nevertheless treated it as a policy determination that, for the purposes of licensing actions, it should be presumed that spent fuel repositories will be available when plant licenses expire. Opponents of the license amendments claimed that the Board had erred in basing its determination of reasonable probability on NRC's "declaration of policy" rather than on evidence presented on the record in the adjudicatory proceedings. The court held that the Commission could properly consider the waste disposal issue in a "generic" rulemaking proceeding and then apply its determination in subsequent adjudicatory proceedings. Because the court then had pending before it the remanded *Vermont Yankee* case and NRC's Table S–3 Rule, it remanded the temporary waste storage matter to NRC for further consideration. However, the court declined to vacate or stay the license amendments permitting expansion of on-site storage capacity at the two plants, since that would effectively shut down the plants. In a concurring opinion, Judge Tamm urged that *both* section 102(2)(C) of NEPA and section 103(d) of the Atomic Energy Act mandate a factual determination of whether it is reasonably probable

[*218*]

that an off-site waste repository will be available when plant licenses expire. In addition, he said, if the Commission determined that the availability of such a repository was not reasonably probable, NRC then was required to determine whether it is reasonably probable that the spent fuel could continue to be stored safely and indefinitely on-site, even after decommissioning of the plants.

In Potomac Alliance v. NRC, 682 F.2d 1030 (D.C.Cir.1982), the same court reiterated that under NEPA the NRC must consider long range effects of allowing plant operators to increase the capacity of on-site spent fuel pools. As in *Minnesota,* the court remanded to NRC but refrained from vacating or staying the license amendment. However, because the Commission had not yet reached a decision on the availability of safe waste disposal methods, the court stated that if NRC failed to reach such a decision by June 30, 1983, the amended license at issue in *Potomac Alliance* would be placed "in jeopardy."

In January 1983 President Reagan signed the Nuclear Waste Policy Act of 1982, P.L. 97–425, 96 Stat. 2201, 42 U.S.C. §§ 10101–10226. It establishes an institutional framework and timetable for the siting and development of repositories for disposal of high-level radioactive wastes from both civilian and defense activities. By January 1, 1985 the Department of Energy is to nominate five potential sites for the first permanent repository; the President then is to make a single recommendation to Congress by March 31, 1987. If the state in which the site is located approves it, DOE must apply for a repository license from NRC, which is allowed three years to review and act upon the application. The Act also provides for a federal interim away-from-reactor storage program, to be conducted only at sites which were already federal facilities in January 1983. An affected state or Indian tribe may object to a site recommended for licensing as a permanent repository or as an interim storage facility; such an objection will eliminate the site from further consideration unless overridden by a resolution adopted by majority votes in both houses of Congress. Costs of the disposal and storage programs are to be borne by benefited nuclear waste generators.

While the search continues at the federal level for a solution to the nuclear waste problem, several states have enacted laws aimed at limiting or banning storage and disposal within their boundaries. Generally these statutes apply only to wastes from reactors outside the enacting state. Are such statutes valid, or are they preempted by federal law or in violation of the Commerce Clause? Illinois v. General Electric Co., 683 F.2d 206 (7th Cir.1982), held that the Illinois Spent Fuel Act, which prohibited transport into and storage within the state of nuclear wastes originating elsewhere, violated both the Commerce and Supremacy Clauses of the U.S. Constitution. The case concerned General Electric's waste storage facility at Morris, Illinois, the only facility in the United States then accepting spent nuclear fuel for storage away from reactor sites. Southern California Edison, a party to the suit, had shipped nuclear fuel to Morris before the Illinois law was passed and had a contract to ship additional amounts to the facility at the time of the statute's enactment. The court held that "to pass laws that arbitrarily burden interstate commerce, by forbidding shipments merely because they originate out of state, violates the Commerce Clause." The court noted that the statute did not limit intrastate movements within Illinois, however lengthy or hazardous, nor even interstate movements so long as they did not end up at Morris. The court also declared that under the Supremacy Clause, state regulation of the storage of spent nuclear fuel was precluded because the Atomic Energy Act establishes "a comprehensive scheme of regulation of atomic energy" administered by NRC. While the Act does not refer explicitly to spent fuel, it does refer to the constituents of that fuel; and the statutory structure and legislative history, according to the court, compel the conclusion that the Act "equally preempts state regulation of the . . . shipment or storage, interstate and intrastate alike, of spent nuclear fuel."

On the other hand, the Supreme Court has upheld a California statute imposing a moratorium on construction of additional nuclear plants until the State Energy Commission finds that adequate storage facilities and means of disposal are available for nuclear waste. In *Pacific Gas & Electric Co. v. State Energy Resources Conservation & Development Commission,* ___ U.S. ___ (1983), the Court accepted California's argument that the statute was directed toward other purposes than protecting against radiation hazards, and thus was not preempted. The Court found that Congress, in the Atomic Energy Act, intended that states retain their "traditional responsibility in the field of regulating electric utilities for determining questions of need, reliability, cost and other related state concerns." The legislative history of the California statute cited uncertainties about permanent waste disposal as making nuclear power uneconomical and uncertain and requiring reliance on other energy sources until the uncertainties were resolved. Saying that it "should not become embroiled in attempting to ascertain California's true motive," the Supreme Court accepted the legislature's "avowed economic purpose" as the reason for the moratorium.

3. LICENSING REFORM

A year before the Three Mile Island accident, the Carter Administration proposed to Congress a bill intended to hasten the licensing of nuclear power plants, S. 2775, H.R. 11704, 95th Cong., 2d Sess. (1978). Principal objectives were to revamp NRC's trial-type permit and licensing proceedings, and to facilitate early site review and approval (site banking) and standardized plant designs. The hope was to reduce by up to 50 percent the ten to twelve years required to bring a new plant on line. Although the bill was not enacted into law, it did highlight some of the major criticisms of the Atomic Energy Act by supporters of nuclear power.

Concerning site banking, the bill would have allowed a utility company to obtain final NRC approval of a specific plant location before applying for a construction permit or obtaining a state or federal determination of the local need for additional electricity. Once approved, a site permit would have been valid for ten years with the possibility of indefinite renewal at NRC's discretion. A major objection to the provision was that once substantial money and governmental review time had been invested in an approved site, the nuclear option would be artificially attractive as against alternative energy sources.

The aim of standardized plant designs was to relieve utilities of the burden of proving environmental and technological acceptability in individual licensing proceedings. Those issues would have been deemed resolved in the earlier design approval proceedings. Design permits would have been valid for five years and subject to an unlimited number of three-year extensions. Opponents argued that by eliminating the existing requirement that a proposed design be certified as harmonious with the topographical, geological, hydrological and other characteristics of a specific site, the bill would entail acceptance of greater environmental risks.

The bill also would have authorized NRC to issue a combined construction permit and operating license (CPOL) which, though not amounting to unconditional authorization to commence operations years in the future, would have allowed resolution of many plant operation questions before construction, facilitating planning and smoothing the transition from construction to operations. Moreover, at the discretion of the NRC, an applicant for a CPOL could have been allowed to begin not only construction but even operations before receiving its license, in response to "urgent public need." Although pre-licensing investment in theory would have been undertaken at the risk of the applicant, environmentalists questioned the likelihood of an unbiased decision thereafter by NRC.

The bill proposed a drastic reduction in the opportunity for public input into the licensing process, particularly concerning issues under NEPA. Hearings would have been mandatory only in connection with applications for early site approval, standardized design approval, or CPOLs. While questions arising under the Atomic Energy Act would have been considered in adjudicatory hearings, those under NEPA were to be considered in rulemaking proceedings or "hybrids" without discovery and cross examination. At any hearing, the issues which could have been raised would have been limited to those for which there was no earlier "opportunity" for a hearing. Thus, if any party to an early site approval hearing could have questioned the geological stability of the site, then even if that issue were not in fact discussed, it could not be raised 10 or 20 years later when the utility sought a construction permit.

Finally, the bill sought to reduce the overlap between federal and state roles in nuclear plant licensing. Interestingly, it would have expanded the permissible scope of state action, rather than preempting it. NRC would have been prohibited from issuing a construction permit prior to a state determination of need for a new source of power at that site, and the state agency would

[*225*]

have been required to conduct hearings comparable to NEPA compliance hearings and to assume responsibility for defending its conclusions in federal court. Moreover, the bill provided authority and strong incentives for a virtually complete transfer from NRC to the states of final decisionmaking on the questions of environmental acceptability and need for power. Whether many states could muster the will, resources and expertise to make tough environmental determinations and defend them in court without participation by NRC or the Department of Justice is at least open to question.

In 1982 the Reagan administration began to talk publicly of new plans for reform of nuclear power plant licensing.

B.   FOSSIL FUELS

1.   OIL

Air pollution from the refining and combustion of oil and gasoline obviously is a major environmental problem associated with the use of petroleum. Various provisions of the Clean Air Act examined earlier were intended to control emissions from stationary sources as well as motor vehicles. Thus, in some geographic areas state implementation plans limit the burning of high sulfur oil in industrial and power plants and require inspection and maintenance of vehicular exhaust systems.

a. Onshore Development

Construction of facilities such as pipelines, terminals and refineries often presents serious problems of conflicting land uses. Projects like the Trans-Alaska and proposed Northern Tier pipelines can scar and disrupt natural areas, while terminal and refining facilities often compete with preservation and recreation values for scenic coastal locations. Without regard for the possibility of oil spills, the mere construction of such facilities in or near sensitive areas can be detrimental to the environment.

Of course, the threat of spills during production, transportation and storage adds another major dimension to the problem of land use conflicts in siting oil-related facilities. While the most dramatic spills to date have involved tankers and offshore wells, spills also have occurred at onshore facilities, affecting natural lands, streams and lakes. For example, in 1982 one of the largest inland spills poured 250,000 gallons of oil from a broken pipeline into an irrigation ditch in northern Wyoming, from which the oil drained into the Shoshone River and through the Yellowtail Habitat Unit, a 19,000 acre state-federal wildlife preserve. Since construction of the Trans-Alaska pipeline there has been concern that a rupture could damage large areas of fragile arctic lands, though to date only minor incidents have occurred.

The proposed Northern Tier pipeline has been a subject of controversy. Since the Alaskan pipeline went into operation in 1977, crude oil has been pumped into tankers at the Valdez terminal for shipment to refineries. Since the supply greatly exceeds the capacity of West Coast refineries, the excess intended for use within the United States must be moved through the Panama Canal to ports located on the Gulf Coast and in the Virgin Islands. From there the oil is refined locally or shipped to refineries on the East Coast. Because of anticipated decreases in oil imports from Canada, which would result in supply shortages for refineries in Northern Tier and other Midwestern states, the Public Utility Regulatory Policies Act of 1978 (PURPA), 43 U.S.C.A. §§ 2001–2012, contained provisions to expedite action on federal permits required for construction of a system to deliver Alaskan crude oil to such states from the West Coast. The statute called for the President to select a particular project and route, based on specified criteria. After considering several applications, President Carter selected the Northern Tier Pipeline Company's proposal to build a pipeline from Port Angeles, Washington, beneath Puget Sound and eastward to Clearbrook, Minnesota, where it would connect with an existing distribution system. However, the President's action by itself did not authorize the company to begin construction. Many federal and nonfederal permits still had to be obtained, the former being subject to PURPA expediting provisions.

Although the pipeline would be nearly 1,500 miles long, controversy has focused on possible degradation of Puget Sound. In a lawsuit brought by the City of Port Angeles and Clallam County, Washington, and by a number of Indian tribes located near Puget Sound, a federal court ruled that President Carter's choice of the Northern Tier pipeline route did not violate PURPA, NEPA, or other federal laws. No Oilport! v. Carter, 520 F.Supp. 334 (W.D.Wash.1981). Early in 1982 the U.S. Army Corps of Engineers issued permits, under the Clean Water Act and the Rivers and Harbors Act of 1899, for construction of an oilport in Port Angeles and the pipeline from there to Minnesota. The Washington State Department of Ecology promptly filed suit against the Corps attacking the validity of the permits. Meanwhile, Governor Spellman of Washington, following advice from the state's Energy Facility Site Evaluation Council, rejected the pipeline company's application for a permit to build the pipeline beneath Puget Sound. He said he was not opposed to the entire project but only to the twenty-eight mile section beneath Puget Sound that would threaten "its delicate ecology and the economy and the lifestyle it supports." The company then sued the Governor, claiming that his refusal to issue the permit violated the Commerce Clause, Supremacy Clause and Fourteenth Amendment of the U.S. Constitution. The actions against the Corps and Governor Spellman remained pending in 1983 when the company announced that it would abandon the project.

b.   Offshore Development

Disputes over the exploration and development of offshore oil and gas deposits have multiplied since the disastrous 1969 blowout and spill in California's Santa Barbara channel, which killed birds and marine organisms, damaged beaches and seafront properties, and impaired fishing and recreational activities over a large area. The disputes most frequently have arisen in connection with federal leasing of tracts in the outer continental shelf (OCS). The United States government, rather than the states, exercises sovereign rights over the seabed and subsoil of the continental shelf beyond three miles from the coastline. United States v. Maine, 420 U.S. 515 (1975); Outer Continental Shelf Lands Act (OCSLA), 43 U.S.C.A. § 1331. Acting primarily through the Department of the Interior, the government leases OCS areas to private firms through a competitive bidding process prescribed by OCSLA.

[*230*]

Leasing and resultant exploration, development, production and transportation of OCS oil and gas also are subject to the mandates of NEPA, the Coastal Zone Management Act (CZMA), 16 U.S. C.A. §§ 1451–1464, and the Clean Water Act.

The process leading to production and transportation of oil and gas from OCS lands involves several stages at which environmental considerations are to be taken into account. As amended in 1978, OCSLA charts a path which begins with promulgation of a five-year leasing program and continues through lease sales and exploration to development, production, and sale of the recovered minerals. 43 U.S.C.A. §§ 1344, 1337, 1340, 1351 and 1353. To insure that the Secretary of the Interior takes into account all relevant policy considerations and the views of all interested persons, the Act provides for participation by Congress, affected state and local governments, other federal agencies, and the public.

Section 18 of the Act, 43 U.S.C.A. § 1344, requires the Secretary to establish a five-year OCS leasing program, consisting of a schedule of proposed lease sales indicating as precisely as possible the size, timing and location of leasing activity which he determines will best meet national energy needs for the five-year period following approval or revision and reapproval. The Secretary must prepare and maintain the program consistent with four basic principles:

[*231*]

(1) Management of the OCS shall be conducted in a manner which considers economic, social, and environmental values of renewable and nonrenewable resources, and the potential impact of oil and gas exploration on other resource values and the marine, coastal, and human environments.

(2) Timing and location of exploration, development, and production among the oil and gas-bearing physiographic *regions* of the OCS shall be based on consideration of an equitable sharing of developmental benefits and environmental risks among the various regions; the location of such regions with respect to, and the relative needs of, regional and national energy markets; the location of such regions with respect to other uses of the sea and seabed, such as fisheries and navigation; the interest of potential oil and gas producers as indicated by exploration or nomination; laws, goals, and policies of affected states which have been specifically identified by their governors for the Secretary's consideration; and the relative environmental sensitivity and marine productivity of different areas of the OCS.

(3) The Secretary shall select the timing and location of leasing, to the maximum extent practicable, so as to obtain a proper balance between the potential for environmental

damage, the potential for discovery of oil and gas, and the potential for adverse impact on the coastal zone.

(4) Leasing activities shall be conducted to assure receipt of fair market value for the lands leased and the rights conveyed by the federal government.

Section 18 also establishes a mechanism for state governments to offer suggestions and comments. The Secretary is required, when preparing a proposed leasing program, to "invite and consider suggestions" from the governors of any states which might be affected. He also is obliged, after he has drawn up the proposed program but before he publishes it in the Federal Register, to submit it to the governor of each affected state for review and comment. If a governor requests modification, the Secretary must reply in writing, granting or denying the request in whole or in part "and stating his reasons therefor." States also may submit comments and recommendations within ninety days after publication in the Federal Register. The Secretary then must submit the proposed program and any comments received to Congress and the President at least sixty days before he approves it, indicating why any specific recommendation of a state government was not accepted.

Following approval by the Secretary, a leasing program is subject for sixty days to judicial review exclusively in the U.S. Court of Appeals for the District of Columbia Circuit, upon suit by any person who participated in the administrative proceedings related to the program and is adversely affected or aggrieved by it.   43 U.S.C.A. § 1349. The court of appeals must consider the matter solely on the record before the Secretary, and his findings are conclusive if supported by substantial evidence.

Having survived all these hurdles, a leasing program achieves important practical and legal significance.   No lease may be issued for any area unless the area is included in the approved leasing program and unless the lease contains provisions consistent with the approved program. The approved program also becomes the basis for future planning by all affected entities, from federal, state and local governments to the oil industry itself.

In California v. Watt, 668 F.2d 1290 (D.C.Cir. 1981), the states of California and Alaska and several environmental groups obtained judicial review of the five-year OCS leasing program approved in 1980 during the Carter administration. Noting that section 18 of OCSLA seeks to assure that the size, timing, and location of proposed lease sales within the program are selected so as to achieve a proper balance among economic, environmental, and coastal state concerns, the court found that Secretary of the Interior Andrus had

[*234*]

erred in failing (1) to specify the location of certain proposed lease sales more precisely than simply "California", (2) to consider the need to share developmental benefits and environmental risks among the various OCS regions, (3) to consider the relative environmental sensitivity and marine productivity of different areas of the OCS, (4) to base timing and location of leasing on some of the standards of subsection 18(2), supra, (5) to strike a proper balance incorporating environmental and coastal zone factors, and not simply administrative and economic factors, and (6) to quantify environmental costs to the extent they are quantifiable. The court remanded the leasing program to Secretary Andrus' successor, James Watt, for reconsideration in connection with a revised leasing program then being prepared.

In 1982 Secretary Watt approved a new 1982–1987 leasing program to offer, in 41 oil and gas lease sales, virtually the nation's entire OCS, almost one billion acres. The program excluded almost no areas for environmental reasons, and clearly evidenced the belief of Watt and others in the Reagan administration that natural resources are best used when in the hands of the private rather than the public sector. On the following day seven environmental groups, the states of Alaska and California, and several local governments in Alaska challenged the program in four separate lawsuits filed in the District of Columbia

[*235*]

Circuit.   The environmental groups' complaint charged that the program did not reflect a proper balance among the potentials for environmental damage, hydrocarbon discovery, and adverse coastal effects, and that it violated the court's 1981 order in California v. Watt.   The suits were still pending early in 1983.

After a five-year OCS leasing program has been approved by the Secretary of Interior and survived judicial review, later steps toward production of oil and gas include the proposal and conduct of lease sales by the Secretary, and proposal by lessees of exploration plans and then development and production plans.   As stated previously, OCSLA requires at all these stages that the Secretary consider environmental factors and the views of other federal officials, state and local governments, and the public.

Related to federal action under OCSLA, there has been extended controversy over the requirements of the Coastal Zone Management Act. CZMA seeks to achieve wise use of coastal land and water resources by providing monetary assistance to states to develop and administer management programs consistent with standards prescribed in sections 305 and 306.   Approval of a state management program by the Secretary of Commerce triggers "federal consistency" provisions in section 307(c), requiring federal agencies, permittees and licensees to show that their pro-

[*236*]

posed developments in or "directly affecting" coastal zones, including the OCS, would be consistent with the state program. In certain instances the consistency requirement is qualified by the phrase "to the maximum extent practicable" or "unless [found by the Secretary of Commerce to be] consistent with the objectives of this title or otherwise necessary in the interest of national security."

California was one of the first states to receive federal assistance to develop a management program under CZMA. In 1976 the legislature enacted the California Coastal Act, and the National Oceanic and Atmospheric Administration (NOAA), the approving agency under the Secretary of Commerce, began working with state officials to assure that the new legislation complied with the requirements of CZMA. In 1977, oil industry trade associations sued to enjoin NOAA's approval of the California management program. They contended, among other things, that it failed to satisfy the requirement of section 306(c)(8) that such a program provide for "adequate consideration of the national interest involved in planning for, and in the siting of, facilities (including energy facilities in, or which significantly affect, such state's coastal zone) which are necessary to meet requirements which are other than local in nature." In American Petroleum Institute v. Knecht, 609 F.2d 1306 (9th Cir.1979), the

[*237*]

court upheld NOAA's approval of the California management program, rejecting plaintiffs' argument that section 306(c)(8) required "explicit commitments" by the state to accommodate new energy facilities.

In 1981, after completion of various environmental studies by his predecessor, and over the protests of state and local officials in California, Secretary of the Interior Watt announced an OCS lease sale of the entire Santa Maria Basin, offshore from an extraordinarily scenic stretch of coastline extending between Big Sur and Santa Barbara. The State of California promptly sued and obtained an injunction directing that certain tracts within the basin be excluded from the sale. The district court held that the final notices of sale were federal activities "directly affecting" the coastal zone of California and therefore, under section 307(c)(1) of CZMA, were required to be conducted in a manner, "to the maximum extent practicable, consistent with" the state's approved management program. On appeal, in California v. Watt, 683 F.2d 1253 (9th Cir.1982), the court held that Secretary Watt had violated section 307(c)(1) by selling tracts without making a determination of consistency, because the sale would "directly affect" the state's coastal zone by establishing "the first link in a chain of events which could lead to production and development of oil and gas on the individual tracts leased."

The consistency provisions of section 307 serve as an incentive for states to develop and carry out comprehensive coastal management programs. In light of the decline in federal funding, the requirement that federal activities be consistent with approved state programs is a major inducement for states to develop and maintain CZMA programs. Therefore, a critical issue now is the meaning of consistency "to the maximum extent practicable." Since CZMA is silent on the meaning of this phrase, it appears that final authority to determine whether a particular proposal satisfies the standard lies with the executive branch of the federal government, subject to judicial review. If a state disagrees with the federal consistency determination, mediation procedures may be invoked by the Secretary of Commerce under CZMA to reconcile the national interest with the concerns of the state.

NEPA frequently serves as the legal base for challenges to proposals for leasing and development of federally owned lands. NRDC v. Morton, 458 F.2d 827 (D.C.Cir.1972), involved a proposed sale of oil and gas leases covering 380,000 acres of OCS lands off eastern Louisiana. Three conservation groups brought suit against the Secretary of the Interior to enjoin the sale. Adjacent to the proposed lease area was the greatest estuarine coastal marsh complex in the United States, some 8 million acres providing food, nursery habitat and spawning ground vital to fish, shellfish and wildlife, as well as food and shelter for migratory water fowl, wading birds and fur-bearing animals. The complex provided rich nutrient systems making the Gulf of Mexico the most productive fishing region of the country. Plaintiffs did not challenge the Department's EIS on the ground of failure to disclose probable environmental impacts of the proposed sale. The EIS acknowledged that both short and long term effects on the environment could be expected from major and minor spills and discharges of wastewater contaminated with oil. It predicted damage to beaches, water areas and historic sights, and to the marine biological community. What plaintiffs objected to was failure of the EIS to discuss the environmental consequences of possible alternative sources of energy. The court held that NEPA required presentation of the environmental risks incident to "reasonable alternative courses of action." In addition, the court rejected the government's contention that the only alternatives required to be discussed were those which could be adopted and put into effect by the official or agency issuing the EIS. While the Department of Interior did not have authority to eliminate or reduce oil import quotas, such action was within the purview of both Congress and the President, to whom the EIS would go. On the other hand, the court held that no additional discussion was required for such alternatives as development of oil shale, desulfurization of coal, coal liquefaction and gasification, tar sands, and geothermal resources. While these possibilities held promise for the future, their impact on energy supply was not expected to be felt for at least a decade, whereas the lease sale in question was proposed to meet a near-term requirement imposed by an energy shortage projected for the mid-1970s.

In County of Suffolk v. Secretary of the Interior, 562 F.2d 1368 (2d Cir.1977), cert. denied 434 U.S. 1064 (1978), the issue was the adequacy of an EIS for a proposed OCS lease sale in the mid-Atlantic area. Earlier, the Department of Interior had prepared a programmatic EIS evaluating the entire area under consideration. The statement had discussed the environmental impacts of oil and gas development and analyzed alternative energy sources such as onshore oil and gas, oil shale, and solar energy. Next, Interior had selected 1,151 tracts, containing 6.5 million acres, and asked industry to specify which were desired for leasing. Industry had nominated 557 tracts, and after further investigation Interior tentatively had announced the choice of 154 tracts located 50 to 90 miles offshore. Then a site-specific EIS was drafted, and the Secretary of Interior approved the lease sale. At that point he was sued. Plaintiffs claimed that the site-specific EIS failed to consider the effect of state and local regulations on the mode of transportation (pipelines or tankers) to be used for oil produced offshore, and failed to project likely pipeline routes and landfalls. The court of appeals concluded that projection of specific pipeline routes was neither meaningfully possible nor reasonably necessary under the circumstances. The EIS, said the court, contemplated that a more specific consideration of and commitment to routes and modes of transportation would occur once it had been determined where, if anywhere, oil or gas existed within the more than 500,000 acres to be leased. The lessee of a tract where oil was discovered would be required, before beginning production and transportation, to present a development plan, including specific pipeline routes, which would be subject to review and approval by both the Secretary and affected coastal states. The Secretary had announced that before he considered whether to approve any such plans, a Development Plan EIS would be prepared, which would include a survey not only of the environmental consequences of specific pipeline corridors but also of any other problems relating to lessee's specific proposals for transportation of oil and gas actually found. The court pointed out that under CZMA the location of pipelines, landfalls and onshore pipeline routes would have to conform to approved management plans of the affected states, and that until the states finished drafting their management plans, onshore pipeline routes could not be determined. The Secretary's decision to lease the tracts for exploration did not preclude him, said the court, from requiring in the future that pipeline routes be modified or altered, or from imposing other conditions and safeguards that would allow pipelining only if environmentally acceptable.

A problem with the decision in *Suffolk* to allow the lease sale to proceed is that the court may not have given sufficient weight to the practical effects of large commitments of resources by oil exploration companies. If the companies were to make discoveries after very large investments, it may be unrealistic to think that the Secretary of Interior would stop development because of environmental problems disclosed in a new EIS.

Both OCSLA and leases issued thereunder by the Secretary of Interior do contain provisions intended to protect against damages from oil spills. The Act confirms that Congress intended to exercise both the proprietary powers of a landowner and the police powers of the legislature in regulating leases of publicly owned resources. Safeguards are not limited to those provided by lease covenants; the Secretary may prescribe at any time rules and regulations which he finds "necessary and proper" for the "conservation of natural resources." 43 U.S.C.A. § 1334(a)(1). Rules in effect at the time a lease is executed are incorporated statutorily into the terms of the lease, and the Secretary may obtain cancellation of the lease if the lessee breaches any such rule. However, violation of rules issued after the lease has been executed does not enable the Secretary to cancel the lease; the property rights of the lessee are determined only by those rules in effect when the lease is executed.

In Union Oil Co. v. Morton, 512 F.2d 743 (9th Cir.1975), four oil companies brought suit to set aside an order of the Secretary denying them permission to construct a drilling platform in the Santa Barbara Channel which they alleged was necessary for full exercise of their lease rights. The lease gave plaintiffs the right to erect floating drilling platforms, subject to the provisions of OCSLA and to "reasonable regulations" not inconsistent with the lease. After the blowout which caused the disastrous 1969 Santa Barbara oil spill, killing birds and marine organizms, damaging beaches and seafront properties, and restricting fishing and recreational activities in the area, the Secretary had ordered all activities on this and other leases suspended pending further environmental studies. A few months later he had issued a regulation authorizing emergency "suspension" of any operation which threatened immediate, serious or irreparable harm or damage to life, including aquatic life, or to property or the environment, and providing that the suspension should continue until in the Secretary's

[*244*]

judgment the threat had terminated. Plaintiffs claimed a distinction between suspension and revocation, asserting that the Secretary had not merely suspended their operations because a suspension by definition was of a "temporary nature." The court held that Congress had intended vested rights under the lease to be invulnerable to defeasance by subsequently issued regulations. Although the regulation in question provided that a "suspension" should be limited in time only by the Secretary's judgment that the environmental threat had ended, and although section 1334(a)(1) authorized regulations providing not only for suspensions but for any other action affecting operations which the Secretary determined to be necessary and proper for conservation of natural resources, the court said that Congress had not intended the granting of leases to be so tenuous that the Secretary could terminate them, in whole or in part, at will. Therefore, while Congress itself could order the leases forfeited, subject to payment of just compensation, without congressional authorization the Secretary had no power to revoke.

The result of the *Union Oil* decision is open to question. *Suffolk* strongly suggested two years later that, after leasing, the Secretary was empowered to take measures necessary to protect the environment. When the *Union Oil* lease was executed, section 1334(a)(1) expressly authorized the Secretary to subject the lease to later regulations necessary for protection of the environment. Clearly the Secretary could not contract away his statutory authority. If an indefinite suspension for environmental protection constitutes a "taking" in violation of the Fifth Amendment, it seems that the Secretary's regulatory power vanishes whenever a pollution problem is so serious that no solution is foreseeable within a reasonable period of time.

c. *Liability for Spills*

Several federal laws impose liability for oil spills. OCSLA amendments of 1978 established liability for clean-up costs and damages resulting from OCS activities and created the Offshore Oil Spill Pollution Fund. The amendments apply to offshore facilities and to vessels carrying oil from such facilities. Strict liability for clean-up costs and damages is imposed jointly and severally on the owner and operator, not to exceed $250,000 in the case of a vessel, or $35,000,000 plus government removal costs in the case of an offshore facility. Such limits, however, are not applicable if an incident is caused by willful misconduct or gross negligence, or by violation, "within the privity or knowledge of the owner or operator", of federal safety regulations. The Fund, which is derived from a fee of 3 cents per barrel imposed on the owner of oil obtained from the OCS, is liable for all losses not otherwise compensated.

The broadest liability for spills is imposed by section 311 of the Clean Water Act. It makes vessels strictly liable for clean-up costs incurred by the government unless the owner proves that the spill was solely a result of an Act of God, an act of war, an act or omission of a third party, or negligence by the federal government. Owners of onshore and offshore facilities also are strictly liable for government clean-up costs. With respect to vessels, the courts have held that section 311 preempts any other remedies which the U.S. might otherwise have, under other statutes or under judge-made maritime law or non-maritime federal common law. In re Oswego Barge Corp., 664 F.2d 327 (2d Cir.1981). Section 311 does place limits on liability thereunder: $125,000 for inland oil barges, $250,000 for other vessels, and $50,000,000 for onshore and offshore facilities. However, the limits are not applicable if the federal government can show that the discharge was due to "willful negligence or willful misconduct within the privity and knowledge of the owner." It also has been held that even if the quoted standard is not satisfied, section 311 does not limit recovery by a state government in an action based upon a state statute imposing liability for clean-up costs. Steuart Transportation Co. v. Allied Towing Corp., 596 F.2d 609 (4th Cir.1979).

The Trans-Alaska Pipeline Authorization Act, 43 U.S.C.A. §§ 1651–1655, and the Deepwater Port Act of 1974, 33 U.S.C.A. §§ 1501–1524, also provide for strict liability and for funds to compensate damaged parties. The Trans-Alaska Act covers only vessels transporting Alaskan pipeline oil to U.S. ports, and it does not recognize the defenses of Act of God or act or omission of a third party. The Deepwater Port Act applies to vessel discharges within "a safety zone" of a deepwater port and allows the same defenses as the Trans-Alaska Act. Both acts set maximum limits on total liability, $100,000,000 for the Trans-Alaska Act and $20,000,000 for the Deepwater Port Act.

A subject of increasing interest is public recovery of damages for injuries to "natural resources." Section 311(f) of the Clean Water Act provides that the costs of removal of oil shall include "any costs or expenses incurred by the Federal Government or any State government in the restoration or replacement of natural resources damaged or destroyed" as a result of the spill. The section further provides that the "President, or the authorized representative of any State, shall act on behalf of the public as trustee of the natural resources to recover for the costs of replacing and restoring such resources. Sums recovered shall be used to restore, rehabilitate, or acquire the equivalent of such natural resources by the appropriate agencies of the Federal Government, or the State government." OCSLA amendments of 1978 also provide for recovery of damages for "injury to", "destruction of", and "loss of use of" natural resources.

Another basis for recovery of damages for injury to natural resources is state statutory law. See Commonwealth of Puerto Rico v. SS Zoe Colocotroni, 628 F.2d 652 (1st Cir.1980), an especially interesting case because it explores various possible measures of damages. The government of Puerto Rico was seeking to recover for injuries to an area of coastal mangrove wetlands. The court rejected a commercial or market-value test as the basis for recovery. The proper measure of damages, it said, was the reasonable cost to restore or rehabilitate the environment to its pre-existing condition. Applying this standard, the court rejected a plan to remove all the oil-impregnated mangrove plants and replace them with containerized plants as too costly and destructive to the remaining natural environment. The court also rejected an abstract calculation of six cents per marine animal killed. The case was remanded for the taking of testimony on a plan that "would have a beneficial effect on the . . . ecosystem without excessive destruction of existing natural resources or disproportionate cost." In reaching these conclusions the court may have been guided more by its sense of reasonableness than by close attention to legislative intent.

2. COAL

Chapter 2 considered various issues bearing on the use of coal as a fuel. New source performance standards (discussed further in subsection *c* below) and PSD requirements under the Clean Air Act obviously could discourage construction of new coal-fired power plants. Similarly, stringent SIP requirements for existing sources could discourage the burning of coal, especially high sulfur coal.

The materials in this section concern primarily the mining of coal and requirements that certain types of facilities use it in lieu of other fuels. The United States has an estimated 1.58 trillion tons of identified coal reserves, approximately half of them located in western states. The federal government owns approximately 60 percent of the western coal reserves, which are predominantly low in sulfur content. Most of the large coal resources in the East and Midwest are privately owned and high in sulfur content.

a. Conversion to Coal

In 1978 Congress enacted the National Energy Act, five statutes intended to reduce dependence on imported oil and domestic natural gas by encouraging the use of more abundant domestic fuels, renewable energy resources, and conservation measures. One of the statutes was the Powerplant and Industrial Fuel Use Act (PIFUA), 42 U.S.C.A. §§ 8301–8483, which requires certain electric power plants and major fuel-burning installations to switch from gas and oil to coal and other alternate fuels. The Department of Energy may order facilities, individually or by category, to convert to coal or alternate fuels if it finds that conversion is financially feasible and that the facilities have the technical capability to convert without substantial physical modification or reduction in capacity. However, PIFUA authorizes both temporary and permanent exemptions upon a demonstration that, despite "diligent good faith efforts," a facility cannot use coal or alternate fuels due to site limitations, inadequate or unreliable supplies of alternate fuels, or applicable environmental requirements under federal or state laws. EPA is required by the Clean Air Act to oppose coal conversions that would cause violations of ambient air quality standards.

Among the environmental hazards of increased coal combustion are "acid rain" caused by sulfur oxide emissions, and possible global climatic changes resulting from carbon dioxide emissions. SO_2 in the atmosphere can be converted by oxidation into sulfates, or sulfuric acid, which may return to the earth in rain or snow. Apparently as a result of this acid precipitation, hundreds of lakes in North America and Scandinavia have become so acidic that they no longer can support fish life. Data related to possible terrestrial impacts are just beginning to be developed. Preliminary research indicates that the yield from agricultural crops can be reduced as a result of both the direct effects of acids on foliage, and the indirect effects resulting from the leaching of minerals from soils. The productivity of forests may be affected similarly.

Concerning possible climatic changes, many scientists believe that CO_2 emissions from the burning of fossil fuels could produce a permanent warming of the atmosphere, accompanied by an even larger change in the temperature differential between the poles and equator, and leading to marked changes in global weather patterns. It is theorized that increases in the concentration of CO_2 in the atmosphere can raise the temperature of the earth's surface because CO_2 gas absorbs and reradiates heat from that surface. A committee of the National Academy of Sciences concluded that a fivefold increase over the next 100 years in the annual amount of fossil carbon fuels burned could roughly double the amount of CO_2 in the atmosphere and produce an increase of 2 to 3° C in mean surface temperatures. Such a change could adversely affect agriculture, particularly in the temperate grain belts. In short, there may be substantial risks for the United

States, and the world, in massive conversions to coal.

b. Surface Mining

In contrast to underground coal mining, which requires removing coal from the earth, surface mining consists of removing earth from the coal. If the size of the coal deposit justifies the cost of large equipment, surface mining operations may penetrate the surface to a depth of 500 feet or more. Equipment depends upon the terrain, the ratio of coal to overburden, and the value of the coal deposit per acre. In general, there are three broad categories of surface mining operations: contour, area, and open pit.

Contour mining occurs on steep terrain. In the mountains of Appalachia where it is prevalent, the operator excavates a portion of the hillside where the coal seam intersects the surface. He then strips off the overburden, following the seam along the contour and excavating as far into the mountain as is profitable. Overburden is cast over the downhill side of the "bench", or flat area from which the coal is removed.

Area mining occurs on flat or rolling countryside. Overburden is piled to one side in a ridge on the area from which coal has been removed. This continous back-filling results in a furrowed mine site terminating in a ditch which marks the

[*253*]

final "cut", usually at the limit of the disturbed area. Area mining is practiced in the western Appalachians and in the Midwest and West.

Open pit mining is similar to area surface mining. However, because the thickness of the coal removed is greater than the thickness of the overburden, the overburden is insufficient to fill the pit, and a depression in the surface remains.

Following removal of the coal, reclamation of the mining site takes place in two phases. First comes the back-filling, drainage and regrading required to achieve the desired surface configuration and removal of excess water. Then comes revegetation: preparation of topsoil, fertilization, cultivation, and seeding or planting desired species. The most serious offsite environmental impacts result from exposure of overburden to the weather with consequent erosion, sedimentation, siltation, acid drainage, landslides, and leaching of toxic chemicals. Good reclamation, therefore, minimizes the time from initial disturbance of the land surface to reestablishment of a vegetative cover. In steep terrain, overburden should be retained on the "bench" to avoid undue offsite impacts and to facilitate regrading. In flat or rolling areas, restoring approximately original contours helps to maintain the prevailing hydrologic pattern. Because low rainfall and soil erodability handicap revegetation in the West, minimizing impacts to the hydrologic balance of the mine site and surrounding lands is especially important.

By the Surface Mining Control and Reclamation Act of 1977, 30 U.S.C.A. §§ 1201–1328, Congress adopted a program of nationwide minimum environmental standards, with enforcement primarily in the hands of the states if they elect to exercise the authority. To assume exclusive jurisdiction over surface coal mining operations on nonfederal lands, a state must submit a regulatory and enforcement program and have it approved by the Secretary of the Interior. If a state fails to submit an acceptable program, the Office of Surface Mining Reclamation and Enforcement, within the Department of the Interior, must create a federal program applicable to that state; and if a state fails to enforce its approved program, the Secretary may provide for federal enforcement. Generally, no person may conduct surface coal mining without a permit issued under a state or federal program. Permit applications must be accompanied by a fee and disclosure of certain information, including a description of the location, type and method of mining proposed, anticipated starting and termination dates, hydrologic information, results of test borings, and a reclamation plan. After a permit has been approved, the applicant must file a bond for performance of all requirements of the Act and permit.

The Act specifies 25 environmental protection performance standards and establishes a two-stage regulatory program: an interim phase, and a permanent phase. The interim program involves immediate promulgation and federal enforcement of some of the performance standards, complemented by continuing state regulation. In the permanent phase, a regulatory program is to be adopted for each state, mandating compliance with the full panoply of federal performance standards, with enforcement responsibility in either the state or federal government.

Under section 1265, the interim program must require mine operators to comply with performance standards governing, among other things, (a) restoration of land to its prior condition; (b) restoration to approximate original contour; (c) segregation and preservation of topsoil; (d) minimization of disturbance to the hydrologic balance; and (e) revegetation of mined areas. The interim regulations were published in 1977 and currently are in effect in most states.

Permanent regulations incorporating all performance standards were published in 1979, but they do not become effective in a particular state until either a permanent state program, submitted to and approved by the Secretary, or a permanent federal program for the state, is implemented. Like the Act, the regulations provide that federal requirements supersede state provisions only to the extent that the latter are less stringent. The regulations also provide that a state, in proposing its program, may request a variance from any federal standard if its proposed alternative "is necessary because of local requirements or local environmental or agricultural conditions"; however, the alternative nevertheless must be "in accordance with the applicable provisions of the Act and consistent with the regulations." It is unclear how this "state window" provision will be applied in practice.

In Hodel v. Virginia Surface Mining and Reclamation Association, Inc., 452 U.S. 264 (1981), discussed in Chapter 4, coal producers, landowners and the State of Virginia sought relief from sections of the Act establishing the interim regulatory program. After rejecting plaintiffs' contention that the provisions violated the Commerce Clause and Tenth Amendment of the Constitution, the Court considered a claim that the steep-slope provisions effected an uncompensated taking of private property by requiring operators to perform the "economically and physically impossible" task of restoring steep-slope surface mines to their approximate original contour, and by prohibiting mining in certain locations and "clearly prevent[ing] a person from mining his own land or having it mined." Because plaintiffs' pre-enforcement suit presented no concrete controversy concerning either application of the Act to particular surface mining operations or its effect on specific parcels of land, the Court rejected the claim, saying that a statute regulating the uses that can be made of property effects a taking only if it "denies an owner economically viable use of his land." The Court noted that there was no indication in the record that plaintiffs had availed themselves of opportunities provided by the Act to obtain administrative relief by requesting either a variance from the approximate original contour requirement or a waiver from the provisions prohibiting mining in certain locations. In short, the taking issue was "not ripe for judicial resolution."

In the companion case, Hodel v. Indiana, 452 U.S. 314 (1981), the Court rejected plaintiffs' pre-enforcement challenge to the Act's "prime farmland" provisions. These provisions state that a permit for surface coal mining on such lands may be granted only if the operator can demonstrate his "technological capability to restore such mined area, within a reasonable time, to equivalent or higher levels of yield as nonmined prime farmland in the surrounding area under equivalent levels of management."

c. Protection of the High-Sulfur Coal Mining Industry

Sulfur dioxide emission limitations under the Clean Air Act increased the attractiveness of low sulfur western coal to public utilities and industrial plants in the East and Midwest. This threat to jobs and local economies in established coal mining areas became a major political issue. One type of reaction was efforts by some states to discourage use of low sulfur coal. For example, Ohio enacted a coal use tax for which the per-ton rate varied inversely with sulfur content. The tax was held invalid in Mapco, Inc. v. Grunder, 470 F.Supp. 401 (N.D.Ohio 1979), on Commerce Clause grounds.

More successful were efforts to include protective provisions in the Clean Air Act amendments of 1977. One, in section 111(a)(1), directed EPA to take a new approach in setting standards of performance for new fossil-fuel fired stationary sources. For each pollutant, including sulfur dioxide, the standard was to reflect both the degree of emission limitation *and the percentage reduction* achievable through application of the "best system of continous emission reduction . . . adequately demonstrated." Thus, the use of low sulfur coal no longer was an acceptable way to reduce SO_2 emissions from new sources, though "cleaning of the fuel or reduction in the pollution characteristics of the fuel after extraction and prior to combustion" was allowed. (Pre-combustion "washing" of crushed coal removes sulfur-bearing particles which are mixed with but not chemically bonded to the coal, and which can con-

[*259*]

stitute 20 to 40 percent of total sulfur content.)
According to the legislative history, essential purposes of amended section 111(a)(1) included the
following: standards should not give a competitive advantage to one state over another in at-
tracting industry; they should maximize the potential for long term individual growth by
reducing emissions as much as practicable; and
to the extent practical, the standards should force
new sources to burn high sulfur fuel, thus free-
ing low sulfur fuel for use in existing sources
where it is harder to control emissions.

In 1979 EPA issued regulations prescribing
NSPSs governing emissions by coal-burning power plants. These standards allowed for a "sliding
scale" of SO_2 emission reductions, depending on
the source's rate of emissions. All sources, regardless of their emission rates, were required to
reduce potential emissions by at least 70 percent,
and those emitting more than 0.6 lbs. per million
British thermal units were required to achieve reductions of at least 90 percent.

In Sierra Club v. Costle, 657 F.2d 298 (D.C.Cir.
1981), the Sierra Club and the California Air Resources Board contested EPA's authority to establish the variable 70 to 90 percent reduction
standard, rather than a single standard reflecting
maximum feasible reduction. Electric utilities,
on the other hand, challenged the 90 percent maximum reduction standard as too stringent. The

court held that, considering all the technical data, the sliding scale reduction formula was reasonable because it would yield the "maximum reduction practicable." Not only would the variable standard achieve the same total emissions reductions nationally as a uniform standard, but it also would permit flexibility in use of either "wet" or "dry" post-combustion "scrubbing" of flue gas, all with less severe long term economic and regional impact than would be the case with a uniform standard. The court also upheld the 90 percent maximum reduction requirement because EPA data showed that it was achievable with a combination of coal washing and flue gas scrubbing.

Section 125 of the Clean Air Act, as modified by section 661 of the 1978 National Energy Conservation Policy Act, Pub.Law 95–619, 92 Stat. 3206, authorizes the President, upon petition of a governor, to prohibit an existing or new major fuel-burning stationary source from using fuels other than "locally or regionally available coal or coal derivatives" to comply with implementation plan requirements. Such action may be taken only if "necessary to prevent or minimize significant local or regional economic disruption or unemployment" which would result from use of other fuels. Action under section 125 was a possibility in 1978 when the governor of Ohio requested EPA to hold public hearings concerning whether plants in that state should be prohibited from using low sulfur coal from Kentucky rather than Ohio coal. Coal companies and public officials from Kentucky and West Virginia intervened, insisting that their states were in the same "regional" market as Ohio and that section 125 was intended to protect them from western coal, not to fragment the area east of the Mississippi into a series of state or local markets. EPA issued a "proposed determination" that significant economic disruption existed in Ohio because of the use of out-of-state coal, and that Ohio utilities should be ordered to buy as much Ohio coal as they had bought previously. A Kentucky coal company then brought suit, claiming that application of section 125 would create a discriminatory trade barrier in violation of the Commerce Clause and would deny equal protection and due process of law under the Fifth Amendment. These claims were rejected in McCoy-Elkhorn Coal Corp. v. EPA, 622 F.2d 260 (6th Cir.1980). However, no order was issued under section 125 because SO_2 emission standards in the Ohio SIP were relaxed to permit the power plants to burn local coal without scrubbers.

3. SYNTHETIC FUELS

Synfuel technologies fall into three classes. First generation processes are those considered to be currently or imminently available for commercial use. They include indirect coal gasification and liquefaction and surface oil shale retorting. Second generation technologies are being demonstrated in pilot plants and nearing commercial readiness. Third generation processes are experimental. The emerging technologies include direct coal liquefaction and *in situ* retorting of oil shale.

A commercial scale synfuels industry could pose potentially serious environmental and social problems. However, since no commercial size plants are in operation in this country, accurate assessment of the problems is difficult. Some of them include siting difficulties, emissions of gases and particulates, disposal of wastewater and solid wastes, health risks to workers, and boom town effects. Since all first generation processes use large quantities of water, its availability could be a serious constraint in arid western states.

A few years ago, as oil prices were rising dramatically, it appeared that commercial production of synfuels was about to be undertaken. Oil shale companies were rushing to obtain facility permits in Colorado to use rapidly dwindling PSD increments. In 1980 Congress enacted the United States Synthetic Fuels Corporation Act, 42 U.S.C.A. §§ 8701–8795. It established a $20 billion federal synfuels development program to be managed by a corporation whose directors would

[*263*]

be appointed by the President, subject to approval by the Senate. National production goals were set at the equivalent of 500,000 barrels per day of crude oil by 1987, and 2 million by 1992. The corporation was to solicit proposals and provide financial assistance for construction and operation of synthetic fuel projects. Price guarantees, purchase agreements and loan guarantees were to be preferred over loans, which in turn had priority over direct participation in joint ventures. Only if the availability of financial assistance failed to attract private firms could the corporation itself own synfuel projects, which had to be constructed and operated by contractors. No action of the corporation except construction and operation of projects was to be deemed a "major Federal action significantly affecting the quality of the human environment" for purposes of section 102(2)(C) of NEPA.

By 1982, expectations had faded before the reality of economic and technological difficulties. The largest projects, involving oil shale development in Colorado, had been canceled or postponed. The Synthetic Fuels Corporation, with resources of more than $15 billion, had not approved assistance to even one synfuel project, and a bill was introduced in Congress to abolish the corporation and use its funds for housing programs.

C. RENEWABLE (SOLAR) SOURCES AND CONSERVATION

In this section we examine legal approaches to encouraging or requiring greater use of renewable energy sources and conservation techniques. Such use is desirable because it would produce far fewer adverse environmental impacts than would construction and operation of more nuclear and coal-fired power plants. As will be shown, the problems to be overcome tend to be more institutional than technological or inherently economic.

1. SOLAR SOURCES

Solar energy sources can be divided into three major groups: (1) *thermal applications:* heating and cooling of buildings, including hot water heating; agricultural and industrial process heating; (2) *fuels from biomass:* plant matter, including wood and garbage; (3) *solar electric:* solar thermal electric, such as the 10-megawatt "power tower" now generating electricity for 6000 homes in the Mojave Desert of California; photovoltaic cells; wind (windmills); ocean thermal electric; and hydropower (dams). Each category can be further elaborated. For example, biomass also includes technologies to improve yields of sea algae farms, and gasification of manure. The unifying concept is that solar energy is the energy

[*265*]

which arrived on the earth from the sun "recently"—during the last hundred years or so.

Much of the technology required to realize solar's potential is already at hand. However,
there are economic and institutional barriers
which must be overcome if solar energy, like conservation, is to have a chance in the marketplace
against conventional sources.

Experience in California shows that governmental intervention can be effective. In 1977 the
legislature passed a 55 percent solar tax credit.
Active and passive systems, as well as solar electricity generating systems, were eligible. The incentives were extended in 1978 to wind and process heating systems, and were supplemented by
laws dealing with financing, utility company involvement, job training, and solar access rights.
Several municipalities adopted ordinances setting
minimum standards for the thermal performance
of buildings. While solar industry growth
slumped nationwide, sales in California soared.
By the end of 1978 California had over 30,000 solar installations. In 1980 the California Public
Utilities Commission ordered the state's four
largest investor-owned utilities to finance some
375,000 solar water heaters during a three-year
demonstration program.

a. Access to Sunlight and Wind

With respect to thermal applications of solar energy, e.g., heating of buildings, assured access to sunlight is obviously very important. Solar installations shadowed by construction of an adjacent highrise, or even by the growth of a neighbor's tree, will function inefficiently or not at all.

The problem of protecting solar access is not new. Obstruction of one landowner's light by another has been a source of litigation for centuries. In ancient Rome, access to light was protected by the doctrine of urban servitudes, which provided "the right that a neighbor shall not raise his building any higher against our will, so as to lessen the amount of light in our house." In England the doctrine of "ancient lights" offered similar protection. If a landowner could demonstrate the existence of lights (windows) overlooking his neighbor's property from "a time whereof the memory of man runneth not to the contrary," he acquired a negative prescriptive *easement* preventing the erection of any structure on the adjoining property that materially diminished the amount of light available to his windows. However, the "ancient lights" doctrine has not been accepted in this country. As a Florida court said some years ago, "No American decision has been [found] in which it has been held that—in the absence of some contractual or statutory obligation—a landowner has a legal right to the free flow of light and air across the adjoining land of his neighbor." Fontainebleau Hotel Corp. v. Forty-Five Twenty-Five, Inc., 114 So.2d 357 (Fla.App. 1959). In that case a Miami Beach hotel sought unsuccessfully to prevent a neighboring hotel from constructing a highrise addition which would cast a shadow upon plaintiff's swimming pool.

Prah v. Maretti, 108 Wis.2d 223, 321 N.W.2d 182 (1982), is the first and only appellate court decision in this country to deal with a claimed right to unobstructed access to sunlight as an energy source. Plaintiff, owner of a solar-heated residence, sought to stop construction of a neighboring house, the specific location of which on defendant's lot would cause it to shade solar collectors on plaintiff's roof. Reversing the trial court's summary judgment for defendant, the Wisconsin Supreme Court held that "unreasonable" obstruction of access to sunlight as a source of energy, rather than of mere aesthetic enjoyment or illumination, could constitute a private *nuisance*; that defendant's compliance with applicable zoning regulations, building codes and deed restrictions did not necessarily make his actions reasonable; and that plaintiff therefore had stated a claim under which relief could be granted. The case was remanded for a full trial, at which the lower court could judge defendant's conduct by the "reasonable use doctrine" set forth in sections 826–828 of the Restatement (Second) of Torts (1977), that is, by balancing the "utility of [defendant's] conduct" with the "gravity of harm" to plaintiff. Meanwhile, spurred by the trial court's initial decision, the Wisconsin legislature joined several other states by enacting a law to facilitate the use of zoning and easements to assure uninterrupted flows of sunlight *and wind*.

b. Interconnection With Utilities

The Public Utility Regulatory Policies Act of 1978 (PURPA) contains provisions favorable to "small power production facilities" which use "biomass, waste, renewable resources [including sunlight, wind and water], or any combination thereof," to produce up to 80 megawatts of electricity. Section 210 of PURPA, 16 U.S.C.A. § 824a–3, requires electric utilities to offer to purchase available electric energy from such facilities (and from "cogenerators", discussed below), and to sell backup power and other services to them on a nondiscriminatory basis. The same section also provides that the Federal Energy Regulatory Commission (FERC) may exempt small power producers and cogenerators from the Federal Power Act and other federal and state laws and regulations respecting rates, finances, and organization of electric utilities. The validity

[*269*]

of section 210 was upheld by the Supreme Court in FERC v. Mississippi, 456 U.S. ___ (1982). The Court had no difficulty in concluding that the statute was within the scope of congressional power under the Commerce Clause, and that there was no violation of the Tenth Amendment in authorizing FERC to exempt qualifying power facilities from state regulation ("nothing more than pre-empt[ing] conflicting state enactments in the traditional way"). Section 210's requirement that "each State regulatory authority shall, after notice and opportunity for public hearing, *implement*" FERC's rules concerning purchases and sales of electricity between utilities and small power producers or cogenerators, was conceded to pose "troublesome" questions under the Tenth Amendment but nevertheless was upheld.

c. *Financing*

The subject of utility financing of solar and conservation measures is receiving increased attention. At least seven states require utility companies to provide such financing. The programs in Iowa, Wisconsin and North Carolina were established by administrative orders of public utility commissions. New York, Ohio, California and Oregon enacted legislation either specifically prescribing financing requirements or giving their utility commissions mandates to do so. There remains some doubt about the legality of state commissions' permitting or requiring solar or conservation financing by utilities in the absence of specific statutory authority. In 1982 an Iowa trial court ruled that the State Commerce Commission lacked a sufficient statutory basis to require utilities to implement financing programs. The counter argument is that utility companies have both a common law and a statutory duty to provide "reasonably adequate service" to their customers, and that this mandate is a proper basis for ordering the financing of solar and conservation measures. The issue is whether such measures are "services" within the meaning of the statutory language, or whether services relate simply to production and distribution of electricity and natural gas.

The Solar Energy and Energy Conservation Act of 1980, 12 U.S.C.A. §§ 3601–3620, established a Solar Energy and Energy Conservation Bank within the federal Department of Housing and Urban Development. Its declared purpose was to "encourage energy conservation and the use of solar energy, and thereby reduce the nation's dependence on foreign sources of energy supplies." The Bank was authorized to make payments to "financial institutions" for the purpose of providing financial assistance to owners of existing buildings for purchase and installation of solar energy systems, and to builders and purchasers of new or substantially rehabilitated

[*271*]

buildings containing solar energy systems. The financial assistance could be in the form of a reduction in the principal obligation of the loan, a prepayment of interest, or a grant. Although the Reagan administration sought to prevent the Bank from beginning operations, Congress appropriated $25 million for it in fiscal year 1982, and a district court placed federal officials responsible for implementation of the Bank under a court-supervised obligation to implement the Act and make the appropriated funds available for expenditure to qualified applicants as expeditiously as possible. Dabney v. Reagan, 542 F.Supp. 756 (S.D.N.Y.1982).

2. CONSERVATION

The traditional response to rising energy prices has been to encourage development of new energy supplies. This approach no longer will lead to reduced costs because most new supplies are significantly more expensive than those already being used. However, the problem of energy inflation can be mitigated if opportunities for cost-effective energy conservation investments are exploited. It is possible to achieve major fuel savings through energy efficiency improvements at much less cost than is required to produce more energy. Although some of the barriers are economic, most are institutional, political and social. Overcoming them may require a public policy which favors conservation, at least temporarily, to give it a fair chance in the marketplace against conventional energy sources.

Experience in Los Angeles from 1973 to 1975 demonstrates the potential of economic incentives for conservation. Utility customers were notified that if they failed to reduce their use of electricity, compared to the same billing period of the previous year, they would have to pay a 50 percent surcharge on their entire bills. Although the aim was to reduce total electricity consumption by 12 percent, the result was a drop of 18 percent: residential use declined by 18 percent, commercial use by 28 percent, and industrial use by 11 percent. Much of the adjustment in commercial establishments, which accounted for 50 percent of electricity usage prior to the cutback, was achieved through better control of lighting and air conditioning. Dramatic results were achieved by a program which required virtually no investment and allowed consumers to decide how and where to make their own cuts.

a. Ratemaking and Conservation Pricing

To understand some of the traditional disincentives for conservation, it is helpful to know how regulated electric utility rates are set. By law they are to allow the company to recover its operating costs and earn a fair return on its rate base. The rate base usually is calculated by reference

[*273*]

to the original cost (in current dollars) of the existing plant, minus accumulated depreciation.

Determination of which consumers pay how much involves two steps. First, the consumers are divided into broad categories, or customer classes, with similar usage and demand patterns. Traditionally the total amount of money to be collected from consumers is allocated among three classes—residential, commercial and industrial—according to the relative costs of serving them. The second step consists of determining the actual rates to be charged within each customer class to insure that the class provides its allocated share of the revenue. Often there is considerable difference in treatment between large users and small users. While some costs of providing service do not depend on how much electricity a consumer uses (e.g., the cost of installing a single line and meter), other costs vary depending upon when the energy is consumed, for how long, and in what amounts. To insure that each customer pays a proper share of fixed costs, even if he uses only a small amount of energy, utilities may price the first units of consumption quite high, or add a separate customer charge to each bill.

Actual costs of providing electricity vary greatly according to the time of day and season of the year. During hot summer days, residential users run air conditioners at the same time as stores, office buildings and industries are making large demands. To meet this demand, the utility must operate older, less efficient generating plants kept in reserve for times of "peak" demand; gas turbine generators, which are cheap to purchase but have high operating costs, also may be used. However, on a winter night, the utility need run only its most efficient baseload plants. Traditionally, utilities have not varied their prices for electricity according to when it is used. As a result, electricity consumed during summer days has been too cheap in relation to generating costs, and that consumed during winter and at night has been too expensive.

Pricing also has failed accurately to reflect variable costs by ignoring the fact that the cost of constructing additional generating capacity is far greater than it used to be. The "marginal" costs of new power are much higher than existing utility rates. This fact, combined with the traditional availability of "declining block rates", or volume discounts for large users, means that utilities have charged such users only a small fraction of the cost per kilowatt hour of providing electricity from new generating facilities.

These practices encourage greater consumption and discourage investments in energy conservation. Because the costs of expensive new sources of energy are "rolled in" with cheaper, older sources, no consumer is confronted with a price that accurately reflects current costs.

Public utility commissions in the United States only recently have begun to deal with these problems. Some have adopted conservation-oriented pricing policies. These have included "peak-load pricing," which charges more for electricity consumed during the daytime, or the summer, than for that consumed at night or in winter. Also, declining block rates have been terminated in some states, and rate structures adjusted in other ways to reflect the marginal or incremental costs of new generating capacity. See Re Madison Gas & Electric Co., 5 PUR 4th 28 (Wis.Pub.Serv. Comm'n 1974). PURPA requires all state utility commissions to "consider" precisely such nontraditional forms of rate design, though four dissenting justices in FERC v. Mississippi, supra, thought this requirement to be impermissible under the Tenth Amendment.

The "second generation" of utility commission actions aimed at promoting energy conservation through ratemaking began in 1975. The California Public Utilities Commission announced that in the future it would make the "vigor, imagination and effectiveness of a utility's conservation efforts a key question" in acting upon requests for rate increases and authority to expand generating capacity. Where possible, quantitative measures of such efforts would be employed, e.g., the number of homes insulated as a result of the company's programs. The Commission expected

[*276*]

utilities not just to advertise and exhort, but "to explore all possible cost-effective means of conservation, including intensive advisory programs directed at large consumers, conservation-oriented research and development, subsidy programs for capital-intensive conservation measures, providing customers with detailed, intelligible information on appliance energy use by brand name ("shoppers guides"), appliance service, repair, or retrofit by utility representatives."

In subsequent proceedings the California Commission showed that it meant business. It denied or reduced requested rate increases because utilities had failed to promote conservation aggressively. In particular, it focused upon utilities' failure to pursue efforts to get "cogeneration" capacity on line.

b. *Cogeneration*

Cogeneration is the combined production of electricity and useful thermal energy, such as heat or steam, with the latter being used for industrial processes or space heating purposes. About half as much fuel is used to produce electricity and heat together as is required to produce them separately. For an industrial firm which generates electricity onsite from heat that otherwise would be wasted, cogeneration also provides a hedge against rate increases and power interruptions. Rather than requiring new technology, cogeneration involves utilizing practices which were widely employed by industrial plants at the beginning of this century, but were given up in response to pressure from the utilities and to the low rates which they offered large customers.

As noted above, PURPA requires utilities to purchase power from cogenerators. However, in American Electric Power Service Corp. v. FERC, 675 F.2d 1226 (D.C.Cir.1982), the court invalidated some of the regulations adopted by FERC to implement this requirement. One of the rules ordered states to set rates for purchases of power from qualifying cogenerators at a level that always equaled the utilities' full "avoided" cost. "Avoided" cost refers to the marginal or incremental cost which a utility would bear if it were required itself to supply—from new generating capacity—the electricity produced by the cogenerator. The purpose of the rule was to create a substantial financial incentive for cogeneration. The other FERC rule which was rejected made a blanket grant of authority to cogenerators to interconnect with utilities without satisfying certain provisions of the Federal Power Act which afford financial and procedural protections to utilities. The rule was intended to save cogenerators time and money, but was found to violate the Power Act. As to the full avoided cost rule, the court found that FERC had not adequately justified its adoption. The court noted that sec-

[*278*]

tion 210 of PURPA not only encouraged cogeneration but also required that the rates paid by utilities for cogenerated power "shall be just and reasonable to the electric consumers of the electric utility and in the public interest." Concerned about a requirement that consumers in all cases must pay the maximum rate (full avoided cost) permitted by PURPA, the court urged FERC to take a "harder look" at whether a rate based upon some *percentage* of full avoided cost should be prescribed. [As this book was going to press, the Supreme Court *reversed* the forgoing decision and upheld both FERC rules in American Paper Institute v. American Electric Power Service Corp., ___ U.S. ___ (1983).]

Even if not under a federal obligation to set rates (for utility purchases of cogenerated electricity) based on full avoided cost, utility commissions nevertheless may adopt such rates if authorized to do so by state law. This is precisely what the California Public Utilities Commission ordered in Re Pacific Gas & Electric Co., Decision No. 91109, OII No. 26 (1979). The Commission held that the price should not be established through negotiation, with the utility paying up to (but not necessarily the full) marginal cost. While a negotiated price might provide savings to the utility and its customers in the short run, the Commission thought it would encourage less than the economically optimal amount of cogeneration in the long run. Consideration of the cogenerator's costs, as in negotiations, would only serve, said the Commission, to place the cogenerator at a disadvantage in obtaining an acceptable price, and delay action on new cogeneration projects.

c. *Financing*

Another conservation measure approved by the California Commission, this time upon request of a utility, was an expanded program of conservation financing, designed to increase the adoption of cost-effective measures by customers. As part of its Weatherization Zero Interest Plan, the company undertook to audit and finance such conservation measures as attic, wall and floor insulation, storm doors and windows, weatherstripping, caulking, water heater insulation, automatic thermostats, insulation of ducts, lighting conversion, and intermittent ignition devices for furnaces.

The mere listing of such measures emphasizes that conservation, like many applications of solar energy, tends to involve decentralized and undramatic actions. Where many individuals and businesses, rather than a few utility companies, are the crucial decisionmakers, institutional factors and plain inerita can discourage adoption of alternatives to the construction of more fossil-fuel and nuclear facilities. This is true even though the nontraditional alternatives are more economical, which is often the case.

As has been shown, subsidized financing is only one of various kinds of incentives and arrangements to encourage the use of conservation and solar sources. Others include tax credits, conservation pricing of electricity, guaranteed markets for power generated by small solar sources and cogenerators, and recognition of solar access rights. Because the success of such devices requires public knowledge and understanding, informational and educational services—whether provided by utilities, government, or equipment suppliers—also are very important.

CHAPTER 6

PRESERVATION OF NATURAL AREAS

Most of the preceding materials in this book have focused on pollution law. Cleaning up our nation's air and water is clearly an important goal of environmental law. There is, however, another strand of environmental law which seeks different, though related, goals. Indeed, this strand may well predate the anti-pollution effort. The reference, of course, is to the goal of preserving wilderness and other natural areas.

Several of the statutes that we have already considered incorporate this goal. For example, NEPA requires the government to "fulfill the responsibilities of each generation as trustee of the environment for succeeding generations," to "assure for all Americans safe, healthful, productive, and esthetically and culturally pleasing surroundings," and to "preserve important . . . natural aspects of our national heritage . . . ." (section 101(b)) Much litigation under NEPA relates to whether factors such as these have been given adequate consideration in environmental impact statements. The Clean Water Act also contains provisions that can be considered preservationist. Section 101 of the Act makes it the national goal "that the discharge of pollutants into the navigable waters be eliminated by 1985" and that by 1983 waters be sufficiently clean to provide "for the protection and propagation of fish, shellfish, and wildlife . . . " Thus, the Water Act aims at a return of the nation's rivers and lakes to their "natural" state. As we will see, the Clean Air Act contains specific provisions relating to the protection of parks and wilderness areas. These statutes all offer some degree of protection to natural areas.

In this chapter, we will be concerned primarily with direct restrictions on land development in natural areas. The effect of these restrictions is to prevent individuals who wish to do so from using certain areas for economically profitable purposes. This chapter will explore the statutory and constitutional implications of these restrictions. We will begin by considering government restrictions on the development of privately owned land. In the second part of the chapter, we will consider restrictions on resource development on publicly owned lands.

A. PRESERVATION AS A GOAL

Before considering these legal restrictions on development, an understanding of their rationale is helpful. A century ago the idea of preventing the development of "useless" wilderness areas would have been widely regarded as completely irrational. Obviously, individuals who share this judgment will regard the legal mechanisms under discussion here as incomprehensible at best and perhaps perverse at worst. What are the arguments in favor of protecting natural areas?

Because the alternative land uses typically are economically profitable, it is useful to begin by examining this question from an economic perspective. As we have seen in the chapter on economics and pollution law, modern economists typically regard the free market as an ideal means of determining resource allocation. It has been argued that this model should be extended to wilderness areas, so that, for example, the Grand Canyon would be sold to the highest bidder. If the highest bidder was the Sierra Club, the Canyon would be saved; if the highest bidder was a strip mining company, the Canyon would be mined. Any attempt to defend wilderness preservation must confront and attempt to refute this position.

Several economic arguments can be made in favor of wilderness preservation. As we saw earlier, the market mechanism breaks down when public goods or externalities are present. Arguably, both are involved in wilderness preservation. Many individuals may consider preservation of wilderness worthwhile even though they have no present plans to use the wilderness. They may be considered as having a so-called "option demand" for wilderness. That is, these individuals

[*284*]

would be willing to pay to preserve the option of using the wilderness in the future for themselves and their descendants. More broadly, some individuals who have no desire to use wilderness at any time may nevertheless have a preference for the preservation of wilderness as an ethical value. These individuals' desire for wilderness preservation converts wilderness areas into public goods. The reason is that if the wilderness is preserved, these individuals cannot be excluded from enjoying the resulting benefit. This "public good" situation is commonly thought to require a non-market solution. Furthermore, externalities are also present. Many biologists would suggest, on the basis of prior studies of ecological changes, that widespread changes in undeveloped areas are likely to have unforeseen negative consequences there and elsewhere. For example, development of estuaries or marsh areas may indirectly affect wildlife and marine life, thereby impinging on the interests of hunters and fishermen. More subtle effects are also possible. The existence of these externalities provides a basis for preserving wilderness areas that is not unlike the basis for preventing pollution.

Moreover, there is also a temporal element to these externalities, for many of the affected individuals belong to future generations. Some economists have argued that these intertemporal effects may be quite large. The amount of

wilderness in the world is limited by present supplies; indeed, the future amount of available wilderness probably will be even less than that existing today. As the supply decreases, the price
individuals would be willing to pay for the use of
any one piece of wilderness will tend to increase.
Moreover, preservation of wilderness seems to be
a "normal" good—that is, a good which is in
greater demand as income rises. If we assume
that economic growth will continue, the result
will be higher individual incomes and therefore a
higher demand for wilderness. Hence, future
generations may have a stronger demand for wilderness areas than current generations. Ignoring the preferences of future generations thus
could result in greatly distorted resource allocation over time. Thus, even from the perspective
of neoclassical economics, a strong argument can
be made for wilderness preservation.

It is also important to acknowledge some of the
limitations of economic analysis. As a descriptive
science, economics can tell us only the consequences of a decision but not its desirability. It
is sometimes argued that economics simply
shows how individual preferences can be combined to maximize the welfare of society. Thus,
under this view, individuals are completely free to
have their own value preferences; economics
merely shows how these can be combined to maximize the satisfaction of everyone. As the Nobel

Prize-winner Kenneth Arrow showed in his book, *Social Choice and Individual Values,* no system of combining individual preferences can lead to a rational decision method. That is, unless some restrictions are placed on which individual preferences are allowed into consideration, it can be mathematically proved that no method of combining those individual preferences can satisfy the customary standards of rationality. (For example, one of these standards of rationality is that if A is preferred to B, and B is preferred to C, then A is preferred to C.) Thus, the market solution cannot be defended as a completely neutral means of combining individuals' value judgments. If it is to be defended, its defenders must either argue that the market system is morally preferable because it promotes human freedom, regardless of the resulting situation of society, or that the market system will produce results which the individual making the judgment finds morally preferable. In either event, the individual must make his own value judgment about these matters. Once individual value judgments are allowed into the analysis, it is hard to see why those judgments should include only those favoring economic freedom or economic prosperity. Other individuals have value judgments in favor of the preservation of wilderness, and these value judgments have as much right to be considered as any other. In short, neoclassical economic theory provides no escape from the necessity of making our own value judgments about the world.

Today's society clearly has made a value judgment in favor of preserving wilderness. This can be seen in the various environmental statutes considered in this chapter. It can also be seen in more direct measurements of public opinion. In 1980, CEQ published a survey of public opinion on environmental issues. One of the questions asked was the following:

> Some people say we should drain more of these areas [marsh and swamp areas] because land for development is becoming harder to find. Other people say that these marsh and swamp areas should be kept as they are because they help maintain nature's balance by providing breeding areas for fish and feeding places for ducks among other things. Who do you agree with most—those who feel these swamp and marsh areas should continue to be drained, *or* those who feel that they should be preserved in their natural state, *or* don't you have a strong feeling one way or the other?

Only 11% of the respondents stated that they had no strong feelings on the question. The preservation of wetlands was favored by 65%, while only 10% supported development. On a related topic, almost 75% agreed that "an endangered species should be protected even at the expense of commercial activity." Thus, whatever might

[*288*]

be argued in general about the defects of the democratic process, the democratically enacted legislation in the environmental area apparently does accurately reflect the opinion of the public.

With this background in mind, we will turn to the problems raised by attempting to prevent individuals from developing privately owned lands.

B. RESTRICTIONS ON DEVELOPMENT OF PRIVATE LAND

Much of the environmentally significant land, particularly in wetlands and coastal areas, is in the hands of private individuals. We will not attempt to survey the various state laws restricting the development of this land. Instead, we will focus on the constitutional issues. We will first consider the extent to which attempts to regulate development of private land may violate the taking clause of the Constitution. We will then turn to the public trust doctrine and some related doctrines that legitimize restrictions which might otherwise be constitutionally dubious.

1. THE TAKING PROBLEM

The Fifth Amendment to the Constitution provides that private property shall not "be taken for public use, without just compensation." This provision applies only to the federal government. The Fourteenth Amendment, which imposes constitutional restrictions on the States, does not contain similar language. The Supreme Court, however, has construed the Fourteenth Amendment as containing a similar requirement by implication from the due process clause. Consequently, courts have not distinguished between the federal and state governments for purposes of taking clause analysis.

As the Supreme Court itself has admitted, it has not succeeded in constructing any clear rules in this area. It is clear that some government activities, falling short of outright condemnation or seizure of land, still may constitute a taking for constitutional purposes. The rationale, apparently, is that otherwise the government could force private landowners to devote their property entirely to public uses—for example, by constructing a school on the property and providing free education to the public—thereby indirectly converting the property to governmental use without paying just compensation. In any event, although some forms of government regulation clearly may be so extreme as to constitute takings, the Supreme Court has given little guidance as to where precisely to draw the line.

Because of the lack of clear doctrines, the taking clause has provided a fruitful ground for litigation and legal commentary. Unfortunately, the resulting literature has done little to clarify

[*290*]

the basic problem. Rather than attempting a new synthesis, it is more useful in the present context to review the most important Supreme Court cases. Given the lack of clear doctrinal guidelines, the best approach for analyzing taking problems may well be the traditional method of case analysis to determine which previous case is most factually similar to a given situation.

The earliest relevant case is Hadacheck v. Sebastian, 239 U.S. 394 (1915). *Hadacheck* involved a Los Angeles city ordinance making it unlawful to operate a brickyard within certain portions of the city. Mr. Hadacheck was the owner of a brickyard in that area. He alleged that he had purchased the land when it was well outside the city limits and not near any residential district. He also alleged that he had had no reason to anticipate that the area would ever be annexed to the city, that much of the property had been excavated for clay, that the land was worth $800,000 if used for brick-making purposes but no more than $60,000 for any other purpose, and that the ordinance would force him to go out of business. He also alleged, although this allegation was rejected by the state courts, that the operation of his business did not have detrimental effects on adjoining property. The real purpose of the ordinance allegedly was to give other brickyards located elsewhere in the city a monopoly in the brick market. (This allegation was also rejected by the state courts.) The Supreme Court decisively rejected the attack on the ordinance:

> We think the conclusion of the [lower] court is justified by the evidence and makes it unnecessary to review the many cases cited by petitioner in which it is decided that the police power of a state cannot be arbitrarily exercised. The principle is familiar, but in any given case it must plainly appear to apply. It is to be remembered that we are dealing with one of the most essential powers of government, one that is the least limitable. It may, indeed, seem harsh in its exercise, usually is on some individual, but the imperative necessity for its existence precludes any limitation upon it when not exerted arbitrarily. A vested interest cannot be asserted against it because of conditions once obtaining. To so hold would preclude development and fix a city forever in its primitive conditions. There must be progress, and if in its march private interests are in the way they must yield to the good of the community.

It should be noted that *Hadacheck* was decided at a time when the Supreme Court was much more willing than it is today to strike down state statutes regulating economic activities. Yet, even in that pro-business period, the Court firmly upheld the *Hadacheck* ordinance.

Hadacheck might seem to suggest that the impact of a regulation on private individuals is irrelevant to determining constitutionality. The theory of the case seems to be that if a statute is otherwise legitimately within the police power— that is, if it is reasonably related to the public health, welfare, or morals—then individuals who suffer severe losses because of the regulation have no remedy. Less than a decade after *Hadacheck*, the Supreme Court drew back from this conclusion in Pennsylvania Coal Co. v. Mahon, 260 U.S. 393 (1922). This case involved a Pennsylvania statute making it unlawful for coal companies to cause the collapse or subsidence of any public building, any street, or any private residence. The Mahons were bound by a covenant to permit a coal company, which had sold to them or their predecessor only the surface rights to their lot, to remove all the coal without liability. The effect of the statute was to annul this covenant. Pennsylvania law recognized three separate property rights: the right to use the surface, the ownership of the subsurface minerals, and the right to have the surface supported by the subsurface earth. The coal company claimed that the statute operated as a taking of both the second and third rights, both of which belonged to them under their deed with the Mahons. In perhaps the most important single decision under the taking clause, Justice Holmes held that the statute was indeed a taking. The heart of the opinion is to be found in the following famous passage:

> Government hardly could go on if to some extent values incident to property could not be diminished without paying for every such change in the general law. As long recognized, some values are enjoyed under an implied limitation and must yield to the police power. But obviously the implied limitation must have its limits, or the contract and due process clauses are gone. One fact for consideration in determining such limits is the extent of the diminution. When it reaches a certain magnitude, in most if not in all cases there must be an exercise of eminent domain and compensation to sustain the act. So the question depends upon the particular facts. The greatest weight is given to the judgment of the legislature, but it always is open to interested parties to contend that the legislature has gone beyond its constitutional power.

In applying this test, the Court stressed that the statute made coal mining in certain areas commercially impracticable and thus had "very nearly the same effect for constitutional purposes as appropriating or destroying it." The Court concluded that so long as "private persons or communities have seen fit to take the risk of acquiring only surface rights, we cannot see that the fact that the risk has become a danger warrants

[*294*]

the giving to them greater rights than they bought." Justice Brandeis filed a strong dissent.

At the very least, *Pennsylvania Coal* makes it clear that *Hadacheck* cannot be taken to its logical extreme. That is, cases exist in which there is a legitimate public purpose for regulation but the regulation falls too heavily on a single individual, who must be compensated under the taking clause. As the Court says in *Pennsylvania Coal*, this is a matter of degree and therefore difficult to predict in advance.

The next case makes it clear, however, that even the physical destruction of property may sometimes be permissible without compensation. In Miller v. Schoene, 276 U.S. 272 (1928), the Court upheld a Virginia statute which authorized the state entomologist to order the destruction of ornamental red cedar trees. The purpose of the statute was to prevent the transmission of a plant disease to neighboring apple orchards. The Court held that the existence of cedars was incompatible with the existence of the apple trees, so that the state was forced to make a choice as to which form of property to preserve. As the Court said, "[W]hen forced to such a choice the state does not exceed its constitutional powers by deciding upon the destruction of one class of property in order to save another which, in the judgment of the legislature, is of greater value to the public."

[*295*]

The most important recent case on the taking clause is Penn Central Transportation Co. v. New York, 438 U.S. 104 (1978). This case marked the Court's only significant attempt to synthesize its taking law opinions. *Penn Central* involved a New York historic preservation ordinance. Briefly, under the ordinance a special commission was empowered to designate buildings as landmarks, subject to administrative and judicial review. After designation, the exterior of a building had to be kept in good repair and exterior alterations had to be approved by the Commission. Development rights lost because of the landmark designation could be transferred to neighboring plots of land, thereby allowing additional development on that land beyond the normal restrictions of the applicable zoning and building codes. Penn Central owned Grand Central Terminal, a designated landmark. A plan by Penn Central to build a multistory office building perched above the terminal was rejected by the Commission. Penn Central then brought suit claiming that its property had been taken without compensation. It conceded, however, that the transferable development rights had some value and that the terminal was still capable of earning a reasonable return on its initial investment.

The opinion of the Court by Justice Brennan begins by reviewing the factors that have shaped prior decisions. The Court conceded that it had been unable to develop any "set formula" for determining when compensation was required. Instead, it referred to the prior cases as involving "essentially ad hoc, factual inquiries." The Court did point, however, to several relevant factors. The most important were (1) whether the regulation had "interfered with distinct investment backed expectations," and (2) whether the government had physically invaded the property or had simply enacted "some public program adjusting the benefits and burdens of economic life to promote the common good." In reviewing the specific regulation before it, the Court concluded that the purposes of the ordinance were permissible because the ordinance was "expected to produce a widespread public benefit and applicable to all similarly situated property." The Court then held that the regulation passed the *Pennsylvania Coal* test because it did not deprive the company of all use of the property, but instead allowed continuation of a past use and more importantly, permitted the company to obtain a "reasonable return" on its investment.

Penn Central can be read as establishing a three-part test for determining the existence of a taking. The first step involves a determination of whether the regulation amounts to a physical invasion of the property in question. If it does, a taking is quite likely to be found. Otherwise, we proceed to the second step, which is to determine

[*297*]

whether a restriction on the use of property is "reasonably related to the implementation of a policy . . . expected to produce widespread public benefit and applicable to all similarly situated property." If this test is passed, we then proceed to the third test, which derives from *Pennsylvania Coal.* This test requires a determination of whether the owner has been denied the possibility of earning a reasonable return on the investment in the property. Because this factor was conceded in the *Penn Central* case, the Court had no reason to address the rather difficult problems of determining an owner's investment basis in the property and deciding what return is "reasonable" under the circumstances of particular cases.

Public utility law may be an appropriate place to look for guidance in making these determinations, particularly since public utility law was once a branch of taking law. Normally, state utility commissions set rates for utilities in order to provide a reasonable rate of return on the original investment (or "rate base"). A considerable body of expertise has been developed for determining the size of the rate base and the rate of return. This expertise may offer the clue to applying *Penn Central.*

A year after *Penn Central,* the Supreme Court decided two additional, significant taking cases. The first case, Andrus v. Allard, 444 U.S. 51

(1979), involved a statute prohibiting commercial transactions in certain "artifacts" such as eagle feathers. The plaintiffs owned bird feathers when the statute was passed and were subject to prosecution for selling them. In rejecting a taking claim, the Court stressed that the plaintiffs retained the rights to possess, donate and devise the feathers. The Court noted that the feathers could conceivably be exhibited for profit, but then went on to add that a loss of future profits, unaccompanied by any physical property restriction, "provides a slender reed upon which to rest a takings claim." The second case, Kaiser Aetna v. United States, 444 U.S. 164 (1979), involved a private fishpond which the owners connected to the ocean and converted into a "marina-style subdivision community." Although the government did not object to this project, it later contended that the marina was subject to a right of public access. The Court held that imposing this right of access would constitute a taking. The opinion does not purport to establish a general test, but instead stresses that the pond was not commercially navigable in its original state, that the government acquiesced in the marina conversion, and that the right to exclude others is a fundamental element of property ownership. We will consider this case again when we discuss the federal navigational servitude.

The taking issue has played a significant role in environmental law. For example, there has been a great deal of litigation, with conflicting results, over the validity of statutes prohibiting the destruction of privately owned swamps and marshlands. It would be extremely helpful if the Supreme Court gave us a clear test for deciding these cases. In the absence of such a test, *Penn Central* appears to be the best formulation of the relevant issues. The post-*Penn Central* cases seem to stress another factor which is only mentioned in passing in *Penn Central.* That factor is the nature of the property interest involved. The Court seems to have in mind a hierarchy of property rights beginning with the most fundamental, the right to exclude others from the property, then proceeding to the right of free physical use of the property and finally down to the least significant right, the right to sell the property. It is not entirely clear what test is used for determining the status of a particular property interest in this hierarchy. Perhaps the Court will clarify these problems in the near future.

Until such judicial clarification is forthcoming, we must continue with the ad hoc process seen in the preceding cases. These cases give some idea of the relevant factors, but the weight to be given these factors remains unclear. It is a fair assumption that the results in particular cases will be largely determined by the extent of judicial sympathy for the statutory scheme in question. A court which believes that a given regulation serves important purposes and prohibits only conduct which is in some sense ethically questionable, will be quite likely to uphold that regulation. On the other hand, a court which believes that a given regulation is simply unjustified meddling with legitimate private activities will clearly be more likely to find a taking.

One response to the taking problem has been to attempt to limit the kinds of interests that can claim the status of property rights. By preventing certain kinds of economic interests from rising to the status of property rights, a court can avoid any taking problem. The court can simply say that whatever was taken was not property and thus not subject to the taking clause. In the next section, we will consider several of the doctrines which have served this function.

2. THE PUBLIC TRUST DOCTRINE

As we shall see, both the federal and state governments possess certain quasi-property rights stemming from their regulatory powers over waterways. These rights have become important in the environmental context because they serve to justify government regulations in coastal and wetland areas which might otherwise be challenged under the taking clause.

[*301*]

At the state level, these quasi-property rights are defined by the public trust doctrine. The leading case concerning this doctrine is the United States Supreme Court opinion in Illinois Central Railroad Co. v. Illinois, 146 U.S. 387 (1892). This case involved the validity of a land grant to the Illinois Central Railroad. In 1869, the Illinois legislature had granted fee title to certain submerged lands under Lake Michigan to the Railroad. (When the bill was introduced, it had conveyed these lands to the City of Chicago, but somehow before final passage the grantee had been changed to the Railroad.) Four years later, the State repealed the prior statute. Illinois then filed a quiet title suit to establish its ownership of the submerged lands. It should be noted that if the 1869 statute was valid, the statute reclaiming ownership of the lands could hardly avoid attack as a taking since it seized title to private property. The Supreme Court, however, avoided any such constitutional problem by holding that the original grant of land to the Railroad was invalid, so that the Railroad never had anything except at most a voidable title to the property. The 1869 Act was invalid because it violated the public trust in which the property was originally held by the State, as the following passage explains:

> That the State holds the title to the lands under the navigable waters of Lake Michigan . . . we have already shown, and that title

necessarily carries with it control over the waters above them whenever the lands are subjected to use. . . . It is a title held in trust for the people of the State that they may enjoy the navigation of the waters, carry on commerce over them, and have liberty of fishing therein freed from the obstruction or interference of private parties . . . . The trust devolving upon the state for the public, and which can only be discharged by the management and control of property in which the public has an interest, cannot be relinquished by a transfer of property. The control of the state for the purposes of the trust can never be lost, except as to such parcels as are used in promoting the interests of the public therein, or can be disposed of without any substantial impairment of the public interest in the lands and waters remaining.

Thus, private property interests in land subject to the public trust are severely limited. To the extent that private individuals can hold title to this land at all, that title is necessarily subject to the requirements of the trust.

The evolution of the public trust doctrine is well illustrated by two cases from California. In a 1928 case, Boone v. Kingsbury, 206 Cal. 148, 273 p. 797 (1928), cert. denied 280 U.S. 517, the California Supreme Court upheld a statute authorizing oil drilling in offshore tidal areas. The court held that this form of development was in the interest of the public and was thus a justifiable exercise of the public trust. Moreover, the court stressed the public interest in encouraging "citizens to devote waste and unused lands to some useful purpose." As an example of such useless lands, the court referred to a prior case involving a salt marsh. By 1971, the court's attitude had changed completely. In Marks v. Whitney, 6 Cal.3d 251, 98 Cal.Rptr. 790, 491 P.2d 374 (1971), the court gave a much more expansive reading to the public trust doctrine. The court stressed that in administering the trust, the state is not bound by traditional classifications of land uses. Instead, the state can give recognition to the need to preserve lands in their natural state, so that they can serve as "ecological units for scientific study, as open space, and as environments which provide food and habitat for birds and marine life, and which favorably affect the scenery and climate of the area." As a result, the court held that a neighboring landowner could sue to prevent tidelands from being filled and developed. The court held that such a suit could be brought even if lands had already been reclaimed with or without prior authorization from the state, since neither reclamation nor prior authorization "*ipso facto* terminate the public trust nor render the issue moot."

The public trust doctrine is not the only property law concept which has been used to uphold restrictions on private land development. In an innovative decision, the Oregon Supreme Court held that fencing beach land violated a property interest on the part of the public deriving from longstanding custom. State ex rel. Thornton v. Hay, 254 Or. 584, 462 P.2d 671 (1969). Opinions such as this, or such as those applying the public trust doctrine, should not be seen simply as a means of finding a technical loophole in taking law. Rather, they are best seen as attempts to adjust the technicalities of taking and property law to the realities of modern life. As a realistic matter, certain activities involve longstanding public interests and therefore must reasonably be expected to be subject to broad government regulation. Given the long history of public control over waterways, no individual claiming to own legal title to a public waterway can really have a firm expectation of uninhibited use of his "property." Thus, the kinds of firm expectations which taking law was intended to protect simply cannot arise in some contexts.

3. THE NAVIGATIONAL SERVITUDE

The same principle is at work in federal law. Like the states, the federal government has a quasi-property interest in navigable waters. The federal interest is called the navigational servitude. The operation of the servitude is illustrated in United States v. Rands, 389 U.S. 121 (1967). The issue in *Rands* was whether the condemnation award for land along the Columbia River should include that portion of the market value of the land which was due to its potential use as a port site. The court held that no individual can own a property interest in the use of navigable waters, for such use is always subject to government control. "Thus, without being constitutionally obligated to pay compensation, the United States may change the course of a navigable stream, or otherwise impair or destroy a riparian owner's access to navigable waters, even though the market value of the riparian owner's land is substantially diminished." Indeed, later in the opinion, the Court referred to the "constitutional power of Congress *completely* to regulate navigable streams to the *total* exclusion of private power companies or port owners." [emphasis added]

The *Rands* case has been somewhat limited by the more recent case of Kaiser Aetna v. United States, 444 U.S. 164 (1979). That case, which was discussed in the previous subsection, involved the private improvement of a pond which was previously incapable of being used for navigational purposes. As a result of the improvements, the pond was to be used as a private marina. The Court acknowledged that the strict logic of

Rands and similar cases might allow the government to require public access to the marina, converting it into a public aquatic park. But, the Court concluded, the facts in the *Kaiser Aetna* case were simply too far removed from previous cases involving navigable waterways. For one thing, the pond was simply too different from the sort of "great navigable stream" that had previously been held "incapable of private ownership." The Court also stressed the government's consent to the marina project:

> We have not the slightest doubt that the Government *could have refused to allow such dredging* on the ground that it could have impaired navigation in the bay, or could have conditioned its approval of the dredging on petitioners' agreement to comply with various measures that it deemed appropriate for the promotion of navigation. But what petitioners *now* have is a body of water that was private property under Hawaiian law, linked to navigable water by a channel dredged by them with the consent of the respondent. While the consent of individual officers representing the United States cannot "estop" the United States, it can lead to the fruition of a number of expectancies embodied in the concept of "property,"—expectancies that, if sufficiently important, the Government must condemn and pay for before it takes over the management of

[*307*]

the landowner's property. In this case, we hold that the "right to exclude," so universally held to be a fundamental element of the property right, falls within this category of interests that the Government cannot take without compensation . . . Thus, if the Government wishes to make what was formerly Kuaapa Pond into a public aquatic park *after petitioners have proceeded as far as they have here*, it may not, without invoking eminent domain power and paying just compensation, require them to allow free access to the dredged pond while petitioners' agreement with their customers calls for an annual $72 regular fee. [emphasis added]

This is obviously a guarded holding. It remains to be seen whether *Kaiser Aetna* will remain a narrow exception to the *Rands* rule or whether it represents a major change in judicial attitude.

It is important to note that the navigational servitude applies only to waters meeting the traditional test of navigability. While statements of the traditional test vary, the central concern behind these tests relates to potential use for navigational purposes. On the other hand, federal regulation has not been limited to this class of waterways. The lower courts have held, with strong support in the legislative history, that the Clean Water Act extends beyond traditional navigable waters to all bodies of water within the

[*308*]

United States. The reason, obviously, is that the purity of navigable waterways cannot be maintained unless other bodies of water which directly or indirectly connect to those navigable waters are also cleaned up. To the extent that Congress has extended its jurisdictional net beyond the traditional navigable waterways, however, it can no longer claim the protection of the navigational servitude as a possible defense to taking claims. Thus, at least some applications of the Clean Water Act possibly might be found to so drastically limit the use of certain parcels of land as to constitute takings.

Perhaps the most significant exercise of congressional authority is section 404 of the Clean Water Act. Section 404 requires permits for the discharge of dredged or fill material. In an important district court opinion, the permit requirement was extended to manmade canals and mangrove wetlands which are periodically covered by tides. The discharges, which ultimately would have resulted in converting these areas into dry land, were held to violate the Act. United States v. Holland, 373 F.Supp. 665 (M.D.Fla.1974). Courts have aggressively enforced the permit requirement, sometimes going as far as to require that land illegally filled be returned to its natural condition.

This tremendous expansion of federal jurisdiction has given rise to some administrative problems. It would obviously be impractical to require a federal permit every time a farmer digs a ditch that connects to an existing drainage system. EPA adopted regulations exempting discharges from agricultural activities, with certain exceptions for relatively major pollution sources. These regulations, however, were held invalid in NRDC v. Costle, 568 F.2d 1369 (D.C.Cir.1977). In that case, the D.C. Circuit rejected EPA's argument that issuing permits for each individual source would be impractical in view of the number of sources involved (around 500,000) and the difficulty of setting effluent limits. Instead, the court held, EPA could issue general permits for whole classes of discharges, setting various limitations on the discharger's actions. The 1977 amendments to the Act exempt a number of "normal farming, silvaculture, and ranching activities" from permit requirements insofar as these activities involve discharges of dredged or fill material. The exemption does not apply to any "activity having as its purpose bringing an area of the navigable waters into a use to which it was not previously subject, where the flow or circulation of navigable waters may be impaired or the reach of such waters be reduced" (section 404(f) (2)).

Because both the federal and state governments, as we have seen, have legitimate interests in regulating the use of water bodies and adjacent lands, a cooperative effort is clearly indicated. A beginning has been made towards such cooperation. The Clean Water Act provides for delegation of the permit system to state governments, subject to certain safeguards. In addition, another statute, the Coastal Zone Management Act, 16 U.S.C.A.˙§§ 1451–1464, attempts to encourage state governments to implement land use plans for coastal areas. The incentive is financial; the requirements are essentially procedural. Congress was less concerned about controlling the eventual form of state regulation than in encouraging the states to engage in some structured form of regulation of coastal areas.

We have seen in this portion of the chapter that certain areas associated with waterways are subject to quasi-public ownership. As a result, governments have unusually broad regulatory powers and are largely free from the restrictions of the taking clause. In the next section, we will consider environmental issues relating to land which is in outright public ownership.

C. PROTECTION OF PUBLIC LANDS

1. PUBLIC LANDS POLICY

Although few individuals in the eastern half of the United States are aware of this fact, the federal government owns vast amounts of land. In 1975, the public lands were estimated at over

740,000,000 acres, an area nearly the size of India or roughly one-third of the land area in the United States. About one-half of this land was located in Alaska. The percentage of federally owned lands, excluding Indian reservations, in the western states ranges from about 30% in Washington to almost 90% in Nevada. The average is close to 50%. Thus federal land policy is of critical importance to the western states.

Land policy is also of great importance to a number of important economic interests. The public lands contain approximately 20% of the nation's commercial forest land, as well as large amounts of minerals such as copper, mercury, and nickel. In addition, federal lands in 1972 accounted for approximately 6% of the nation's production of oil and gas, with another 12% coming from offshore lands. Thus, the federal lands also have tremendous economic importance.

Of course, the public lands also have tremendous importance to conservationists. In perhaps the single most important conservation act of this century, Congress in 1980 set aside vast tracts of land in Alaska as national monuments, parks, and wilderness areas. Roughly 30,000,000 acres were added to the national parks system alone. Even before this legislation, over 180,000,000 acres had been reserved for national forests and parks. It takes little imagination to foresee the possibility of considerable conflict between environmentalists and resource developers. Until the last decade, the developers clearly had the upper hand in this struggle. Since 1970, however, there has been a considerable shift in the balance of power. In this section, we will explore the resolution of these conflicts under current federal statutes.

In order to understand the environmental aspects of public land law, a basic understanding of the non-environmental aspects is necessary as background. Unfortunately, there is no comprehensive statutory scheme governing federal lands. The numerous existing statutes are complicated and poorly coordinated. We will not attempt here to cover them in detail since to do so would require an undue amount of space. Nevertheless, we will attempt to give a basic outline of public land law.

Until the Twentieth Century, the federal government's main purpose with respect to public lands was to dispose of them as quickly as possible. This policy was evidenced by several homestead acts which conveyed large portions of land to farmers and ranchers. The most important survivor from this period is the Mining Law of 1872, 30 U.S.C.A. §§ 22 et seq. The Act allows private purchase of "all valuable mineral deposits in lands belonging to the United States." (This statute does not apply to certain important minerals such as oil, gas, coal and oil shale.) Any individual who discovers a valuable mineral deposit on public lands can obtain a mining claim for that deposit.   The locater of the minerals acquires a possessory interest in the claim, which is a form of transferable property.   Beginning at the time of location, this property interest gives the holder the right to extract, process and market the minerals.   In addition, the holder of the claim has the right to obtain title to the land on which the claim is located.   The locater of the minerals is not required to apply for a government patent to the land, but if it chooses to do so, the Secretary of the Interior has no discretion about issuing the patent.   The sole purpose of this statute is to promote mining.   Thus, under the statute, the federal government has little power to control mining.

In 1976, mining activities were finally subjected to some degree of governmemt control.   As part of the Federal Land Policy and Management Act, Congress provided that in "managing the public lands" the Secretary "shall, by regulation or otherwise, take any action necessary to prevent unnecessary or undue degradation of the lands." 43 U.S.C.A. § 1732(b).   The preceding sentence in the statute makes it clear that this provision is applicable to mining.   Until this statute was passed, however, the government was essentially powerless to deal with environmental problems relating to mining, and even today its power is limited.

As mentioned earlier, some important natural resources such as oil have been exempted from the 1872 statute. Under the Mineral Leasing Act of 1920, the Secretary of the Interior was empowered to issue prospecting permits and leases for certain minerals such as oil and gas. Unlike the limited government role under the Mining Act, the government's powers to control mineral leasing are quite broad because of its discretion over the issuance of permits and leases.

The other major resource use with which we will be concerned is logging. Since 1891, the President has been authorized to set aside land as national forests. See 16 U.S.C.A. § 471. Under an 1897 statute, the purposes of establishing national forests were declared to be water control and "a continuous supply of timber." 16 U.S. C.A. § 475. The motivation for the statute was the fear that forest lands might soon disappear, leaving the United States with a shortage of timber and of watersheds needed to control stream flows. The Supreme Court has recently made it clear, as we shall see later, that it regards these as the exclusive purposes of the 1891 and 1897 Acts. In 1960, Congress broadened the purposes of the national forest system by passing the Multiple-use Sustained Yield Act, 16 U.S.C.A. §§ 528–531. This statute provides that national forests shall be administered for various purposes, including outdoor recreation, timber, and wildlife purposes. Because the Act gave the administrator no guidance as to what weight to give these various purposes, the Act was held to leave the administrator almost complete discretion. In 1974 and 1978, Congress called upon the Secretary of Agriculture to establish land management plans for national forests. This new legislation also addresses matters such as clearcutting, a logging practice which had previously given rise to considerable controversy. See 16 U.S.C.A. §§ 1601 et seq. In 1976, the Federal Land Policy and Management Act was passed, which calls for similar planning on the 450,000,000 acres administered by the Bureau of Land Management. See 43 U.S.C.A. §§ 1701–1784.

2. EXECUTIVE WITHDRAWALS

Historically, resource development on public lands has been the rule rather than the exception. Most public land law was geared toward encouraging resource development, while preservation was an exception. Thus, historically, preservation of public lands has taken place when either the executive or the legislature took action to withdraw lands from the normal development process.

Presidential authority to withdraw land from development was upheld by the Supreme Court in United States v. Midwest Oil Co., 236 U.S. 459 (1915). Because of the encouragement offered by the public land laws of the time, a race among oil companies arose in California to remove as much oil as possible as quickly as possible, with each company attempting to pump out the oil before owners of nearby wells could do so. In 1909, the Director of the Geological Survey reported that all the oil lands might be in private hands within a few months. This, in turn, might jeopardize the Navy's fuel supply. In response, the President issued an order "in aid of proposed legislation" withdrawing certain public lands from disposal to the public. The oil companies argued strenuously that the President lacked statutory authority to take this action. The Court held, however, that Congress had been aware of numerous prior instances of similar Presidential actions. Because Congress did not repudiate these previous withdrawals and indeed acquiesced in the practice, Congress was held to have impliedly consented to the Executive practice. The Court stressed the need for flexibility in administering the public lands:

> These rules or laws [passed by Congress] for the disposal of public land are necessarily general in their nature. Emergencies may occur, or conditions may so change as to require that the agent in charge [the President] should, in the public interest, withhold the land from sale; and while no such expressed authority has been granted, there is nothing in

the nature of the power exercised which prevents Congress from granting it by implication just as could be done by any other owner of property under similar conditions.

The Presidential power at issue in *Midwest Oil* was confirmed by the Pickett Act. The Act authorized the President "in his discretion" to "temporarily withdraw from settlement . . . any of the public lands of the United States . . . and reserve the same for water-power sites, irrigation, classification of lands, or other public purposes to be specified in the orders of withdrawal, and such withdrawals shall remain in force until revoked by him or by an Act of Congress." Such withdrawals did not affect the application of the mining laws to metallic minerals on withdrawn land. Despite the use of the word "temporary", a temporary withdrawal remained in effect until expressly revoked, even though the result is that such a "temporary" withdrawal may in fact last 50 years or more, long after its original purpose has ceased. In part, the rationale for this rule was the need for certainty in the determination of property claims with respect to public lands.

In 1976, the Pickett Act was repealed. The power of the Secretary of the Interior to withdraw public lands is now governed by 43 U.S.C.A. § 1714. The goal of this legislation was to give Congress greater control over Executive withdrawals. Withdrawals of large tracts of land (over 5,000 acres) can be made only for 20-year periods, subject to a legislative veto by concurrent resolution of both houses. The Secretary is authorized to make smaller withdrawals for various periods of time, the period varying from 5 years to infinity, depending on the reason for the withdrawal. The statute does provide for emergency 3-year withdrawals, which must be made when either the Secretary or the Interior Affairs Committee of either house of Congress determines that "an emergency situation exists and that extraordinary measures must be taken to preserve values that would otherwise be lost." This provision was utilized on December 1, 1978, to make an emergency withdrawal of 105,000,000 acres in Alaska. The legislative history shows that the 1976 legislation was intended to eliminate the President's implied withdrawal power under the *Midwest Oil* doctrine. The President does retain withdrawal power under certain other statutes, such as the Antiquities Act, 16 U.S.C.A. § 431, which was also used by President Carter with respect to large tracts of land in Alaska.

3.   LEGISLATIVE WITHDRAWALS

The most important legislative land withdrawal, apart from the 1980 Alaskan Lands Act, was the Wilderness Act of 1964, 16 U.S.C.A. §§ 1131–1136. This statute created the National Wilderness Preservation System. The Act defines a wilderness as having four characteristics: (1) unnoticeable human impact, (2) outstanding opportunities for solitude or primitive recreation, (3) an area of at least 5,000 acres or a sufficient size to make preservation practicable, and (possibly but not necessarily) (4) ecological, geological, or other value.   Section 1132 of the Act designates certain lands as wilderness areas and provides for review of other national forest lands to determine the desirability of further legislation adding them to the wilderness system.

The most important effect of wilderness designation is found in section 1133 of the Act, which sharply restricts the use of wilderness land.   Section 1133 makes the agency administering any wilderness area "responsible for preserving the wilderness character of the area" and for insuring that these areas are devoted to "the public purposes of recreational, scenic, scientific, educational, conservational, and historical use."   Except where the Act expressly so provides, no commercial enterprise and no permanent roads are allowed within any wilderness area.   Mineral use remains a major exception, with the mining laws remaining applicable to wilderness areas until 1983.   One area of uncertainty is the relationship between the Wilderness Act and other previous legislation, since the Act sharply changes the status of these lands but purports not to repeal such previous legislation.

Apart from its impact on land already designated as wilderness, the statute also has some effect on federal land under study for wilderness designation. In Parker v. United States, 448 F.2d 793 (10th Cir. 1971), cert. denied 405 U.S. 989 (1972), the Tenth Circuit held that timber sales were barred on land of "predominantly wilderness value" adjacent to a designated wilderness area. The Court's rationale was that logging activities would irrevocably destroy the land's wilderness nature and thus deprive Congress of the opportunity to consider its inclusion within the wilderness system. The 1976 Federal Land Policy and Management Act requires an inventory by 1991 of all roadless areas of 5,000 acres or more outside of the national forest system. The Act codifies the *Parker* approach by requiring that, subject to existing rights, areas under study be managed "in a manner so as not to impair the suitability of such areas for preservation as wilderness." In a recent case, this provision was held to apply to mineral leasing, except for activities actually underway when the 1976 Act was passed. Rocky Mountain Oil & Gas Association v. Watt, 696 F.2d 734 (10th Cir. 1982).

Particular problems have arisen under the Wilderness Act with respect to the Boundary Waters Canoe Area in northern Minnesota. The Wilderness Act contained a special provision for the BWCA requiring that it be managed "in accor-

[*321*]

dance with the general purpose of maintaining, without unnecessary restrictions on other uses, including that of timber, the primitive character of the area." 16 U.S.C.A. § 1133(d)(5), repealed 92 Stat. 1650 (1978). This provision gave rise to a great deal of litigation. Ultimately the Eighth Circuit upheld extensive logging activities in the BWCA, but Congress then passed a special statute relating to the BWCA to terminate all logging activities. Interestingly, the statutory language which now defines the areas in which logging was banned refers to the district court injunction overruled by the Eighth Circuit. This is an important example of the novel relationships between courts and Congress which have evolved in the environmental area.

4. PREVENTION OF CONFLICTING PRIVATE USES

In addition to limiting development of public lands themselves, preservation of these lands often requires restrictions on activities on private lands. For example, preserving a water supply for public lands may be critical if they are to fulfill their purposes. Other public lands cannot be effectively used for their intended purposes without clean air and good visibility. In the remaining part of this chapter, we will briefly consider the statutory and common law doctrines which protect public lands from conflicting uses of adjacent private lands. As we saw in Chapter 4, congressional power under the property clause to regulate the use of private lands is not altogether clear. This has not proved a major problem with respect to the restrictions we are about to discuss. Restrictions on water use have been considered to be federal property rights reserved when lands were originally granted to private individuals. The restrictions relating to air pollution are part of a general statute clearly authorized under the commerce clause.

To understand the federal government's special prerogatives in water law, it is necessary to recall some basic facts about western water law. In much of the western half of the country, water is a scarce commodity. To allocate this commodity, the western states generally use a priority system based on order of use together with some kind of filing system. Generally speaking, individuals who first appropriate part of a water supply have prior claim over those whose appropriation is later in time. Of course there are numerous complications and local variations, but this is the general scheme. The federal government has often failed to comply with the state priority systems. The question that arises is whether the federal government can claim a greater right to the use of water than it is given by state law.

As Cappaert v. United States, 426 U.S. 128 (1976), illustrates, the federal government does indeed have special prerogatives in water law. *Cappaert* involved an underground pool in the Devil's Hole Cavern in Nevada. The land surrounding Devil's Hole is part of the Death Valley National Monument. In a pool within the cave, the Devil's Hole pupfish live and breed. If the water level falls below a certain level in the pool, uncovering a rock shelf, the fish cannot breed. Nearby landowners began pumping operations which resulted in declining water levels in the pool. The Court held that the Presidential proclamation establishing the cave as part of the national monument had the effect of reserving the necessary underground water required to fulfill the purposes of the reservation. One of the purposes of the reservation was preservation of the pool and the fish that live within it. Thus, although it had failed to qualify under state law, as a matter of federal law the government was entitled to insist that sufficient underground water be left to maintain the pool level.

Some of the limitations of the implied reservation doctrine became clear in United States v. New Mexico, 438 U.S. 696 (1978). The question in that case was whether the creation of a national forest reserves water for recreation and wildlife-preservation purposes. In an opinion by Justice Rehnquist, the Supreme Court held that the sole purposes of creating national forests were to preserve timber supply and watersheds. Although a secondary purpose of preserving wildlife may later have developed, according to the Court such a secondary purpose does not suffice to trigger the implied-reservation doctrine. The Court's opinion shows great sensitivity to state's rights in the water law area. Four justices dissented, arguing that the Congressional desire to "improve and protect" the forests included a desire to preserve the wildlife that inhabit those forests. Even after *New Mexico,* apparently it is open to the federal government to prove that preservation of wildlife is necessary to preserve the vegetation in the forest and is therefore part of the primary congressional purpose. Such a showing presumably would be sufficient to justify use of the impliedreservation doctrine.

The implied-reservation doctrine has deep historical roots. A much more recent protection for federal lands is to be found in the Clean Air Act. Section 162 designates major national wilderness areas and parks as Class I areas. These Class I areas are subject to special protection under the PSD (prevention of significant deterioration) provisions of the Act. As we saw in Chapter 2, air in Class I areas must be kept cleaner than would otherwise be required by the national air quality standards. To implement this clean air requirement, the Act contains special permit provisions and requires changes in state implementation plans.

Under section 165, a facility can receive a permit even if its emissions would violate the Class I limits, if the manager of the affected federal lands certifies that there will be no adverse impact on the federal lands. Even if the federal land manager refuses to issue the permit, the state governor may request a limited Presidential exemption. On the other hand, even if a facility does meet the Class I requirements, it may be denied a permit if it will have an adverse impact on visibility or other "air quality-related values" in a Class I area. Another significant provision of the Clean Air Act is found in section 169A. This section is designed to maintain high visibility in mandatory Class I areas. To some degree, retrofitting is required in the interests of improved visibility, although major weight is given to the cost factor.

This concludes our survey of protection of natural areas. The reader should be cautioned that we have only scratched the surface of the problems involved in this area of the law. Courses in land use regulation consider the problems of preserving privately owned lands in far more detail than we have attempted here. At many law schools, public lands and water law are also the subjects of separate courses.

INDEX

INDEX

INDEX

References are to Pages

NUCLEAR ENERGY—Continued
Plant siting,
    Consideration of alternative sites, 207–208
    Low population zone, 203
Plutonium, weapons manufacture, 197, 214
Preemption, 192–193, 198–199, 221–222
Price-Anderson Act, 7–8
Reactor accidents,
    Classes, 49, 201
    Discussion in EIS, 49, 201, 204
        Emergency plans, 205
Risk assessment, 49
Terrorism, 214
Thermal pollution, 22
Three Mile Island, 28–30, 49, 201–206

NUCLEAR REGULATORY COMMISSION
See Nuclear Energy

NUCLEAR WASTES
See Nuclear Energy

NUISANCE
Air pollution, 59, 62
"Coming to the nuisance" doctrine, 63
Federal common law, 63, 64
Noise pollution, 190–191
Obstruction of sunlight, 268
Private, 61
Public, 61
Remedies,
    Injunctions, 57, 59, 60, 63
    Permanent damages, 60
Standing, 61
Water pollution, 121

OIL
Coastal areas, public trust, 304
Federal lands, 312
    Mineral Leasing Act, 315
Offshore production,
    Coastal Zone Management Act, 236–239
    Discussion of alternatives in EIS, 45, 240
    Discussion of effects in EIS, 240–243

INDEX
References are to Pages

INDEX
References are to Pages

[*342*]

†